AN ILLUSTRATED BIO-BIBLIOGRAPHY OF

Black Photographers

1940 – 1988

Garland Reference Library of the Humanities

(Vol. 760)

AN ILLUSTRATED BIO-BIBLIOGRAPHY OF

Black Photographers

1940—1988

Garland Publishing, Inc.
NEW YORK & LONDON 1989

LIBRARY OF CONGRESS CATALOGING-IN-PUBLICATION DATA

Willis-Thomas, Deborah, 1948–
An illustrated bio-bibliography of black photographers, 1940–1988
Deborah Willis-Thomas.
p. cm.—(Garland reference library of the humanities ; vol. 760)
Bibliography: p.
Includes index.
ISBN 0-8240-8389-X (alk. paper)
1. Photography—Bio-bibliography.   2. Afro-American photographers.
I. Title. II. Series.
TR139.W55   1989
770'.92'2—dc19   88-11200

Design by ALISON LEW

MANUFACTURED IN THE UNITED STATES OF AMERICA

For

RUTH,
TOM

and

HANKIE

ACKNOWLEDGMENTS

When I was asked by Garland Publishing, Inc., to create a companion volume to *Black Photographers, 1840–1940: An Illustrated Bio-Bibliography*, published in 1985, I was elated. I thought that the information available on the contemporary black photographer would be accessible, well supplied with critical analysis, and abundant. I began to review notes and clippings that I had saved since my undergraduate years at the Philadelphia College of Art to find names to include and research. I then realized the complexity of my task. I was overwhelmed!

I want to thank a number of individuals and institutions. It is impossible to thank individually every institution, curator, photographer and librarian who assisted me in all phases of research and compilation. However, a number of friends and colleagues assisted me in identifying photographers across the country; I am especially grateful to Moneta Sleet, Edmund Barry Gaither, Robert Sengstacke, Francis Giles, Lou Draper, Kellie Jones, Sharon Howard, Vance Allen, Anne Tucker, Val Wilmer, Sule Wilson, Charles Blockson, Danny Dawson, Isabelle Fambrough, Joe Crawford and Cynthia Badie-Rivers.

I also want to thank the photographers themselves who agreed to assist me in making this contemporary history come alive—by sending samples of their work and, in turn, sending me letters of thanks and support.

I particularly wish to thank Kathe Sandler, Cheryl Shackelton, Diana Lachatanere, Mary Yearwood and James Briggs Murray who provided assistance in teaching me the value of computer technology, as well as Eleanor Hartsfield, Tei Sing Smith, Janet Rodriguez, Sydney Kamlager and Joyce Lee who assisted me in organizing my files, notes and mailings. At Garland I would like to thank Phyllis Korper, Kennie Lyman, Alison Lew and Henry Babcock.

What really kept me going was the understanding, encouragement and support I received from my son, Hank Sloane Thomas, Donald Bogle, Howard Dodson, Catherine

Lenix-Hooker, John Pinderhughes, Bert Andrews, Dick Newman, Claudine Brown, Clarissa Sligh, and my sisters Melvina Lathan, Yvonne Brooks and Leslie Willis.

Finally, I am grateful to Lillian Foreman Holman (the matriarch) and to my loving family and friends for always providing what I needed to hear—advice, criticism and cheers!

CONTENTS

Foreword   *ix*

Introduction   *xi*

The Photographers   *1*

The Photographs   *161*

Afterword   *163*

Bibliography   *167*

Exhibitions, 1969–1987   *171*

FOREWORD

Photography as a documentary resource and art form dates back to the nineteenth century. Almost from the origin of this revolutionary reproduction technique, blacks have figured prominently in its history—as documentarians, journalists, artists, studio photographers and subjects. A free man of color, Jules Lion, introduced the daguerreotype to New Orleans as early as 1840. Blacks appeared frequently as subjects and objects of nineteenth-century photographers—black as well as white—in Africa and throughout the Americas. During the first four decades of the twentieth century, black photographers made significant contributions to preserving aspects of African American history and culture through the photographic medium.

In her first book, *Black Photographers, 1840–1940: An Illustrated Bio-Bibliography* (New York: Garland Publishing, Inc., 1985), Deborah Willis-Thomas rescued many of the pioneering nineteenth- and early twentieth-century black American photographers from oblivion. The sixty-five selected individuals included therein worked during the first hundred years of the development of the medium, capturing poignant aspects of the rural and urban worlds in which the black American community came of age. The product of more than ten years of research, this work has become an essential resource for the study of the lives and work of these black pioneers in photography. In it one finds basic biographical information on the selected photographers, source information on their collections, exhibitions, publications and representative samples of their work.

An Illustrated Bio-Bibliography of Black Photographers, 1940–1988 brings this fifteen-year project to a conclusion. Necessarily more selective than the first volume, it is, nevertheless, the only resource of its kind available to researchers and others seeking information on black involvement in the profession over the last half century. As she did with the previous volume, Ms. Willis-Thomas has had to mine a plethora of scattered, uneven and disparate sources in order to bring together this concise, selected guide to the lives and works of black photographers of our own times. As such, it does not purport to be

FOREWORD

the definitive work on the subject or the period. It is, however, the most comprehensive survey available to date. And, like its predecessor, it lays the foundation on which a new field of critical inquiry can be based.

Relatively little is known, for instance, about the influence of race or sex on photography as an art form and medium of documentation. While we have begun to see systematic studies of the work of such masters as James Van Der Zee, Gordon Parks, Roy DeCarava and P. H. Polk, we know relatively little about how their work compared with that of their peers—or with one another. Are there discernible commonalities and differences in technique and subject matter between the work of nineteenth-century black photographers and these twentieth-century masters? Are the themes/subjects chosen by black women different from those highlighted by black men? Are there recurring themes in the work of black photographers that cut across gender, nationality or geographic boundaries? What aspects of their biography distinguish the photojournalist from the documentarian; the documentarian from the creative artist; the black photographer from the photographer who just happens to be black? Critical studies of these and other provocative questions are suggested by the information and images contained in this work—questions that frequently could not be raised, much less answered, previously because we had so little information about the identity and work of black photographers.

An Illustrated Bio-Bibliography of Black Photographers, 1940–1988 and its companion volume are at one and the same time source books for the study of individual black photographers and aids (indeed inspirations for) the study of black photography—the unique and universal aspects of the creative genius of people of African descent working through the photographic medium.

Ms. Willis-Thomas is the head of the Photographs and Prints unit of the Schomburg Center for Research in Black Culture, The New York Public Library. She has relied heavily on the resources of the Schomburg Center in locating and knitting together the textual information contained in these volumes. The works of many of the photographers identified here are also found in the center's collection of over 300,000 images by and about blacks from the nineteenth century. This research collection that is being preserved at the Schomburg Center, a research library, is committed to promoting the study and interpretation of black life using the photographic image as a primary resource document and as a medium of artistic, cultural and historical interpretation. Ms. Willis-Thomas is to be commended for helping to introduce practitioners, scholars and the general public to little-known facts and insights into the work of black photographers. It is our hope that others will be inspired to use these leads to refine our current understandings of these artists and their works and venture into new frontiers of knowledge about the nature of the human experience as recorded by black photographers.

HOWARD DODSON, Chief
Schomburg Center for Research in Black Culture
The New York Public Library

FOREWORD

INTRODUCTION

The world's first photograph was taken in 1826 by Joseph-Nicéphore Niépce. He directed his camera—made by a Parisian optician—out of an attic window overlooking his country estate in eastern France. Eight hours later he closed the shutter, and the world's first photograph had been taken. It showed a courtyard in blurred shades with a pigeon hole on the left and pear tree on the right with patches of sky peeping through the branches. The long exposure produced a strange effect—the sun seemed to be shining on both sides of the courtyard.

Niépce, in 1829 almost financially ruined, signed a contract to share his secret with Louis Jacques Mandé Daguerre, a theatrical designer with an interest in photography. Daguerre saw the advantages of photography, and it was he who adapted Niépce's original invention so that photography became practical. Niépce died in 1833; Daguerre renegotiated Niépce's contract with his heirs, and within months the invention had been recognized by the French government. Experimenting from 1833 to 1839, Daguerre reduced the exposure time from eight hours to thirty minutes, found a way of fixing the images and called his new process the "daguerreotype."

Jules Lion, a free man of color, is credited with introducing the daguerreotype to New Orleans in 1840. Between 1840 and 1940, hundreds of black photographers were being listed in major city directories, advertising in newspapers, and attending conferences and photography schools.

This book is a continuation of *Black Photographers, 1840–1940: An Illustrated Bio-Bibliography*, a selective overview of photographers active during the profession's first hundred years. Photographers Roy DeCarava, Gordon Parks, Austin Hansen, P. H. Polk, James Van Der Zee and the twin brothers Morgan and Marvin Smith, were included in that book, although all of them were active well beyond the 1940s.

An Illustrated Bio-Bibliography of Black Photographers, 1940–1988 is intended as an introduction to the achievements and activities of black photographers not listed in the earlier book, who were studio owners, photojournalists, and commercial and fine art photographers during the past fifty years.

This book is organized to assist the reader in identifying photographers to encourage further study, exhibitions or research in the contemporary black photography movement. Where possible, I have included works by individual photographers. The brief biographies describe the activities of each photographer, the type of work he or she produced and, when found, critical articles and reviews. Most entries consist of the photographer's name, birth and/or active dates, biographical data, a listing of public repositories where the photographs are housed, a selected list of exhibitions and a selected bibliography.

Photographers included are not always well known, but references to their activities are as inclusive as possible. Selected international photographers of Africa and its diaspora outside of the United States have been included in this bibliography. I have also identified significant events that were documented by black photographers in Africa, the Caribbean and North and South America.

Most of my information came as a result of my activity as a free-lance curator and specialist in photography at the Schomburg Center for Research in Black Culture. The Schomburg Center has a substantial collection of books, articles and original works by photographers active between 1940 and 1988. This book will also serve as a guide, survey and/or directory to the holdings in the Schomburg Center's collections of both primary and secondary sources about this topic, as well as being a reference source to other repositories.

Over the past two years I have also depended on friends and associates to keep me informed of related activities throughout the African diaspora. One may think that my references are eclectic. They are! My sources included books, articles in periodicals and newspapers, material identified in a special finding aid called The Ernest D. Kaiser Index to Black Resources at the Schomburg Center, citations in exhibition catalogs, invitations to exhibitions, portfolios and personal interviews.

Unfortunately, there are very few good or retrospective books, bibliographies or indices dedicated to the black photographer. Of note in this area, photographic historian Dr. Rodger Birt of San Francisco State University is currently completing a critical study of the work of James Van Der Zee.

A few notable publications have appeared during this time: Jeanne Moutoussamy-Ashe's *Viewfinders: Black Women Photographers* (1986); the reprint of Roy DeCarava's and Langston Hughes' *The Sweet Flypaper of Life* (1986); the *Black Photographer's Annuals* and *A True Likeness: The Black South of Richard S. Roberts: 1920–1936*.

The Black Photographer's Annuals represent a fantastic source. Begun as an annual in 1972 by Joseph Crawford and other black photographers, they list over 200 photographers from around the country, often with portfolios and biographical data about a particular photographer.

Another important tool for identifying black photographers in the 1970s was the *Photo Newsletter* published by the James Van Der Zee Institute and edited by Vance Allen and Jerome Tucker. The director of the institute was Reginald McGhee.

Ebony and *Our World* magazines from the 1940s through the 1960s have been extremely helpful in locating names and events that have marked photographic history from World War II homefront activities to the civil rights movement. Popular subjects documented by the photographers are musicians, local and national celebrities, neighborhoods and the visual arts movement of the 1970s.

Black photojournalists of the 1940s through the 1960s were employed by such black publications as *Ebony, Flash, Our World* and *Sepia* magazines. Magazines born in the post–civil rights movement era, like *Encore, Essence* and *Black Enterprise* provided additional work opportunities. Very few black photojournalists found work with the larger, mainstream magazines such as *Life, Look* or *Newsweek,* or with the major city daily and weekly newspapers. Many of the photojournalists during this period learned photography in schools of journalism and the military as well as in workshops.

A landmark photographic exhibition of the 1950s was the Museum of Modern Art's "Family of Man," which included the works of only a few black photographers.

One of the more controversial exhibitions that affected the contemporary black art movement was the Metropolitan Museum of Art's exhibition "Harlem on My Mind" in 1968. Heralded in the mainstream media as an in-depth historical examination of the Harlem community, the exhibit, among other things, brought the works of the then-little-known Harlem photographer James Van Der Zee to the attention of the international public. It also drew protests from many black artists, photographers and activists who felt that the show had been organized and conceived with little input from the black arts community.

More recently, several important group exhibitions have toured the country. They include: The Black Photographers' Annual Touring Exhibition in the 1970s; The Rhode Island School of Design's "A Century of Black Photographers: 1840–1960"; the Smithsonian Institution's "We'll Never Turn Back" (civil rights photographs) and "The Tradition Continues: California Black Photographers" at the California Museum of Afro-American History and Culture.

In response to the need for black representation and mobilization in the art world, artists and photography groups were organized in major cities. Community and institutional resources such as the Kamoinge Workshop in New York City and the Organization of Black American Culture in Chicago were established. Black museums also became more prominent around the country. The following institutions were and still are a haven for the exhibiting photographer: the California Museum of Afro-American History and Culture (Los Angeles), the Afro-American Historical and Cultural Museum (Philadelphia), the Studio Museum in Harlem (New York), the Texas Institute of Culture, the Banneker-Douglass Museum (Annapolis, Md.), the University Museum at Hampton Institute (Virginia), the Smithsonian Institution's Anacostia Museum (Washington, DC), the DuSable Museum (Chicago), the Museum of the National Center of Afro-American Artists (Boston), the Museum of African American History (Detroit), Bishop College's Museum of African American Art (Dallas), Rhode Island Black Heritage Society (Providence), Howard University Museum (Washington, DC), the Los Angeles African American Art Museum, En Foco (the Bronx), the Fourth Street Photo Gallery, the Urban League's Gallery 62, The New York Public Library's Schomburg Center for Research in Black Culture and the Countee Cullen Branch Library.

During the civil rights movement a large number of socially committed men and women became photographers. Over the past twenty years photography synthesized art and politics. Many socially conscious photographers emerged during the mid-1960s through the early 1970s and set a new standard in artistic and documentary photography.

Since 1970 fine art photographers have been actively exhibiting and studying photography in workshops, museums, art schools and universities. The fine art photographers are exploring and defining their works under two major categories—photograph as metaphor and photograph as document.

Black photojournalists have won fellowships and awards. Between 1969 and 1986, six black American photojournalists—Ovie Carter, Michel du Cille, Matthew Lewis, Ozier Muhammad, Moneta Sleet, and John White—have won the coveted Pulitzer Prize.

Preservation activities have gained some recent momentum due to the efforts of librarians, curators and photographers themselves. A number of significant collections have been placed in institutions and stock agencies for archival and research purposes, including Austin Hansen's collection at The Schomburg Center; Richard S. Roberts' photography at The South Caroliniana Library in Columbia; Herbert Collins' work at The African Meeting House in Boston; and John W. Mosley's collection at Temple University in Philadelphia.

Unfortunately, this type of activity is still rare. Far too often, the legacies of studio photographers or community oriented photographers are either being destroyed, tucked away or lost.

Many of the organizations and groups formed and active in the 1960s through the 1980s are now defunct. Their aims and mission are a memory retained by just a few. I hope that this book stimulates interest in the reader, photographer, collector, hobbiest, curator and librarian to document the activities of contemporary photographers and to preserve their photographs whether they are viewed as document, art, snapshot or material culture.

Collecting the twentieth century in photographs will provide the historian, archivist, filmmaker, student and the general public with visual testimony of the black community through the photographer as witness, documenter, artist and recorder.

THE PHOTOGRAPHERS

ABBOTT, RANDY
active New York City, 1960s

ABEL, O'NEAL LANCY (1941–   )
active New York City

Abel began photographing in 1963 while working with the Harlem Education Project. His initial interest began at the age of sixteen when his father bought him a camera. Abel studied graphic design, photography and fine arts at New York City Community College in the early 1960s.

Abel's early work, like that of the Civil Rights photographers of the period, documented the activities of student protest marches, political leaders and outdoor rallies in Georgia and New York. Included in his portfolio are Malcolm X, Adam Clayton Powell, Jr., Dick Gregory and the photojournalist Gordon Parks on assignment.

His contemporary images are photographs of social and political events in the Harlem community. His work has been published in *Jet* and *Crisis* magazines.

SELECTED EXHIBITIONS

1987. "Home," 23rd Annual Art Show, Goddard-Riverside Community Center, New York, New York

1987. "Coast to Coast," National Conference of Artists, California Museum of Science and Industry, Los Angeles, California

1986. "East Meets West," Houston Art Gallery, University of Pennsylvania, Philadelphia, Pennsylvania

1985. "Reflections of Dr. Martin Luther King, Jr.," Adam Clayton Powell State Office Building Gallery, New York, New York

See photographs pages 163–164.

ABERNATHY, BILLY "FUNDI"
active Chicago, 1950s–present

Billy Abernathy (Fundi) is best known for his collaboration with Amiri Bakara on the publication *In Our Terribleness*. Abernathy's documentary style surveyed serious, happy, sad and tender moments. His observations and the writings of Amiri Baraka offered an insider's view of the black community in Chicago.

Abernathy began photographing in the late 1950s. He influenced the next generation of social landscape photographers in Chicago, such as Robert Sengstacke, Ozier Muhammad, Frank Stewart and Roy Lewis. Recognized for his activities as a photojournalist as well as a mentor, Abernathy photographed political and religious groups such as the Black Panthers and the Black Muslims in Chicago.

SELECTED BIBLIOGRAPHY

Abernathy, Billy, and Baraka, Imamu Amiri. *In Our Terribleness*, New York/Indianapolis: Bobbs-Merrill, 1970.

Stewart, Frank, "Two Schools: New York and Chicago" (exhibition catalog) Kenkeleba Gallery, New York, 1986.

See photographs pages 165–166.

ADAMS, GENE
active New York City, 1980s

ADAMS, HARRY (1918–   )
active Los Angeles

Harry Adams' work concentrates on the black social life of Los Angeles. As a photojournalist, Adams worked for a number of years for the *California Eagle* and later for the *Los Angeles Sentinel*. As a studio photographer, he documented the families, school children and entertainers who frequented the Los Angeles area. Born in Arkansas, Adams became interested in photography at the age of twelve, however, his career began after he completed his tour of duty in World War II and attended the California Graphics School of Art.

SELECTED EXHIBITIONS

1983–84. "California Black Photographers: The Tradition Continues," The California Museum of Afro-American History and Culture, Los Angeles, California

AJANIKU, IFE
active Washington, DC, 1970s

ALEXANDER, JIM
active Atlanta, 1970–present

ALI, SALIMAH
active New York City, 1976–present

A teacher and freelance photographer, Ali studied fashion photography at the Fashion Institute of Technology. She has worked as a photo editor, photographer's assistant and darkroom technician for commercial studios in New York City. Her photographs have been published in *Ms., Encore, Black Enterprise, Essence* and *Rock and Soul* magazines.

SELECTED EXHIBITIONS
1984. "Art Against Apartheid", Jamaica Art Center, Jamaica, New York
1982. Columbia Law School, Columbia University, New York, New York
1980. "Self-Portrait", The Studio Museum In Harlem, New York, New York (traveling exhibition organized by *Black Enterprise* magazine)
1978. "Directions", The Roosevelt Public Library Art Workshop Gallery, Roosevelt, New York

SELECTED BIBLIOGRAPHY
Moutoussamy-Ashe, Jeanne. *Viewfinders: Black Women Photographers.* New York: Dodd, Mead and Co., 1986.

See photograph page 167.

ALLEN, JULES (1947–   )
active San Francisco and New York City

Jules Allen studied photography at San Francisco State University, where he received a B.F.A. in Photography. Early in his photographic career he worked as a Mental Health Specialist (he holds an M.S. in Counseling). Upon moving to New York City in the late 1970s, he returned to freelancing and teaching photography.

In his personal work Allen explores realism in photography, juxtaposing popular cultural artifacts with his subjects. Critic Sherry Turner DeCarava states that Allen's pictures achieve a crucial balance between form and content in their rich explorations of the perceptual world.

Currently, Allen is teaching photography at the Queensborough Community College (New York City). He continues to produce fine art photographs and exhibits in the New York area. In 1980 he received the Creative Artists Public Service Award in New York City. Allen holds an M.F.A. in Photography from Hunter College (New York City) where he studied with Roy DeCarava.

COLLECTIONS

Schomburg Center for Research in Black Culture, The New York Public Library, New York, New York

SELECTED EXHIBITIONS

1982. "Image and Imagination," Jazzonia Gallery, Detroit, Michigan
1980. "Self-Portrait," Group show, Studio Museum in Harlem, New York, New York
1980. "Photographs: Beuford Smith, Frank Stewart, Jules Allen," Gallery 62, New York, New York

SELECTED BIBLIOGRAPHY

"Photographic View: 'Mixed Bag,'" *New York Times*, January 18, 1981.
Black Photographer's Annual, Vol. 4, New York: Another View Publishing, 1981.
"*Photographs: Beuford Smith, Frank Stewart, Jules Allen* (exhibition catalog), New York: National Urban League, 1980.
"New Rituals—New Visions," *Black Enterprise*, December 1980.
"Black Eyes/Light: Photos by Frank Stewart and Jules Allen," *New York Amsterdam News*, February 17, 1979.
"Images of Human Awareness," *Artweek*, November 27, 1976.
"Jules Allen Opens Charles Turner Art Gallery," *The Sun Reporter*, November 25, 1976.

ALLEN, VANCE (1939–)
active New York City

Vance Allen has been active in photography since the mid-1960s. Born in Asbury Park, New Jersey, he studied photography at Pratt Institute. He began his career as a freelance photographer working for large publishing houses in New York City. His photographs have been published in *Artweek, The New York Times*, and *Black Enterprise*. In 1971 Allen became editor of the *Photo Newsletter* of the now defunct James Van Der Zee Institute. Allen is a member of the National Press Photographers Association, Inc., the American Society of Picture Professionals, Inc., and has exhibited his photographs at the Brooklyn Museum, The Schomburg Center for Research in Black Culture, the Metropolitan Museum of Art, and the Studio Museum in Harlem in New York City. His reviews of photography books appear in national publications.

COLLECTIONS

Schomburg Center for Research in Black Culture, The New York Public Library, New
    York, New York
Private Collections

SELECTED EXHIBITIONS

1986. "Two Schools: New York and Chicago," Kenkeleba House Gallery, New York, New
    York
1978. One-man show, "The Black Male Nude," Studio Five, New York, New York
1971. "Eye Rap," Studio Museum in Harlem, New York, New York

SELECTED BIBLIOGRAPHY

Growing Up Black, South Carolina University Medical Center (film strip).

See photographs pages 168–171.

ALLEN, WINIFRED HALL
active New York City, 1940s

ANDERSON, BILL
active New York City, 1950s

ANDERSON, GORDON
active New York City, 1946–present

Gordon Anderson's chief subject matter has been the performers and personalities who
frequented the Apollo Theatre during its heyday.

Anderson began photographing the entertainers on stage as well as backstage at the
famed Apollo Theatre on West 125th Street in Harlem in 1948. He became known as "Doc
Anderson," the unofficial Apollo photographer.

Anderson's first creative interest was in music; he played the piano in local clubs in his
native Baltimore. He became interested in photography around the same time. Anderson
was photographing the entertainers at Baltimore's Royale Theater when Frank Schiffman,
owner of the Apollo, invited him to visit the Apollo Theatre. After his arrival in New York in
the late 1940s, Anderson embarked on his career as unofficial Apollo photographer, taking
candid photographs of virtually every performer who appeared on stage there: Josephine
Baker, Richard Pryor, Johnny Mathis, Billie Holiday, Ella Fitzgerald, The Supremes, James
Brown, Ethel Waters and Dizzy Gillespie to name a few.

Anderson's photographs were used in Ted Fox's book, *Showtime at the Apollo*, a popular history of the Apollo. Since 1981, Anderson has exhibited and lectured widely.

COLLECTIONS

Schomburg Center for Research in Black Culture, The New York Public Library, New York
Private Collections

SELECTED BIBLIOGRAPHY

Fox, Ted, *Showtime at the Apollo*, New York: H. Holt, 1983.
"He Shot the Stars at the Apollo," *New York Daily News*, February 20, 1984.
"Memories Live on in His Photographs," *New York Daily News*, July 18, 1982.
"Gordon Anderson Memories of the Apollo," *Class*, July, 1985.

ANDRADES, ERNEST
active Boston 1970s–present

After studying art with George Demetrios of Gloucester, Massachusetts, and at the Museum School of Fine Arts in Boston, Andrades (a painter and sculptor) began taking photographs in the mid-1970s. Andrades credits his trip to Ecuador as a turning point in his coming to photography as an art form. It was there that his photographs of everyday subjects began to stand by themselves as expressions of his artistic vision rather than simply serving as the source material for his paintings. He comments, "I simply take photographs of what's already there." A purist, he desires to present moments in the world exactly as he sees them—he photographs with a 55mm. normal lens and presents his photographs uncropped.

Andrades has won numerous awards, scholarships and fellowships for his painting and sculpture. In 1969, he traveled to Europe after becoming the eighty-sixth recipient of the Clarissa Bartlett Traveling Scholarship awarded him by the Museum School of Fine Arts. His photographs, paintings and sculpture has been exhibited at the Copley Society, Massachusetts Institute of Technology's Hayden Gallery, the Museum of the National Center of Afro-American Artists, the Boston Museum of Fine Arts, and he has had shows in both Munich and Frankfurt, Germany.

SELECTED BIBLIOGRAPHY

"Ernest Andrades, Recent Color Photographs," (exhibition brochure), the Museum of the
    National Center of Afro-American Artists, Boston, Massachusetts.

ANDREWS, BERT (1931–   )
active New York City

Bert Andrews is renowned for his powerful and extraordinary documentation of over thirty years of black theatrical productions. Among the production companies whose plays he has photographed are the Negro Ensemble Company, New Federal Theatre, and the Frank Silvera Writers' Workshop. Andrews' collection is considered to be the largest visual documentation of the contemporary black theater movement. He has photographed two Pulitzer Prize winning productions: *The Subject Was Roses* with Martin Sheen and Jack Albertson, and playwright Charles Fuller's *A Soldier's Play*. His subjects include film and screen stars such as Cicely Tyson, Theresa Merritt, Robert Hooks, Louis Gossett, Jr., Billy Dee Williams, Diana Sands, Adolph Caesar, and Phylicia Ayers-Allen.

Andrews' interest in photography began while in the U.S. Army during the 1950s. He credits photographer Chuck Stewart as being his mentor and teacher in the early years. He is currently working on a book entitled, "Bert Andrews: A 20-Year Retrospective of Blacks in American Theatre." He was also a photographer for the Actor's Equity Association. His photographs appear in John Willis' volumes *Theatre World* and are found in a number of theater anthologies that have been published over the last twenty-five years.

In 1985 over 100,000 prints and negatives representing thirty years of his life's work were destroyed by a fire in his studio. Andrews is attempting to restore the collection by making copies of the original prints which are held in private and public collections.

COLLECTIONS

Schomburg Center for Research in Black Culture, The New York Public Library, New York, New York
Negro Ensemble Company, New York, New York
Private Collections

SELECTED BIBLIOGRAPHY

"Black Theater in America: 20 Years" *Delegate*, 1983, pp. 306–307.
Jasiri, Libre, "Black Theater," *Dawn*, April 1983, pp. 17–18.
Interview with Deborah Willis-Thomas in *Scenes from the 20th Century Stage*, Exhibition Catalog, New York: Schomburg Center for Research in Black Culture, 1983.
Easy (The Black Arts Magazine), October 1980, pp. 18–19.

See photographs pages 172–174.

ANTHONY, DARIUS
active Los Angeles, 1980s

AUSTIN, GENE
active New York City, 1970s

AYORINDE, OMOBOWALE (1945–)
active Rochester, New York

Omobowale Ayorinde is known for his photographic profile of the Rastafarians in Jamaica. The photoessay entitled "A Sense of Rasta" documents the private life of the movement through the eyes of a New York Rastafarian. He writes, "my personal interest in photography could be described as cultural ethnology using the medium as a means of exploration. This lineage of Rasta, this linkage to East Africa is but yet another umbilical cord in the vast African diaspora. It is with this continued interest that I resume exploration of what I've come to know as 'Black Pulsations.'"

Ayorinde received a B.F.A. in photography and cinematography in 1975 from the Massachusetts College of Art and an M.F.A. in photography from the Rochester Institute of Technology in 1977. A photography instructor at the Rochester Institute of Technology, Ayorinde has worked as a curator, film and video producer/director, freelance photographer and staff photographer for various museums and corporations. He has also been an architectural photographer and a counselor for teenagers in Boston and Rochester.

COLLECTIONS
Schomburg Center for Research in Black Culture, New York, New York

SELECTED EXHIBITIONS
1985. "A Sense of Rasta," Museum of National Center of Afro-American Artists, Boston, Massachusetts
1984. Group Show, Gallery 4 Eleven, Rochester, New York
1984. "Black Photographers from South Africa to South Carolina," Otto Rene Castillo Gallery, New York, New York
1984. "14 Photographers," Schomburg Center, New York, New York
1983. "To Each His/Her Own," Sibley's Ward Gallery, Rochester, New York
1983. One-man show, Community Folk Art Gallery, Syracuse, New York
1977. Group Show, Museum of Modern Art, Sao Paulo, Brazil
1976. "Looking Back," Wilson Commons, University of Rochester, Rochester, New York

See photographs pages 175–178.

BAILEY, J. EDWARD
active Detroit, 1950–1980

Educator, author, photographer and photojournalist, J. Edward Bailey became interested in photography in the early 1950s. In 1952 he won a prize in a *Life* photo contest and tried to get employment in *Life*'s bureau office in Detroit. Unsuccessful in getting assignments from the bureau chief after winning the prize and told to take his work to black publications, Bailey was determined to break into the mainstream publications. For the next seven years, he studied the art of photography, lighting, photographic theory and chemistry. He had his first big break in 1958 when *Time*'s assistant bureau chief gave him freelance assignments in Detroit.

Bailey credits his *Time* cover photograph of John F. Kennedy kicking off his presidential campaign in Detroit as the turning point in his career. From that time on, he shot major stories for *Time*, *Life*, *Fortune*, and *Sports Illustrated*. He was also hired by the auto manufacturers in the city to photograph for them.

He was commissioned by the Detroit Institute of Arts to do a photo essay entitled, "The City Within" in 1968. The photo essay became a touring exhibition throughout the state of Michigan and the country for four years. Concerned about the development of young people and education, Bailey lectured throughout the United States. He won awards for his photography; one of particular merit is the John F. Kennedy Award for Excellence in Photojournalism. He won this in 1961, when he was the only black journalist on Kennedy's campaign train.

Bailey taught photojournalism at Wayne State University and in 1976 as a bicentennial-initiated project organized, researched and photographed "Living Legends in Black." This project, funded by the Ford Motor Company, profiled 200 outstanding black Americans in the business, art, social sciences and music fields. His portraits are concerned with formal visual relationships of the subject and his/her environment/occupation. The exhibition and subsequent publication included sports figures Muhammad Ali, Arthur Ashe; photographer Griffith Davis; art historian Edmund B. Gaither; political leaders John Conyers, Barbara Jordan; journalist Ida Lewis, Carl T. Rowan; and civil rights leaders Bayard Rustin, Rosa Parks, Vernon Jordan, Roy Wilkins and Andrew Young.

SELECTED BIBLIOGRAPHY

Bailey, J. Edward, III, *Living Legends in Black*, Detroit: Bailey Publishing Company, 1976.

Baker, Tracy, "He Remembers Where He Comes From," *News Photographer*, September 1980, pp. 44–46.

BARBOZA, ANTHONY (1944–   )
active New York City

Anthony Barboza is most renowned for his innovative commercial work—advertising, fashion and editorial photography. He has created strongly realized work in several distinctly different areas.

Born in New Bedford, Massachusetts, Barboza left New Bedford for New York City at the age of nineteen, after reading an advertisement for a photography course there. He studied photography at night and worked as a messenger during the day for Hearst Magazines. Shortly after, he met the noted fashion photographer, Hugh Bell, and studied the art of printing and photography with him. Around the same time he became acquainted with a group of black photographers who met frequently to critique works and discuss photography and the role of the black photographer. The group, whose members included Roy DeCarava, Jimmie Mannas, Lou Draper, Daniel Dawson, Adger Cowans, Albert Fennar, Shawn Walker, Ray Francis and others, was known as the Kamoinge Workshop.

In 1965, Barboza joined the Navy. He worked part-time as a photographer for the base's newspaper in Pensacola, Florida, and continued to make reportage photographs. As a result of his commitment to the art he had two one-man shows. Upon returning to New York after his stint in the Navy, Barboza opened his first studio where he has become a successful fashion, advertising and editorial photographer.

Barboza's personal work is an extension of his commercial work. He uses images to make statements and to entice viewers to create and explore their own personal reactions. Commenting on his portraits of artists, intellectuals, models, boxers and other sports figures, he says: "When I shoot a portrait, I meet another person's space. I interpret it and define it."

In 1975, Barboza pursued portraiture as a hobby, primarily taking portraits of close friends and admired artists. By 1980, and with the assistance of a National Endowment for the Arts grant, Barboza published his first book; *Black Borders*, which includes 30 portraits of the 150 images he took during this five-year period.

Frontality is a trend in portraiture that only a few photographers have used successfully: because of his sensitivity to the medium and to his subjects, Barboza is one of the few. Barboza wrote of his portraits, "I am not showing their faces and bodies and other elements that indicate what their work looks like—to catch not the outward appearances, but the essences of their work—and getting into the photograph forms exemplifying their work."

Characteristic of Barboza's work is the love he has for his art. He has synthesized all of his interest in his art. Barboza is a poet, a short story writer and a collector of nineteenth-century photographic images produced by black photographers. He is one of the early founders and officers of the International Black Photographers (IBP), a group of contemporary black photographers dedicated to acknowledging the contributions of living black photographers who were active before the 1960s. He has been on a number of photographic panels, among them the Creative Artists Public Service Program (CAPS) New York, National Conference of Artists, the Massachusetts State Council on the Arts, and the National Endowment for the Arts.

COLLECTIONS

Howard University, Washington, DC
Museum of Modern Art, New York, New York
Orleans Public Library, Orleans, New York
Schomburg Center for Research in Black Culture, New York, New York

Studio Museum in Harlem, New York, New York

University of Ghana, Accra, Ghana

University of Mexico, Mexico City, Mexico

SELECTED ONE-PERSON EXHIBITIONS

1982. "Introspect: The Photography of Anthony Barboza," Studio Museum in Harlem, New York, New York

1974. James Van Der Zee Institute, Friends Gallery, New York, New York

1974. Light Gallery, New York, New York

1973. Light Impressions Gallery, Rochester, New York

1969. Jacksonville Art Museum, Jacksonville, Florida

1967. Emily Lowe Gallery, University of Miami, Miami, Florida

1966. Pensacola Art Museum, Pensacola, Florida

SELECTED GROUP EXHIBITIONS

1982. "Photography: Image and Imagination," Jazzonia Gallery, Detroit, Michigan

1982. "Recent Acquisitions," Schomburg Center for Research in Black Culture, New York, New York

1981. "Self-Portrait," Studio Museum in Harlem, New York, New York

1979. "9 Contemporary Photographers," Witkin Gallery, New York, New York

1978. "Mirrors and Windows," Museum of Modern Art, New York, New York

1975. International Center of Photography, New York, New York

1974. Columbia College, Chicago, Illinois

1972. Floating Foundation of Photography, New York, New York

1972. Studio Museum in Harlem, New York, New York

1971. Addison Gallery of American Art, Andover, Massachusetts

SELECTED BIBLIOGRAPHY

Introspect: The Photography of Anthony Barboza (exhibition catalog), New York: Studio Museum in Harlem, 1982.

Thornton, Gene, "Two Approaches to the Portrait Genre," *New York Times*, December 19, 1982.

"The World of Commercial Photographers," *Black Enterprise*, February 1982.

Gardner, Roberta, "Spatial Relations: Portraits by Anthony Barboza," *Camera Arts*, 1981.

"Anthony Barboza," *Camera*, June 1980.

Barboza, Anthony, *Black Borders*, New York: Anthony Barboza, 1980.

Black Photographers Annual (Vols. I–IV), New York: Another View Publishing (1972–1980).

Edelson, Michael, "The Four Faces of Barboza," *35MM Photography*, Spring 1977.

"Anthony Barboza," *Creative Camera*, May 1975.

Time–Life Photography Annual, New York: Time/Life Publishers, 1974.

See photographs pages 179–184.

BARCLAY, CONRAD
active New York City, 1980s

BARNES, DONNAMARIE
active New York City, 1970–present

Barnes studied art and photography during the Sarah Lawrence College Junior year abroad program in France, at The Boston Museum School, and at Cooper Union in New York. She is currently teaching photography at Hunter College and City University of New York and works as a photo editor for an international photo news service based in New York City. Barnes has also worked as a photojournalist and photo archivist for the James Van Der Zee photograph collection at the Studio Museum in Harlem.

Barnes' images of the city and its teenagers are conceptual in nature. Her photographs seek to heighten the relationships of young adults and their environment. Strange relationships between people and structure develop into elements of design and surrealism.

SELECTED EXHIBITIONS

1981. Emerson College, Massachusetts
1980. Cooper Union, New York, New York
1979. Cinque Gallery, New York, New York

SELECTED BIBLIOGRAPHY

Arts in the Schools, A Study of Art Programming in the New York Public School System,
New York: New York City Board of Education, 1977.

BARNES HILLIAN, VANESSA
active Washington, DC, 1980s

BARNETT, ARZA
active Huntington, West Virginia, 1970s

BARNETT, EDWARD
active France, 1950s

BECKLES, KEN
active New York City, 1970s

BELL, HUGH
active New York City, 1956–present

Advertising and documentary photographer Hugh Bell has been active in the medium since the mid-1950s. Initially a fashion photographer, Bell is credited by a number of the next generation of photographers as a mentor and teacher. He has a B.A. from New York University in filmmaking. His style of advertising and editorial photography is reportage. His photographs are published in journals, magazines and books such as the exhibition catalog "The Family of Man," *Bird, Legend of Charlie Parker* and *Jazz Past.* Over the years, Bell's photographs have appeared in *Popular Photography, Black Enterprise, Esquire, Essence* and *Newsweek.*

His subjects range from jazz photography to the corporate board room. Bell's ads for Coca-Cola, Eastern Airlines and IBM have appeared on billboards and in trade magazines.

See photographs pages 185–186.

BELLAMY, FAY D.
active Atlanta, 1970s

BELLAMY, LISA
active Staten Island, New York, 1970s

BERNARD, DONALD (1943–   )
active Los Angeles

Donald Bernard photographs people young and old, the famous and the unknown in the Los Angeles area. His images are straightforward and relaxed; his subjects look comfortably at the lens. Bernard says that he likes to make eye contact: "It's the same as when you are talking to someone, we need to look at their eyes, find out something about them."

Bernard became interested in photography while studying art at California State University, Los Angeles, eventually taking photography classes at the Otis Art Institute. He has exhibited widely in the Los Angeles area, and his photographs of artists and writers have included such artists as Varnette Honeywood and sculptor Marsha Johnson.

SELECTED EXHIBITIONS

Los Angeles Photography Center, Los Angeles, California
California Afro-American Museum, Los Angeles, California

SELECTED BIBLIOGRAPHY

Gunther, Darlene, "Photographs Try to Capture Inner Beauty of Women," *Los Angeles Times*, March 6, 1985.

BEY, DAWOUD (1953–)
active New York City

Dawoud Bey records the ordinary, daily occurences in his own life, especially the streets of Harlem.

Bey's interest in photography began in 1967 when he was given an Argus C3 35 mm. rangefinder camera. In 1969, he went to the Metropolitan Museum of Art to view the exhibition "Harlem on My Mind." In an interview Bey stated that the exhibition, which was the first photography exhibit he had seen, had a profound effect on him. "What impressed me the most about the 'Harlem on My Mind' exhibition was that it contradicted everything I had been taught to believe Harlem was." The spirit of that exhibition stayed with him over the years and has become the cornerstone for the works in one of his many photographic essays, "Harlem U.S.A."

Dawoud Bey, an accomplished writer as well as a photographer, studied photography at the School of Visual Arts (New York). His vision is of the contemporary style of documentary photography. He believes that "it is important, if a photograph is to succeed, that it cease to be merely a record of a person, place or thing. It must transcend that. To be a photographer one must be in love with life. And light. The kind of light I am concerned with in these photographs is that which imbues the environment with a sense of abstraction."

Bey has received numerous grants and fellowships; among them are the New York Foundation for the Arts (1986), Light Work, Syracuse, New York (1985), New York State Council on the Arts (1984).

COLLECTIONS

Brooklyn Museum, Brooklyn, New York
International Center of Photography, New York, New York
Schomburg Center for Research in Black Culture, New York, New York
Studio Museum in Harlem, New York, New York
Fogg Art Museum, Cambridge, Massachusetts
Atlanta Life Insurance Company, Atlanta, Georgia

SELECTED EXHIBITIONS

1987. "New American Photographs," Fogg Art Museum, Cambridge, Massachusetts

1986. "Dawoud Bey," Light Work, Syracuse, New York

1985. "Honey! I'm Home!," Midtown Art Center, Houston, Texas

1984. "The Lower East Side: A Portrait in Photographs," City Gallery, New York, New York

1983. "Five Photographers from the Visual Arts Referral Service/CAPS," Midtown Y Photography Gallery, New York, New York

1982. "Photography: Image and Imagination," Jazzonia Gallery, Detroit, Michigan

1980. "Self Portrait," Museum of Fine Arts, Springfield, Massachusetts

1979. "The Black Photographer," San Francisco Museum of Modern Art, San Francisco, California

1977. "Photographs," Louis Meisel Gallery, New York, New York

SELECTED BIBLIOGRAPHY

De Carava, Sherry Turner, "Dawoud Bey's Harlem," *Amsterdam News* (New York), February 3, 1979.

White, Phoebe, "Good Documents, Bad Fantasies," *Folio*, March 1979.

Lifson, Ben, "The Heirs of Robert Frank," *The Village Voice*, February 12, 1979.

Stout, Ruth, "Negatives Positive for Jamaica," *The New York Daily News*, August 19, 1980.

Sunbury 9, New York: Sunbury Press, Inc., 1980.

Schoener, Allon, *Harlem on My Mind, 1900–1978*, New York: Dell Publishing Co., 1979.

Black Photographers Annual, Vol. 4, New York: Another View Publishing, Inc., 1981.

See photographs pages 187–189.

BIBBS, HART LEROY (1930–   )

active Paris, France, and Kansas City, Kansas

Hart Leroy Bibbs was born in Kansas City, Kansas. During the late 1940s and early 1950s he worked as a commercial photographer in the Kansas City area. Interested in music, he moved to Europe in the late 1950s and settled in Paris, where he began to photograph the jazz musicians who performed in the nightclubs throughout Europe. He lived in Paris for many years photographing poets, writers and musicians in his studio and in the local nightclubs.

Bibbs' photographs are not straightforward portraits—they are experimental, lucid and often unrecognizable color images of such jazz legends as Archie Shepp and Rassan Roland Kirk. He says that his experiments are emotional and expressive, suggesting the rhythm of the jazz sounds.

COLLECTIONS

Schomburg Center for Research in Black Culture, The New York Public Library, New York, New York

SELECTED EXHIBITIONS

1983. Kodak Center, Paris, France
1980. Museum of Modern Art, New York, New York
1971. Gallery Ranson, Paris, France

See photograph page 190.

BLACK, BOB
active Chicago, 1960s

BLUE, CARROLL
active San Diego, 1980s

BONAIR, ANTHONY
active New York City and Trinidad, West Indies, 1975–present

Anthony Bonair became interested in photography while working as a laboratory technician at Wometco Photographic Services. He moved to the United States from his native Trinidad in 1968. A graduate of Hunter College, City University of New York, Bonair studied photography with Roy DeCarava.

Bonair's interest is in dance, whether formal or on the streets at Carnival. He has exhibited in galleries in the New York area. His photographs have been published in *Dance Magazine, Dance World* and the *Caribbean–American Carnival Journals.*

See photograph page 191.

BOUGH, MARTIN
active New York City, 1970s

BOURNE, ST. CLAIR
active New York City, 1960s

BRAITHWAITE, HILTON
active Newark, New Jersey, 1980s

BRANCH, HARRISON (1947–   )
active Oregon

Born in New York City, Harrison studied photography at the San Francisco Art Institute (B.F.A.) and Yale University School of Art (M.F.A.). He is currently professor of Art at the Oregon State University at Corvallis. He has exhibited widely for the last fifteen years and is working with a large format camera capturing the beauty and mysteries in nature.

COLLECTIONS
Bibliotheque Nationale, Paris
Oakland Museum, Oakland, California
Seattle Arts Commission, Seattle, Washington
International Museum of Photography at George Eastman House, Rochester, New York

See photographs pages 192–193.

BRANCH, WALLACE
active Hartford, Connecticut, 1980s

BRATHWAITE, KWAME (1938–   )
active New York City

Born in New York, Brathwaite began photographing in the early 1960s. Influenced by the political leaders and rallies in Harlem during this period, Brathwaite photographed events and political leaders in Harlem. In 1962, he began photographing the "Naturally" shows, where models did not straighten their hair, a pioneering effort for models during this period.

In 1968, he traveled to Africa, visiting and photographing the people of West and East Africa. As a result of this trip, a photo essay was televised on ABC's television program "Like It Is" with Gil Noble. During the 1970s he covered activities in the United States and Africa: the funeral of Kwame Nkrumah, the Ali-Foreman Heavyweight Championship fight in Zaire, "Wattstax '72," conventions, etc. His files include portraits of such African and Caribbean Heads of States as Sekou Torre, Julius Nyerere, Thomas Sankara, William Tubman, Maurice Bishop and Michael Manley.

He has photographed for the Black Music Association, the Apollo Theatre and the Harlem Urban Development Corporation.

COLLECTIONS

Schomburg Center for Research in Black Culture, The New York Public Library, New York, New York

See photographs pages 194–196.

BRATHWAITE, RONNIE
active New York City, 1970s

BRISSET, BONNIE
active New York City, 1970s

BROOKS, JOE (1948–   )
active Washington, DC

Brooks, a photographer for the United States Information Agency, has been working in the field since 1977. His mentor, former USIA photographer Richard Saunders, trained and guided Brooks' career as a photojournalist. He also credits Johnson Publications' photographer Maurice Sorrell as a strong influence in his life. In addition to working for the USIA's *Topic* magazine, Brooks has had work published in *Jet* and *Ebony* magazines.

SELECTED PUBLICATIONS

Cupples, Cynthia, "Focus on Photography," *USIA World*, United States Information, September 1982, Vol. 1, No. 4.

SELECTED EXHIBITIONS

1982 "F-4: Four Washington Photographers", Martin Luther King Memorial Library, Washington, DC

See photographs page 197.

BROWN, BARBARA
active Washington, DC, 1970s

BROWN, ED
active New York City, 1970s

Brown, Emmett   (1918–1959)
active Indianapolis

After studying at Tennessee State University, Emmett I. Brown, Jr., opened The Brown Show Case photographic studio in the late 1940s on Indiana Avenue in Indianapolis. The studio was located in a popular area of town where well-known musicians played in the local clubs. Brown's photographs of the social activities of Indianapolis included church groups, street scenes, sports figures such as Joe Louis and Sugar Ray Robinson, and musicians Dizzy Gillespie and Buddy Parker.

Brown moved to Chattanooga, Tennessee, in the mid-1950s where he became the editor of the *Sepia Fame* magazine. Returning to Indianapolis in 1956, he opened a new studio specializing in portrait photography.

COLLECTIONS
Indiana Historical Society Library, Indianapolis, Indiana
Mrs. Alta Jean Bellinger, Indianapolis, Indiana

SELECTED BIBLIOGRAPHY
"Emmett Brown: Indiana Avenue Photographer," *Indiana Historical Society Library,* Volume 2, February 1980.

Brown, John A.
active Atlanta, 1970s

Brown, Larry
active Brooklyn, New York, 1980s

Brown, Lisa
active Seattle, Washington, 1970s

Brown, Owen
active New York City, 1970s

Brown, Shelly
active New York City, 1970s

BROWN, TREVOR
active New York City, 1970s

BUNYON, CURTIS
active New York City, 1970s

BURNETT, SPENCER
active New York City, 1970s

BURNS, MILLIE
active New York City, 1980–present

Millie Burns studied art and photography at the Rochester Institute of Technology, Parsons School of Design and the School of Visual Arts. As a photographer and advocate for the arts, she has lectured and exhibited widely. Her photographs of her travels, particularly Morocco, have received critical acclaim.

Burns' recent work includes hand-colored abstractions of the commonplace. She describes her photographs: "My personal photographs express my visions of solitude, seasons and time, of scenes left to themselves when man has departed or not been there at all. Photography is a continual process of anticipation and discovery, exploring new places or seeing familiar scenes in a new light."

Burns has received grants from the New York Foundation for the Arts and the Artists Space/Artists Grants for her photography. She is a member of the American Society of Magazine Photographers and the Professional Women Photographers.

COLLECTIONS

King Hassan II of Morocco
Price Waterhouse & Company, New York, New York
Museum of the Hudson Highlands, New York (slides on file)
Studio Museum in Harlem, New York, New York
Percent for Art Program, Pennsylvania
Rotunda Gallery, Bronx, New York
Art Information Center, New York

SELECTED EXHIBITIONS

Bronx Museum of the Arts, New York, New York
Rotunda Gallery, Bronx, New York

Museum of Science and Industry, Chicago, Illinois
Gallery III, New York, New York

SELECTED BIBLIOGRAPHY

Rauschenbush, Stephanie, "Photographs by Women Artists at Rotunda Gallery," *The Prospect Press*, April 2–15, 1987.

Schiller, Marlene, "Refreshing Talent in 2 Snug Harbor Exhibits," *Staten Island Advance*, August 14, 1984.

The Zaner Corporation, *Small Works*, Zaner Gallery, Rochester, New York, 1982.

See photographs pages 198–199

BURTON, AUKRAM
active Boston, 1977–present

Photographer and media specialist Aukram Burton studied film and video at the Massachusetts Institute of Technology and photography at the New England School of Photography. He holds a B.A. and a M.A. from the University of Massachusetts. He has produced a number of photographic essays on the countries he visited such as China, Cuba, Nigeria and Japan. His images are not the straightforward travel photographs of foreign countries normally published in magazines. The subjects are posed as naturally as possible, and the photographs juxtapose doorways and outdoor sculpture with human figures.

Burton's film and video productions include such titles as "Rainbow in China" (1984), "Rhumba Sabado" (1983) and "The Griot: A Portrait of Allan Rohan Crite" (1981).

SELECTED EXHIBITIONS:

1987. "Glimpses of the Middle Kingdom—Photographs of the Peoples Republic of China," The Museum of the National Center of Afro-American Artists, Boston, Massachusetts

1986. Guangdong Fine Arts Academy, China

1986. Harriet Tubman Gallery, Boston, Massachusetts

1985. Yunnan Institute of Nationalities, Kunming, China

1980. Grinnell Galleries, New York, New York

1979. Piano Craft Guild Gallery, Boston, Massachusetts

BUSH, MURIEL AGATHA FORTUNE (1910–1983)
active Atlantic City, New Jersey

Born in New York, Bush developed an interest in photography in the late 1920s. As a teenager, she had two aspirations—to be a model and journalist. Unable to pursue a career in modeling, she attended Miner Teachers College in Washington, DC. Graduating from college in the mid-1920s she moved to Atlantic City, New Jersey, and was hired as a grade school teacher at the Indiana Avenue School.

Bush attended photography workshops in the area and began to photograph visitors on the Boardwalk in the 1920s, continuing through the mid-1940s. Married in 1947, she set up a photo studio on the Boardwalk with her husband. Bush won first place in a photography contest, and her photograph was published in a local magazine. Her photographs include families and couples on the Boardwalk, school children and social events. As a commercial feature in her studio, she offered season greeting cards with images of her subjects in family settings. Her portrait work is pictorial in nature, with soft focus and soft lighting.

See photographs pages 200–201.

BYRD, LEONARD
active New York City, 1975–present

Leonard Byrd, a fine art photographer, is a native of New Jersey. He attended Parsons School of Design, The Educational Alliance and the City University of New York. He has a B.A. in film. Byrd is presently working in photo assemblages and constructing graphic patterns of nature scenes.

In his own words, "The technique of photo-assemblage affords me the means to explore different framing ratios to capture the feeling and mood of a place. By using standard photographic equipment and commonly available services, I can make a picture almost any shape or size, thereby giving me the artistic freedom of choice to capture the essence of a scene as I see and feel it. The process also forces me to establish the form so that I can control the piece and/or series with predictable results."

SELECTED EXHIBITIONS
Borough of Manhattan Community College, New York, New York
Richmond College, Staten Island, New York
Cinque Gallery, New York, New York
Rotunda Gallery, Bronx County Building, Bronx, New York
Brooklyn Botanic Gardens, Brooklyn, New York

See photograph page 202.

CALLENDAR, RUPPERT
active New York City, 1970s

CALLWOOD, DENNIS OLANZO (1942–   )
active California

Dennis Olanzo Callwood was born in St. Thomas, Virgin Islands. He received a B.A. from the University of California at Santa Cruz and studied photography at the University of Veracruz in Mexico. He later attended the University of Southern California and earned a M.F.A. in photography.

Callwood has always experimented freely with new techniques such as his most recent project, "Autofocus: The Development of a New Photographic Language." Explaining this theory he writes, "My portfolio is an exploration of new technology—the autofocus camera. The point here is not that the portfolio was made using an autofocus camera; the point is what occurs between the photographer and the subject when the need for looking through the viewfinder is eliminated. In autofocus work, the camera need not be held up to the eye. Framing and composition are not under tight control. It is the emotional content of the situation that matters, and recording it becomes a matter of intuition. I found that using this technique made the act of making photographs increasingly part of my life—a twenty-four hour activity. It became an adjunct to perception, rather than deliberate art-making." About his imagery he writes, ". . . I work to produce bodies of work that have not only artistic merit, but also social and cultural ramifications."

An active exhibitor, Callwood's photographs are of people of the Los Angeles area—a multi-cultural city and its rituals, which include weddings and other celebrations.

SELECTED EXHIBITIONS

1987. "Autofocus," West Los Angeles Municipal Gallery, Los Angeles, California

1986. "America—Another Perspective," New York University, New York, New York

1986. The Lloyd Gallery, Spokane, Washington

1986. Cosejo Mexicano de Fotografica, AC, Mexico

1986. University of Vera Cruz, Xalapa, Vera Cruz, Mexico

1986. Photovision, Madrid, Spain

1985. Los Angeles Center for Photographic Studies, Los Angeles, California

1984. Museo Nacional de Bellas Artes de la Habana, Habana, Cuba

SELECTED BIBLIOGRAPHY

KNBC-TV, Los Angeles, CA. "Expressions in Black," in "Slices of Life from the Black Experience," February 1985

"Black Women: Achievements Against the Odds," Washington, DC, Smithsonian Institution Traveling Exhibition (SITES), 1984

Fabricius, Klaus & Red Saunders, editors. *24 Hours in the Life of Los Angeles*, New York: Alfred Van der Marck Editions, 1984

A Day in the Life of London, Sydney, Australia: McGregor Publishing, 1984

"Contemporary Black Photography," *Obscura Magazine*, Los Angeles: Los Angeles Center for Photographic Studies, November 1982 [Reviews]

Rosas, Alejandro, "Siete Fotografos Latinos en Los Angeles," *La Communidad*, no. 219, March 1984

Berland, Diana, "On Photography, Facing up to a Challenge in Exhibit," *Los Angeles Times* Calendar, January 6, 1985

Nicholson, Chuck, "Defining the Portrait," *Artweek*, vol. 16, no. 2, p. 12

See photographs pages 203–205.

CARTER, DWIGHT
active New York City, 1980s

CARTER, OVIE (1946–   )
active Chicago

Ovie Carter began his photographic career in 1969. Born in Indianola, Mississippi, he studied photography in Chicago. Working as a staff photographer at the *Chicago Tribune*, he produced a photo essay (1970) on the effects of drug addiction in the Chicago community. In 1975 he won the coveted Pulitzer Prize for International Reporting for his photographs of famine in Africa and India. He was cited by the Pulitzer committee for using his camera with "rare sensitivity to show to an unheeding world the faces of hunger as he saw them." The same year he won the Overseas Press Club award for best newspaper photography from abroad. He also won the first prize in the prestigious World Press Photo Contest in Amsterdam, Holland.

Carter is a member of the Black Journalists Association and the Chicago Press Photographers Association and was twice honored by holding the title of Illinois Press Photographer of the Year.

SELECTED BIBLIOGRAPHY

"Under 30 and Moving Up," *Black Enterprise*, August 1975, p. 20.

Stein, M. L., *Blacks in Communication*, New York: J. Messner, 1972.

"Selected by Jurors for the Pulitzer Prize for 1975," *New York Times*, May 6, 1975.

Chicago Tribune, May 7, 1972, section 1, p. 3

CHARLES, ELLIOT
active Los Angeles, 1970s

CHARLES, ROLAND
active Los Angeles, California, 1970–present

Born in New Orleans, Charles is a fashion and editorial photographer in the Los Angeles area. His professional career began in 1970 in New Orleans. His photographs have appeared in such national magazines as *Newsweek, Ebony* and *US* as well as in trade magazines.

Charles is the president and founder of Black Photographers of California and co-director of the Black Gallery, a multi-ethnic photography exhibition space. As a curator, he has coordinated photography exhibitions at the Black Gallery, Los Angeles City Hall Bridge Gallery, the Hollywood Bowl Museum and the California Afro-American Museum. He is the host and associate producer of a ninety-minute video documentary sponsored by Eastman Kodak Company entitled, "The Legacy Continues: Black Photographers," which profiles pioneering and contemporary photographers and their work during the last 60 years.

In 1975, Charles received a B.A. in Communications from Windsor University, Los Angeles, California, and has studied photography at the University of Southern California, Otis Parson School of Design and California State University at Los Angeles.

SELECTED EXHIBITIONS

1987. "Through Ebony Eyes," Santa Barbara Arts Council Gallery 10, Santa Barbara, California

1987. "The Legacy Continues," Long Beach Public Library, California

1987. "Horizons," Museum of Science and Industry, Los Angeles, California

1986. "Black Hollywood: Artists and Entertainers," Hollywood Bowl Museum, California

1986. "Black Photographers Exposition," Bridge Gallery, Los Angeles, California

1985. "Immigrants and Minorities in LA—The New International City," Southern California Library for Social Studies and Research, Los Angeles, California

1985. "Cameras Four," Black Gallery, Los Angeles, California

1984. "The Tradition Continues: California Black Photographers," Museum of Afro-American History and Culture, Los Angeles, California

1983. "Our Point of View," William Grant Still Community Art Center, Los Angeles, California

1981. "The Black Photographic Experience in LA," Watts Towers Art Center, Los Angeles, California

SELECTED BIBLIOGRAPHY

"Afro-American Community Visible in Exhibits," *Santa Barbara News Press,* January 19, 1987.

"A Studio 10 Special: Through the Ebony Eye," *Santa Barbara Arts Magazine,* December–January 1987.

"Black Gallery Features Face of the Earth," *Los Angeles Sentinel,* May 8, 1986.

"Kodak Sponsors Black Photographers Exhibit," *Herald Dispatch,* February 20, 1986.

"Photography Featured in Documentary," *Los Angeles Metropolitan Gazette*, October 24, 1985.

"The Legacy Continues," *Los Angeles Metropolitan Gazette*, October 17, 1985.

"Black Photography Gallery Opens," *Southwave*, June 27, 1984.

See photographs pages 206–208.

CHATMAN, LARRY
active Milwaukee, Wisconsin, 1980s

CHENET, JACQUES
active New York City, 1980s

CHISELY, ARTHUR "CHILLY"
active Chicago, 1970s

CHONG, ALBERT (1958–   )
active New York City

Chong lives and works in the New York metropolitan area. Born in Jamaica, West Indies, and a graduate of the School of Visual Arts, New York, Chong works primarily with cultural icons commonly found in Jamaican society. Curator and critic Kellie Jones writes of his works: ". . . Elements of landscape are a part of Chong's work. He collects pieces of nature and brings them back to the studio, arranging the elements carefully before photographing them. Through the juxtapositions Chong creates still lifes reminiscent of shrines."

Described as a photographic shaman, Albert Chong composes his photographs from a personal source emanating from his experiences in his Jamaican homeland. Chong, also a lecturer, teaches photography at the School of Visual Arts and has received the Silver and Bronze Medal for Photography from the Jamaica Festival for the Arts (Kingston, Jamaica, 1977) as well as the C.A.P.S. Photography Fellowship for two consecutive years (1982 and 1983).

COLLECTIONS

Schomburg Center for Research in Black Culture, The New York Public Library, New York, New York

Oberlin College, Oberlin, Ohio

Erie Art Museum, Pennsylvania
Catskill Center for Photography, New York

SELECTED EXHIBITIONS

1987. "Large as Life: Contemporary Photography," Jamaica Arts Center, Jamaica, New York

1986. "We Follow the Dream," BACA Downtown, New York, New York

1985. "Another World," Bronx River Gallery, Bronx, New York

1985. "Seeing is Believing?," Alternative Museum, New York

1984. "Photonational/84," Erie Art Museum, Pennsylvania

1984. "Caribbean Influence," Rotunda Gallery, Brooklyn, New York

1984. "14 Photographers," Schomburg Center for Research in Black Culture, New York, New York

1983. "Under Currents," Just Above Midtown/Downtown, New York, New York

1983. "People of Color," William Paterson College, New York

1982. "Image and Imagination," Jazzonia Gallery, Detroit, Michigan

1981. "Dread in Exile," School of Visual Arts, New York, New York

See photographs pages 209–212.

CLARK, ARNOLD
active New York City, 1980s

CLARK, BOB
active New York City, 1970s

CLARKE, BOB
active 1960s–1970s

Photojournalist Bob Clarke's essay on the Detroit riots is a poignant study of the dangers and sensitivities of an active photojournalist. His style of reporting is an important contribution to the field. Clarke worked for the Black Star Photo Agency during the 1960s.

SELECTED BIBLIOGRAPHY

Clarke, Bob, "Nightmare Journey: Photographer Covering Detroit Riots," *Ebony*, October, 1967.

COATS, NOAH
active Los Angeles, 1970s

COBB, VANDELL
active Evanston, Illinois, 1970s

COLE, ALLEN EDWARD   (1893–1970)
active Cleveland, Ohio

Cole opened his studio in Cleveland, Ohio in the early 1920s. He is noted for being one of the first black studio photographers in the area. He studied photography in exchange for work in a white-owned commercial studio. His first studio was in his own home where he began making portraits of the men, women, children, organizations and businesses in his community. His collection consists of group portraits, weddings, entertainers and street scenes.

SELECTED EXHIBITIONS/BIBLIOGRAPHY

1980. "Somebody, Somewhere, Wants Your Photograph," Western Reserve Historical Society, Cleveland, Ohio (exhibit catalog).

1983. "A Century of Black Photographers: 1840–1960," Museum of Art, Rhode Island School of Design, Providence, Rhode Island (exhibit catalog).

COLLECTIONS

Western Reserve Historical Society, Cleveland, Ohio

See photographs pages 213–216.

COLE, CYNTHIA D.
active Atlanta, 1980s

COLE, ERNEST   (1940–   )
active South Africa

South African photojournalist and documentary photographer Ernest Cole produced his most powerful photo essay depicting life under apartheid rule in South Africa, one of the richest nations of the world. Cole's photographs reflect his deep emotional commitment to telling the story of the struggle for freedom by the 13 million black South Africans.

Born in Pretoria, Cole took his first photographs at the age of fifteen with a borrowed camera. Early in his career, he worked as a darkroom technician for *Drum* magazine. He later got freelance positions for newspapers and magazines. In 1959, he read two books written by the French photographer, Henri Cartier-Bresson, *The Decisive Moment* and *People of Moscow*. Both books had a profound effect on his political and artistic aesthetic. He stated in an article that he decided to make photojournalism his life's work. He felt that through his pictures he could lift the "curtain hiding what life was really like for the black man under the apartheid system." He decided to do a book of photographs depicting life in South Africa. He knew that the government would jail him or censor or prevent the book's publication and that he would have to leave the country to publish it. Nevertheless, from 1959 to 1962, he photographed the miners, the schools, the police, segregation signs and conditions throughout South Africa for the book. While he was in self-imposed exile in 1967, Random House published his book, *House of Bondage* with text by Thomas Flaherty, an associate editor for *Life* magazine.

SELECTED BIBLIOGRAPHY

Cole, Ernest, *House of Bondage*, New York: Random House, 1967.
———, "My Country, My Hell," *Ebony*, February 1968.

COLE, JUANITA
active New York City, 1980s

COLLIER, JAMES W. (1942–   )
active New York City

A native New Yorker, Jim Collier has used photography as an extension of his art and design interest since high school. Receiving his A.A.S. degree in Advertising Design from New York City Technical College, he worked in advertisting agencies while studying commercial photography at night. In 1965, Collier became an assistant at Bert Stern's studio, where he learned the business of photography. He opened his first studio in 1968 with the help of employer and friend, director Harry Hamberg.

Collier credits Bert Stern, Harry Hamberg, Eugene Smith and Rev. Rooks of Harlem as influential in his career as an artist, photographer, and educator. His recent images explore the changes, growth, and diversity of the family unit. He is currently chairperson for the photography department of the Fashion Institute of Technology in New York City where he has taught since 1970. Collier is a member of the American Society of Magazine Photographers, an Examiner for the New York City Board of Education in photography and is a former member of the now disbanded organization International Black Photographers.

SELECTED EXHIBITIONS

1987. "Five Viewpoints on Black America," African American Museum, Hempstead, New York

1981. "Teaneck Places" (one-person show), United Jersey Bank, Teaneck, New Jersey

1980. "Portraits of the Faculty" (one-person show), Fashion Institute of Technology, New York, New York

1976. "Advertising Photography," Rhode Island School of Design, Providence, Rhode Island

1972. "Black Americans" (two-person mini-exhibit), Metropolitan Museum of Art, New York, New York

See photographs pages 217–218.

CONNER, JAMES
active New York City, 1980s

See photograph page 219.

COOPER, FRED (1907–   )
active Los Angeles

Cooper first became acquainted with photography while living in Chicago in the 1930s, where he apprenticed with a number of studio photographers. In 1945 Cooper moved to California where he became active in photographing night clubs and performers such as Ethel Waters and Count Basie. He concentrates on the beauty and style of the musicians and singers who frequented California. Cooper freelanced for many years with black newspapers such as the *Pittsburgh Courier*, New York's *Amsterdam News* and the *California Eagle*.

SELECTED BIBLIOGRAPHY

The Tradition Continues: California Black Photographers (exhibition catalog), California Museum of Afro-American History and Culture, November 10, 1983–January 16, 1984.

COTTMAN, WILLIAM J.
active Minneapolis, 1980s

COWANS, ADGER W.

active New York City, 1960–present

Adger W. Cowans attended Ohio University, where he studied photography with Clarence H. White, Jr. He moved to New York City in 1959 and later became acquainted with *Life* photographer Gordon Parks, whom he assisted for a period of time. He also worked with fashion photographers, among them Henri Clark. During this period Cowans was a member of "The Heliographer's," a group of photographers that included such notables as Paul Caponigro and Jerry Ullsman.

During the early 1960s, Cowans photographed the activities of the civil rights movement, particularly the Student Non-Violent Coordinating Committee (SNCC) and the Congress on Racial Equality (CORE). In 1962, he won the coveted John Hay Whitney Fellowship for creative photography, and in 1963 he won the award for best photography at the Yolo International Exhibition in California.

Cowans was one of the founding members of the International Black Photographers; he was also a member of the Kamoinge Workshop and AFRICOBRA and is currently a member of International Photographers Local 644. His works have appeared in *Harper's Bazaar, Esquire, The New York Times, Look, Essence, Modern Photography,* and *Paris Match.*

For the past 15 years Cowans has been working as a still photographer for the motion picture industry. His credits include, *The Cotton Club, On Golden Pond, The Way We Were, Cotton Comes to Harlem,* and *Nothing but a Man.*

SELECTED EXHIBITIONS

1981. "Moments," Greenespace, New York, New York

1977. FESTAC, The Second World Black and African Festival of Arts and Culture, Lagos, Nigeria

1975. International Center for Photography, New York, New York

1974. Chicago Institute of Design, Chicago, Illinois

1969. "New Trends in Photography," University of New Hampshire, Durham, New Hampshire

1968. "Photography U.S.A.," Decordova Museum, Lincoln, Massachusetts

1968. "Photography in the Fine Arts," Metropolitan Museum of Art, New York, New York

1967–68. USIA Traveling Exhibit

1966. First World Festival of Negro Arts, Dakar, Senegal

1965. Heliography Gallery, New York, New York

1963. George Eastman House, Rochester, New York

SELECTED BIBLIOGRAPHY

"Adger Cowans, Photographer" (transcript of interview with Shawn Walker, March 3, 1985). In *Artist and Influence,* New York: Hatch-Billops Collection, Inc., 1986.

Moments, Exhibition Catalog, New York: Greenespace Gallery, 1981.

Bearden, Romare, "Adger Cowans," *The Drum,* Vol. 15, No. I & II, 1987.

See photographs pages 220–223.

CRAWFORD, ROBERT
active Chicago, 1970s

See photograph page 224.

CRAWFORD, JOE
active Brooklyn, New York, 1970s

CREIGHTNEY, DARRELL
active Chicago, 1970s

CRYOR, CARY BETH (1947–)
active Baltimore

Cary Beth Cryor is best known for her photographs of the birth of her own child. In addition to pursuing her personal photography, Cryor has been active as a teacher, librarian and film editor. Cryor has a M.L.S. from the University of Maryland at College Park, a M.F.A. from Pratt Institute in Photography and a B.S. in Art Education from Morgan State University. Currently she is a professor at Coppin State College in Baltimore, Maryland.

Since 1986 she has been spending her summers in West Africa photographing. In 1987 she received a Fulbright-Hays Group Study Abroad Fellowship to assist her in her documentation project of Senegal, Ivory Coast, Togo, Sierra Leone and Benin. While in Africa she became interested in textiles and is currently writing an article entitled "Tie-Dyeing and Country Cloth Weaving: The Functional and Aesthetic Use of Natural Forms in African Ritual and Visual Art."

As a photo-archivist, she is working with the Baltimore Afro-American newspaper, assisting them in setting up an archive of their photographs, clippings and personal correspondence.

SELECTED EXHIBITIONS

1984. "Mayor's Ball for the Benefit of the Arts," Baltimore Convention Center, Baltimore, Maryland

1981. "Quilts Inspired by Traditional African Weave," Coppin State College, Baltimore, Maryland

1980. "Mayor's Ball for the Benefit of the Arts," Baltimore Convention Center

1979. "Rites of Passage: A Photographic Exploration from the Mother's View," Gallery 409, Baltimore, Maryland

1979. "Guyana and Back: Another View," Dundalk Community College and Gallery 409, Baltimore, Maryland

1976. "In Expression of Gratitude and Pride to Ancestors Who Have Carved My Future," Minden Civic Center, Minden, Louisiana, and Morgan State University, Baltimore, Maryland

SELECTED BIBLIOGRAPHY

Moutoussamy-Ashe, Jeanne, *Viewfinders: Black Women Photographers*, New York: Dodd, Mead & Company, 1986.

The Black Photographers Annual, Vol. 4, New York: Another View, Inc. Publishers, 1980.

Beckles, Frances, *Twenty Black Women*, Baltimore, Maryland: Gatewood Publishers, 1976.

The Black Photographers Annual, Vol. 2, New York: Another View, Inc. Publishers, 1974.

See photographs pages 225–226.

CUESTA, TERE L.
active New York City, 1980–present

A graduate of Long Island University, Cuesta studied photojournalism and anthropology. She is the recipient of the George Polk Student Award which is "presented to the senior, who by way of personal integrity, dedication to the highest journalistic standards, and exceptional achievements in formal studies and extracurricular activities, most effectively encourages university-wide respect for journalism as a discipline and a career.

As a result of her interest in photographing in Cuba, Cuesta has a distinguished body of work. She writes of the experience, "Photographing subjects in Cuba allowed me to make discoveries about my personal experience as an American-born Cuban and about the diversity of racial and ethnic groups in the Americas. Seen through a lens, there is no typical appearance for the Cuban. . . . Modern generations derive their energies from their ancestors: indigenous Asiatic Indians, European settlers and imported African slaves. The photographs emphasize the array of skin tones of the people of the island. Therein lies their beauty." In addition to other exhibitions, she has exhibited her series "Images of Cuba" in galleries in the New York area.

See photograph page 227.

CUMBO, FIKISHA
active Brooklyn, New York, 1972–present

Born in Houston, Texas, Cumbo was a science major at Texas Southern University (B.S.) and received an M.S. from the City University in New York. Her early work included nature scenes and images of her newborn baby son. While interviewing Maurice White from the musical group Earth, Wind and Fire, for a book project, she photographed him, which led to other assignments interviewing and photographing musicians such as Bob Marley, Peter Tosh and Stevie Wonder. Her work has appeared on the album jacket for "Equal Rights" (Peter Tosh, Columbia Records), and in newspapers and magazines such as *The Daily Gleaner* (Jamaica, West Indies) and the *Caribbean Voice*. Cumbo's works have been included in exhibitions in the New York area.

See photograph page 228.

CUNNINGHAM, COOPER
active New York City, 1970s

CUNNINGHAM, DONNIE
active Los Angeles, 1970s

CUNNINGHAM, PHYLLIS
active New York City, 1970s

DALEY, MICHAEL
active Washington, DC, 1970s

DAVIS, CLARENCE
active Hillburn, New York, 1970s

DAVIS, COLLIS H., JR.
active New York City, 1965–present

Davis, a photographer and filmmaker, received an M.F.A. in Film and Television Production from New York University in 1975 and a B.S. in Political Science from the University of Wisconsin, Madison in 1966. He is best known for his forceful and innovative portraits of jazz musicians who frequent New York nightclubs. As a photojournalist, Davis has worked for local newspapers in the New York City area and *Downbeat* magazine. He has taught photography at Pratt Institute, Queensborough Community College, City University of

New York and at the Hampton (Virginia) Association for the Arts and Humanities. He also gained considerable experience as an intelligence photographer for the United States Army, 1966–69.

As a filmmaker and videoartist, Davis has produced and directed numerous productions. He has received awards for his efforts, such as the 1984 CEBA Award of Excellence for *Voyage of Dreams*. This production, which received critical acclaim, was also noted by the New York State Associated Press Broadcasters Association, received Honorable Mention for Best Feature, WNET-TV's Television Laboratory's Artist-in-Residence Award, 1982, and received Honorable Mention in the National Black Programming Consortium/PBS Prize Pieces Competition.

A specialist in videodisc operation and computer graphics, Davis has been a consultant and lecturer. He is a member of the Association of Independent Video and Filmmakers, and New York SIGGRAPH, a computer graphics professional organization.

SELECTED EXHIBITIONS

1986. "Harlem on the Hudson," Harlem Urban Development Corporation, New York, New York

1986. "Give Me Your Tired, Your Poor . . . ? Voluntary Black Migration to the United States," Schomburg Center for Research in Black Culture, The New York Public Library, New York, New York

1981. "Blacksilver Riffs: Solo Photography by . . . ," (an exhibition of jazz photography) Soundscape Music Space, New York, New York, December 1981–March 1982

1969. "Korea: Impressions/Expressions: A GI's Vision of South Korea," Main Service Club, 2nd Infantry Division, USARPAC

FILM AND VIDEO PRODUCTIONS

1984. "Cavity-Free," Video documentary on the Oral Health Education Program of the William F. Ryan Community Health Center

1983. *Voyage of Dreams*, Video documentary/essay on the plight of Haitian refugees

1981. "Fishing Story," Documentary film on the spiritual meaning of traditional fishing in West Africa

1973. "A Silent Rap," Dramatic short on interracial relationships

SELECTED BIBLIOGRAPHY

Feather, Leonard, *The Passion of Jazz*, New York: Horizon Press, 1981.

See photographs pages 228–231.

DAVIS, DARRYL
active Los Angeles, 1980s

DAVIS, GRIFFITH J. (1923–)
active Washington, DC.; Atlanta; Africa

Griffith Davis' reputation rests largely on his professional activities with the U.S. Agency for International Development (AID). As an advisor to African governments such as Liberia, Tunisia, Nigeria, and for the Bureau for Africa and the Bureau for Population and Humanitarian Assistance, he had the fortuitous opportunity to document in still photographs and motion pictures the life and activities of the many African governments between 1952 and 1980.

Davis, born in Atlanta, Georgia, began working with AID in 1952 and retired in 1985. He received his B.A. from Morehouse College and an M.A. in journalism from Columbia University in 1949. Before beginning his successful and active governmental career in the foreign service, Davis worked as a roving editor for *Ebony* magazine (1947–48) where he wrote and photographed his own articles. He later moved on to work as a photojournalist for the Black Star Publishing Company, a stock photo agency (1949–52). As a freelance photojournalist for Black Star and a stringer for *The New York Times*, he photographed extensively in Africa, Europe and parts of the United States.

In 1981 Davis donated 7,000 photographs and negatives documenting social and economic development in Liberia to Howard University's Moorland-Spingarn Research Center. In donating the photographs, Davis said that "the prints and negatives should be placed in the public domain and made available to serious researchers probing into this epoch of West African affairs." Included in his collection are portraits of Kwame Nkrumah, Haile Selassie, William Tubman, Dr. Albert Schweitzer, Langston Hughes and poet William Stanley Braithwaite.

Davis is a member of the American Society of Magazine Photographers, the Washington Film Council, and the International Committee on Visual, Auditory Materials for Distribution Abroad, USA.

COLLECTIONS

Moorland-Spingarn Research Center, Howard University, Washington, DC
Ebony Magazine, Johnson Publications, Inc., Chicago, Illinois

SELECTED EXHIBITIONS

1983. "A Century of Black Photographers: 1840–1960," Rhode Island School of Design, Museum of Art, Providence, Rhode Island
1952. "Liberia 1952," American Museum of National History, New York, New York

SELECTED BIBLIOGRAPHY

A *Century of Black Photographers: 1840–1969* (exhibition catalog), Providence: Rhode Island School of Design, 1983.
Bailey, J. Edward, III, *Living Legends in Black*, Detroit: Bailey Publishing Co., 1976.

"Global Honeymoon: Photographer Takes His Own Pictures of Travels on Three Continents," *Ebony* Magazine, September 1952.

Pepperbird Land, Film for the Republic of Liberia (producer), 1952.

Davis, Griffith J., "Iron Boom in Liberia," *Steelways*, September 1951.

Davis, Griffith J., "Haile Selassie's Son: A Shutterbug," *Modern Photography*, September 1952.

"Haile Selassie," *Der Spiegel*, July 1951.

Davis, Griffith J., "The Private Life of Emperor Selassie," *Ebony*, November 1950.

See photographs pages 232–238.

DAVIS, JACK
active Los Angeles, 1949–present

Davis emerged as a free-lance photographer in the late 1940s, some years after his arrival in Los Angeles from Waco, Texas in 1939. His early photographs were of local night club scenes. In 1950 he began taking classes in photography, learning the rudiments of commercial photography, and opened his first studio shortly after. For more than thirty-five years, the Davis Modern Arts Studio was noted for its fine portrait and commercial work.

Jack Davis teaches photography in local high schools and junior colleges. A "photographer's photographer," Davis is a founding member of the Photo Hobby Club, a thirty-year-old organization of black professional and amateur photographers.

SELECTED EXHIBITIONS

"The Tradition Continues, California Black Photographers," California Museum of Afro-American History and Culture, Los Angeles, November 1983–January 1984

DAVIS, PAT
active New York City, 1970–present

Pat Davis was born in New York City. She studied art and photography at the Brooklyn Museum Art School, City University of New York and the New School for Social Research (New York).

Davis' images are analytical. She photographs her subjects at odd angles, e.g., high or low views. In 1976 she wrote about her work, "Using the controlled technique of the camera, and the free spirit of the mind—I have tried to interpret the human figure through light, space and time—making a realistic and surrealistic expression of form."

Davis is a freelance photographer and gallery owner. She has taught photography in workshops and has had numerous exhibitions in the New York metropolitan area. Her work has appeared on book jackets, in *Freshtones: Women's Anthology*, and in *Encore* Magazine. She has exhibited in a number of shows organized by the National Conference of Artists of which she is a member.

See photographs pages 239–240.

DAWSON, C. DANIEL (1944–   )
active New York City

A curator, filmmaker and photographer, Dawson became interested in the medium while studying zoology at Columbia University. In the 1960s he studied photography with Paul Caponigro, Ralph Hattersley and Lizette Model, and became involved in the 1970s with the Kamoinge Workshop, a black photographers group in New York City that sponsored exhibitions of the members' work and provided a forum for discussion of photographic issues.

A fine art photographer, Dawson works primarily in color. His works are abstractions of reality, mysterious and ambiguous.

Influential as a filmmaker, writer and photographer, Dawson is active in the arts. He has received numerous awards for his diverse talents including the Blue Ribbon (citation) from the American Film Festival (1983) for the film *Capoiera*; an award from the Art Libraries Society of New York for curating the exhibition, "The Sound I Saw: The Jazz Photographs of Roy De Carava" (1984); the Oscar Michaux Award for Best Documentary and Best Film of the Year for *Head and Heart* (1980); and in 1984, a grant to photograph and document Brazilian culture.

Dawson has worked as a photo editor, still photographer and cameraman for commercial and scholarly magazines and films. His works have been published in *Black Photographers Annual, Jet* and *Essence* as well as the *Philadelphia Tribune, Amsterdam News* and *The New York Times*. Dawson has worked for numerous publishers, including Doubleday, Viking, Grove and Third World.

SELECTED EXHIBITIONS

1984. "Summits of Expression," Nassau Community College, New York, New York

1983. "14 Photographers," Schomburg Center for Research in Black Culture, New York, New York

1980. "Self-Portrait Show," *Black Enterprise* Magazine/Studio Museum in Harlem Traveling exhibit, New York, New York

1975. "Kamoinge Workshop," International Center of Photography, New York, New York

1973. "Kwanza," Studio Museum in Harlem, New York, New York

1965. "Blackamerica Photo Exhibit," Black Arts Gallery, New York, New York

EXHIBITIONS (Curator)

1983. "The Sound I Saw: The Jazz Photographs of Roy De Carava," Studio Museum in Harlem, New York, New York

1982. "Image and Imagination," Jazzonia Gallery, Detroit, Michigan
1981. "Extensions: Nonconventional Photographic Imagery," Studio Museum in Harlem, New York, New York
1976. "Light Textures/3," Just Above Midtown Gallery, New York, New York

See photographs page 241.

DAY, WINIFRED
active Chicago, 1970s

DECARAVA, ROY
active Brooklyn, New York, 1950s

DE JESUS, CARMEN
active New York City, 1980s

DENTE, AMARTEY
active Long Island, New York, 1970s

DIXON, MEL
active New York City, 1970s

DOGGETT, BILL
active California, 1980–present

Raised in Los Angeles, California, Doggett became interested in photography in the 1980s. Basically self-taught, he has been influenced by German filmmakers. Doggett says of his color photographs, which have a surreal quality, "'seeing' has increasingly become the art of perceiving, constructing and presenting an experience that not only communicates the immediate elements photographically captured, but as well has become the art of having that experience transcend its denotative representation and become an abstracted reality that is in itself a new experience."

Interested in experiments with neon photography, Doggett has been working within this area of photography for the past few years.

SELECTED EXHIBITIONS

1983–84. "California Black Photographers: The Tradition Continues," The California Museum of Afro-American History and Culture, Los Angeles, California

1983. "Cities," Gallery Space Somar, San Francisco, California

1983. "Our Point of View," William Grant Still Community Art Center, Los Angeles, California

1983. "1983 All-California Biennial Competition," Riverside Art Center and Museum, Riverside, California

See photographs pages 242–243.

DOUGLAS, DAVID
active New York City, 1970s

DOUGLAS, LYDIA ANN
active New York City, 1982–present

Douglas is a fine art/portrait photographer based in New York City. She received a B.F.A. in photography from the University of Bridgeport. She has taught photography locally. She is currently working on a project entitled "Women of African Music", a photo/documentary, which covers women of African descent involved in all areas of music with a distinct African influence. Douglas received a Ludwig Vogelstein grant for this project. She states, "The idea of photographing Black women performers grew from my desire to capture their unique qualities as artists."

SELECTED EXHIBITIONS

1985. Museum of the Americas, Leon, Nicaragua (permanent installation)

1983. Ansonia Community Action, Inc., Ansonia, Connecticut (permanent installation)

1982. Gallery 5, University of Bridgeport, Bridgeport, Connecticut

SELECTED BIBLIOGRAPHY

Photographer's Forum Magazine, Best of College Photography Annual, 1983.
The Middle East, March, 1983.

See photograph page 244.

DOZIER, CILE
active Los Angeles, 1980s

DRAPER, LOUIS (1935–   )
active New Jersey; New York

A professor at Mercer County Community College (New Jersey), Draper has been active in photography since 1960. A founding member of the Kamoinge Workshop, he has been instrumental in initiating workshops, critiques, and exhibitions of photographers for over thirty years. A contributor and consultant for the *Black Photographer's Annual*, Draper reviewed works and interviewed photographers for the editors.

Born in Richmond, Virginia, he attended Virginia State College (B.A.). An exhibiting and active photographer, Draper has been a guiding light for young photographers. Draper is one of the early "street photographers" committed to documentation and integrating conceptual concerns while telling his visual story of a particular community. He has exhibited widely, and his work has been published in numerous publications.

See photographs pages 245–248.

DU CILLE, MICHEL
active Miami, Florida

A 1985 Pulitzer Prize winner, duCille won the award with his colleague Carol Guzy for their coverage of the Colombian earthquake. duCille graduated from Indiana University, and is a photographer for the *Miami Herald*.

SELECTED BIBLIOGRAPHY

Hesterman, Vicki, "Pulitzer Roundup in Ohio" by *News Photographer*, May 1987.

DUMETZ, BARBARA
active California, 1970–present

Commercial and advertising photographer Barbara Dumetz began her career in photography in the early 1970s. Born in Charleston, West Virginia, she graduated from Fisk University and studied photography at the Art Center in Pasadena, California. Dumetz's interest in photography began in childhood; her grandfather was a professional photographer. Her first job in photography came when she worked as a photo illustrator for *Essence* magazine.

Dumetz's portfolio includes images of celebrities and sports figures, such as Kareem Abdul Jabbar, Olivia Newton-John, Nancy Wilson, Al Jarreau and Lou Rawls. Her ads for Toyota, Miller Brewing Company, J. P. Martin Associates, Carnation Company and the Coca-Cola Bottling Company have appeared in magazines and on billboards.

SELECTED BIBLIOGRAPHY

Moutoussamy-Ashe, Jeanne, *Viewfinders: Black Women Photographers*, New York: Dodd, Mead, 1986.

Bentley, Kenneth W., "Barbara Dumetz," in *Beyond a Dream: Black Women in the Arts.* Los Angeles: Carnation Company, 1985.

EASTMOND, CLARENCE E.
active Brooklyn, New York, 1970s

EDA, JOAN
active New York City, 1965–present

Born in Washington, DC, Joan Eda has a B.A. from Howard University and an M.A. in media studies from the New School for Social Research. She has exhibited her photographs in group and solo exhibitions. Her work has been included in multi-media performances at Long Island University and the American Museum of Natural History in New York, and her photographs have been published on record albums and in magazines and books. She has won an award for her photography from the New Jersey State Council on the Arts. An audiovisual librarian for the Brooklyn Public Library, Eda is a member of the American Society for Picture Professionals.

SELECTED ONE-PERSON EXHIBITIONS

1987. "Autobiography: Her Story," Rotunda Gallery, Brooklyn, New York

1985. John Jay College of Criminal Justice, New York, New York

1979. Carl Van Vechten Gallery, Fisk University, Nashville, Tennessee

1977. Soho Photo Gallery, New York, New York

SELECTED GROUP EXHIBITIONS

1986. "Reflections of Self: Women Photographers," Fordham University at Lincoln Center, New York, New York

1986. "America: Another Perspective," New York University; New York State Office Building in Harlem; Gallery 62, National Urban League, New York, New York

1985. The Otto Rene Castillo Gallery, New York, New York

1985. Rotunda Gallery, Bronx County Building, Bronx, New York

1984. The Otto Rene Castillo Gallery, New York, New York

1980. "Women on the Scene," Brockman Gallery and The Woman's Building, Los Angeles, California

1978. Gallery 84, New York, New York

1978. New York Arts Consortium, New York, New York

1976. "Washington, D. C. Photographers," Martin Luther King Public Library, Washington, DC
1975. Group Exhibit, Washington Project for the Arts (WPA) Gallery, Washington, DC
1971. Lorraine Hansberry Center for the Arts, Princeton, New Jersey
1968. Group Exhibit, Corcoran Gallery of Art, Washington, DC

PERFORMANCES AS A PHOTOGRAPHER

"The Ladies and Me" and "A Friend," multi-media performances directed by Blondell
 Cummings. New York, 1980
"Friends, II," by Blondell Cummings, Black Theatre Alliance, New York, 1980
"Inner Space/Outer Space," a multi-media performance by Ellsworth Ausby. Long Island
 University (Brooklyn Campus) and Museum of Natural History, New York City,
 1978. CETA Artists Project Production.
"Cycle," a multi-media performance by Blondell Cummings. New York, 1978

SELECTED BIBLIOGRAPHY

Public Productivity Review, 1980
Bell, Roseann, P., Bettye J. Parker and Beverly Guy-Sheftall (eds.), *Sturdy Black Bridges,*
 Visions of Black Women in Literature, New York: Doubleday, 1979.
SohoCamera 3, New York: Soho-Photo Foundation, 1978.

See photographs page 249.

ELLISON, SULAIMAN (1951–   )
active New York City

Sulaiman Ellison has been active in photography since 1972. His work consists of two main
themes—the African diaspora and jazz musicians. He frequently travels to Africa (Ethiopia,
Ghana, Mali, Niger, Egypt and Nigeria) photographing the countryside and its people.
Ellison's jazz photographs are of musicians and performances on stage in night clubs and
the concert stage. A notable characteristic of Ellison's work is his confidence in and respect
for the medium as well as his subjects.

Ellison trained and worked as an electrical engineer, then studied photography at the
School of Visual Arts (New York) and at the New School for Social Research (New York)
with Benedict Fernandez. He has been a member of a number of photography clubs and
organizations, including Collective Black Photographers, Higher Ground Cinema, and The
Photographer's Forum.

COLLECTIONS

Schomburg Center for Research in Black Culture, The New York Public Library, New
 York, New York
Performing Arts Research Center, The New York Public Library, New York, New York

SELECTED EXHIBITIONS

1983. "African Mosaics," The 4th Street Photo Gallery, New York, New York
1982. "Fourteen Photographers," Schomburg Center for Research in Black Culture, The New York Public Library, New York, New York
1978. "ACIA Permanent Collection Exhibition," ACIA, New York, New York
1977. "Jazz Improvisations," The 4th Street Photo Gallery, New York
1975. "Visions of Black Classical Musicians," The East Cultural Center, Brooklyn, New York

See photographs pages 250–251.

FANI-KAYODE, RUTIMI
active Washington, DC: Nigeria, 1980s

FARMER, SHARON
active Washington, DC 1975–present

Sharon Farmer is a free-lance photojournalist and fine art photographer. Her free-lance clients include IBM corporation, the Southern Christian Leadership Conference, *The Washington Post* and *The Washington Informer*, and the Delta Sigma Theta Sorority. She is a member of the Washington Women's Art Center and is on the advisory board of Roadwork, Inc. An activist in the women's art movement, Farmer has organized exhibitions and lectures in the Washington, DC, area.

SELECTED EXHIBITIONS/BIBLIOGRAPHY

1983. "For Women Only: An Exhibition of Local Black Women Photographers," (exhibition catalog), Moorland-Spingarn Research Center, Howard University, Washington, DC.
Moutoussamy-Ashe, Jeanne. *Viewfinders: Black Women Photographers*, New York: Dodd, Mead, Inc., 1986.

See photographs pages 252–253.

FARRIS, PHOEBE
active, Washington, DC 1975–present

A fine art photographer and art therapist, Phoebe Farris studied at the City University of New York, Pratt Institute and the University of Maryland. She has exhibited her photographs in galleries in New York and Washington, D.C., such as the Castillo Center, Gallery 10, Northern Virginia Community Gallery and the Art Barn.

SELECTED EXHIBITIONS/BIBLIOGRAPHY

1983. "For Women Only: An Exhibition of Local Black Women Photographers" (exhibition catalog), Moorland-Spingarn Research Center, Howard University, Washington, DC.

FEARING, JEFFREY JOHN
active Washington, DC 1968–present

A bio-medical and free-lance photographer since 1968, Fearing's personal work includes landscape and portrait photography.

See photographs pages 254–255.

FENNAR, ALBERT
active Englewood, New Jersey, 1970s

FERRILL, VALERIA "MIKKI" (1937–   )
active Chicago and San Francisco

Interested in graphic arts, lapidary, gold and silversmithing, filmmaking and photography since high school, Mikki Ferrill continued her studies in art at Wilson City College, the Art Institute of Chicago, and in workshops with photographer Ted Williams. She spent several years travelling and photographing in Puerto Rico, Chicago, Philadelphia, Mexico City, Senegal, Jamaica, northern California, and Canada. Ferrill is best known for her compelling, sensitive and often humorous photographs of life in the inner city and in small communities.

Ferrill has taught photography at Columbia College, Malcolm X College, Urban Gateways Artists-in-Residence Program and at Northeastern University's Inner City Studies/Cook County Jail. Her work has appeared in group and solo exhibitions in New York, Chicago, Washington, DC, San Francisco, Los Angeles and Moscow.

Over the past twenty years, Ferrill has worked as a photojournalist for *Time, The Chicago Tribune, The Chicago Defender, Muhammad Speaks, Ebony, Jet, California Monthly* and *The San Francisco Examiner*. Her photographic essays have appeared in *Life, Downbeat* and *The Black Photographer's Annual*.

Mikki Ferrill continues to work as a photojournalist, to teach, to exhibit and to produce powerful photo essays. "Upon embracing photography as my medium," she remarks, "I realized the vast scope of being able to record the present as it is. Not what one would imagine, want, or think things should be but to actually capture and freeze life in a second as it is."

"In my work," Ferrill once said, "I have always strived to capture the unveiled moments when one's defense or guard is down. That moment of truth. In recognizing my ability to reveal that truth, I've also accepted the responsibility to my subjects of making sure they are never depicted in a derogatory way. I must say that my concern for my subject matter has sometimes earned me the title of 'being uncompromising,' which at times has led to periods of hunger; however, hunger is a temporary condition. Compromising one's creative values can be a permanent state of dissatisfaction. Needless to say, my goal is to continue my work uncompromised. . . ." A curator as well as a consultant, Ferrill has organized photographic exhibitions in Washington, D.C. and Chicago. Currently she lives and works in Berkeley, California.

SELECTED BIBLIOGRAPHY

On Freedom: The Art of Photojournalism, Exhibition Catalog, New York: Studio Museum in Harlem, 1986.

Moutoussamy-Ashe, Jeanne, *Viewfinders: Black Women Photographers*, New York: Dodd-Mead, 1986.

See photographs pages 256–259.

FLETCHER, BOB
active New York City, 1963–present

Born in Detroit, Michigan, Bob Fletcher attended Fisk University (Nashville) and Wayne State University (Detroit) majoring in English and history. Fletcher became active in the civil rights movement in 1963. That same year he began to take photographs while administering the National Student Association's Detroit Tutorial Program. A self-taught photographer, he moved to New York City to work at the Harlem Education Program, setting up a photographic workshop.

Concerned about the struggle for human and civil rights, Fletcher moved to Mississippi in the summer of 1964 to teach in the Freedom School. "I became a photographer during the time of the struggle for civil rights. Like many people around the world, I was very affected by photographs like the one of a policeman holding a brother with one hand, while he let the dog on a leash in his other hand attack him." Also in 1964 Fletcher joined the Student Nonviolent Coordinating Committee (SNCC) staff as a photographer documenting the civil rights activities throughout the South, especially Mississippi, Alabama and southwest Georgia. His photographs were published in community newspapers, *Muhammad Speaks, The Student Voice,* and distributed through the SNCC photo agency and Black Star.

In 1969 Fletcher moved back to New York City where he set up a photography workshop at the Henry Street Settlement. An exhibiting photographer as well as an instructor, he exhibited his photographs in two SNCC exhibits, "US" (1965) and "Now" (1968). Images from his trip to Cuba in 1968, where he attended the Cultural Congress International Conference, were shown in a travelling exhibit organized by the James Van Der Zee Institute. His work has appeared in *Jet, Ebony, Ms, Redbook, Life,* and the *Black Photographer's Annual*.

Also active in cinema, Fletcher worked with journalist Robert Van Lierop on two films about the Angolan Revolution, codirecting *A Luta Continua* ("The Struggle Continues") and *O Povo Organizado* ("The People Organized"). Additionally, he has done photographic work for the films *The Wiz* and *The Freddi Prinz Story*. In television, Fletcher has worked as a cameraman for *Black Journal* and *Interface*, both produced by PBS.

SELECTED EXHIBITIONS

1982. "Image and Imagination," Jazzonia Gallery, Detroit, Michigan
1980. "We'll Never Turn Back," Smithsonian Institution, Washington, DC

SELECTED BIBLIOGRAPHY

We'll Never Turn Back, Exhibition Catalog, Washington, DC: Smithsonian Institution, 1980.

"Focus on Bob Fletcher," *Photo Newsletter*, New York: James Van Der Zee Institute, Vol. I, Issue 2, 1972.

Black Photographer's Annual Vol. II, New York: Another View, Inc. Publishers, 1973.

See photograph page 260.

FORD, JOHN
active St. Louis, 1970s

FOURNIER, COLLETTE V. (1952–   )
active Rochester, New York

Collette Fournier studied photography and biomedical communications at the Rochester Institute of Technology, receiving a B.S. degree in 1978. An exhibiting photographer, Fournier has worked as a staff photographer for a Rochester magazine and has had numerous free-lance assignments for such organizations as the National Black Network, the Democratic National Convention and the Urban League.

Fournier, a recipient of two awards for her photography, teaches photography in a local high school and art workshops, teaching all aspects of photojournalism and camera techniques.

She often photographs in the Caribbean, documenting the activities of the women, and she is currently photographing black motorcyclists throughout the United States. In her own words she states, "These people are a closer knit group than many of the social, fraternal and professional organizations. They are a rich part of a black history who served their community and organized themselves in an era when there were no integrated clubs. Some groups are strictly male, others coed, some strictly female; some groups social, others road groups with individual members who have traveled throughout the country. In essence, some of these members represent a 'cowboy' image, which America is striving to hold onto through popular movies and books."

SELECTED EXHIBITIONS

1987. "The Family," Bedford-Stuyvesant Restoration Corporation, Brooklyn, New York

1986. "Honoring the Arts of Harlem," Harlem Urban Development Corporation, New York, New York

1984. One-person show, Eisenhart Museum, Rochester Museum of Science, Rochester, New York

1984. Group exhibition, Allofus Art Gallery, Rochester, New York

See photographs pages 261–263.

FRANCIS, RAY
active New York City, 1970s

FRANKLIN, JACK (1922–   )
active Philadelphia

A prolific photographer since the early 1940s, Jack Franklin cannot be easily classified. Franklin began photographing while in high school. A self-taught photographer, he produced a sizable collection of over 200,000 images of every aspect of city life in Philadelphia.

For over forty years, he photographed political and social movements, including rallies, protest marches and leaders of the civil rights movement, in Philadelphia as well as in the South. Franklin's photographs of performing artists who frequented the theaters and night clubs in Philadelphia are an extraordinary record of entertainers such as Nat King Cole, Ella Fitzgerald, Lionel Hampton, and George Kirby, among others. His photographs of ceremonies—christenings, weddings, anniversaries and funerals—depict his deep dedication to photographing significant personal events as well as public and political events.

Franklin has worked for such major black newspapers as *The Philadelphia Tribune, The Afro-American,* and *The Pittsburgh Courier.* In 1986, the Afro-American Historical and

Cultural Museum in Philadelphia acquired more than 200,000 prints and negatives from Jack Franklin.

Franklin acquired specialized photographic skills while in the U.S. Army. He studied photography at the U.S. Signal Corps Photo Center in New York. Among his other achievements, he was the official yearbook photographer for many schools and universities in the Philadelphia metropolitan area, such as Cheyney State College, Temple University and Lincoln University. His free-lance assignments include photographs of former President Lyndon Baines Johnson's Inauguration, the March on Washington in 1963 and the "Poor Peoples March" in Philadelphia, among others.

COLLECTIONS

Afro-American Historical and Cultural Museum, Philadelphia, Pennsylvania

See photographs pages 264–266.

FREDERICK, MONROE
active New York City, 1980s

FREEMAN, ROLAND (1936–   )
active Washington, DC

Influential as both a photographer and folklorist, Freeman made his first photographs in 1963. Moved by the enormous crowds and the determination of the participants of the 1963 March on Washington, as well as the speeches of Dr. Martin Luther King, Jr., Freeman decided to become a photographer to document his personal experiences and the activities of the civil rights movement. He was influenced by the photographs of Gordon Parks, Roy DeCarava and Burk Uzzle. Freeman was born in Baltimore and began his photographic career with a borrowed camera. He started taking pictures as a hobby while he was in the U.S. Air Force (1954–58).

Viewing the camera as a research tool, Freeman became a free-lance photographer for major publications such as *Time, Newsweek, Paris Match* and the London *Sunday Times.* In 1967, he began photographing for the *D.C. Gazette* and for the following seven years, he worked as its photo editor. Freeman was the first photographer to receive a National Endowment for the Humanities fellowship (Young Humanist) in 1970. In 1971, he taught a documentary photography course at George Washington University in Washington, DC. A recipient of a number of research grants from the National Endowment for the Humanities, Freeman had the opportunity to research and document the rural South and its retention of African culture and rituals such as cooking, sewing, religious practices and herbal medicines.

In 1974, he visited Mississippi as a field research photographer in folklore for the Smithsonian Institution's Festival of American Folklore. Working with folklorist Worth Long, he surveyed and documented black folk culture in Mississippi. Between 1975 and 1977, Freeman was the Director/Photographer for the Mississippi Folklife Project. He was elected to the Executive Council of the Association of African and African-American Folklorists in 1976.

Photographing the Southern Christian Leadership Conference's Poor People's March from Marks, Mississippi, to Washington, DC, Freeman was struck by the warmth and determination of the marchers. His life's work became capturing African-Americans in the South as well as in the North who shared similar traditional folkways.

Freeman is a member of a number of organizations, including the American Society of Magazine Photographers, U.S. Senate Press Photographers Gallery, White House News Photographers Association and the National Conference of Artists.

SELECTED EXHIBITIONS

1983. "Contemporary Afro-American Photography," Oberlin College, Oberlin, Ohio

1981. "Southern Roads/City Pavements," International Center of Photography, New York, New York (Traveling exhibition: 10-City/3-year tour)

1980. "We'll Never Turn Back," Smithsonian Institution, National Museum of History, Washington, DC

1979. "A Baltimore Portfolio, 1968–1979," University of Maryland, Baltimore County Library, Baltimore, Maryland

1978. "City Pavements/Country Roads," Antioch University, Philadelphia, Pennsylvania

1977. "Folkroots: Images of Mississippi Black Folklife (1974–76)," Mississippi State Historical Museum, Jackson, Mississippi

1975. "Crossroads: Black America," Massachusetts Institute of Technology, Boston, Massachusetts

1974. "Black Photographer's Exhibit," Southside Community Arts Center, Chicago, Illinois

1972. "Countryside/Inner City," Smithsonian Institution's National Collection of Fine Arts, Washington, DC

1971. "Eleven Washington Photographers," Corcoran Gallery of Art, Washington, DC

1969. "Cross Currents, Roland Freeman," Gallery de Gaines, Washington, DC

SELECTED BIBLIOGRAPHY

Contemporary Afro-American Photography (exhibition catalog), Allen Memorial Art Museum, Oberlin College, Oberlin, Ohio, 1983.

We'll Never Turn Back (exhibition catalog), Smithsonian Institution, National Museum of History, Washington, DC, 1980.

"Focus on Photographer," New York *Daily News*, April 1, 1981.

Southern Roads/City Pavements: Photographs of Black Americans by Roland Freeman (exhibition catalog), International Center of Photography, New York, 1981.

"A Harrowing World Versus the Good Life" by Gene Thornton, *The New York Times*, April 26, 1981.

"How the March on Washington Shaped A Man's Life" by C. Gerald Fraser, *The New York Times*, April 18, 1981.

See photographs pages 267–269.

FRYE, VINCENT
active New York City, 1980s

GAIRY, JOHN
active New York City, 1980s

GARDNER, KENLEY A.
active Philadelphia, 1970s

GARNER, GIL
active Los Angeles, 1980–present

An exhibiting fine art photographer, Garner is a successful commercial photographer with clients throughout the United States. Garner graduated from the Herron Art School in Indianapolis, Indiana, and has taken photography and art classes at the Art Center School of Design and the Otis Art Institute in Los Angeles. His works have been published in numerous periodicals throughout the country.

SELECTED EXHIBITIONS/BIBLIOGRAPHY

1983–1984. "California Black Photographers: The Tradition Continues" (exhibition catalog), The California Museum of Afro-American History and Culture, Los Angeles, California.

GEORGE, RENNIE
active Bronx, New York, 1970s

GEORGIOU, TYRONE (1947–   )
active Buffalo, New York

Tyrone Georgiou is known for his constructed photosculptures incorporating photographic images displayed as dioramas. He uses painting, architectural installations, polaroid and silver gelatin prints to create environmental photographic images. He states about his recent work that the diaoramas, which he started in 1985, began "as a way for me to personally discuss the mythology of photography and photo history. . . . I have become even more interested in exploring my relationships (both emotionally and psychologically) to the real world of life and society. This is most ironic since my interest in photographing originally grew out of my political involvement in the radical movement of the 1960s. Perhaps photography has served as the religion in which I managed to calm my confusion and hostility toward the world."

Georgiou, interested in design, architecture, photography and history, studied at Yale University's School of Art and Architecture, receiving a B.F.A. and M.F.A. He bought his first camera in 1966 and was committed to photographing the sociopolitical atmosphere of the time. In the late 1960s, he worked as a photographer, graphic artist and draftsman in Harlem and in the black community of New Haven.

As a photography professor at the State University of New York at Buffalo, he received numerous awards and grants in photography, including a National Endowment for the Arts grant and a research fellowship from the State University of New York Research Foundation. In addition to his teaching responsibilities at SUNY, Buffalo, Georgiou gives workshops in Photographic Techniques at the Firehouse Art Center (Norman, New York), CEPA Photo Workshop, and the Albright-Knox Art Gallery in Buffalo, New York, among others.

A lecturer and panelist, Georgiou has served on the New York Foundation for the Arts and the Creative Artists Public Service Grants Committee and has given numerous lectures on early photographic processes. He is featured in Michelle Auer's *Photographers Encyclopedia International 1839 to Present*, published in 1985 by Editions Camera Obscura.

COLLECTIONS

George Eastman House, Rochester, New York
Polaroid Print Collection, Cambridge, Massachusetts
Burchfield Center, Buffalo, New York

SELECTED EXHIBITIONS

1987. "New American Photographers," Fogg Art Museum, Harvard University, Cambridge, Massachusetts

1987. "Afro-American Artists, New Images," James Howe Gallery, Kean College, Union, New Jersey.

1986. "Photography in Western New York: A Regional Survey," Visual Studies Workshop, Rochester, New York

1982. "Images of Niagara Falls," Buscaglia-Castellani Gallery, Niagara Falls, New York

1980. "The Painterly Photograph," Washington Project for the Arts, Washington, DC

1979. "One man show: Contemporary Photography Series," International Museum of Photography at the George Eastman House, Rochester, New York

1976. "Five Western New York Photographers," CEPA Gallery, Buffalo, New York

SELECTED BIBLIOGRAPHY

"Afro-American Artists: New Images," Kean College of New Jersey (exhibition catalog), 1987.

"The Taking of Niagara, a History of the Falls in Photography" by Anthony Bannon, *Afterimage*, October, 1982.

American Photographer, September, 1980.

"Graphic Plus," (exhibition catalog), Ithaca: Herbert Johnson Museum, Cornell University, 1981.

"In Western New York, 1979" (exhibition catalog), Albright-Knox Art Gallery, Buffalo, New York.

Essence Magazine, Vol. 1. No. 4, August, 1970, p. 29.

The Metropolitan Museum of Art Bulletin, Vol. XXVII, No. 5, New York, New York.

See photographs pages 270–271.

GIBSON, BERNADETTE F. B.
active California, 1979–present

Originally a psychology major (B.A.), Gibson received a B.F.A. in photography from the California Institute of Arts and a M.A. in photography from California State University. As a free-lance photographer, she has worked with galleries and theater groups.

SELECTED EXHIBITIONS

1986. "Alumni Exhibition," California Institute of the Arts, Los Angeles, California

1986. "If it's Friday, it must be Fish" (solo exhibition) California State University, Fullerton, California

1984. "Olympic Pretensions," Los Angeles Photography Center, Los Angeles, California

1984. "Strictly Pictures/No Rhetoric," Black Gallery, Los Angeles, California

1983. "The Tradition Continues: California Black Photographers," California Museum of Afro-American History and Culture, Los Angeles, California

1981. "Aesthetics of Dance," Nassau County Museum of Fine Arts, Hempstead, New York

See photograph page 272.

GIBSON, RAY
active Brooklyn, New York, 1970s

GIBSON, SAM
active New York City, 1970s

GILES, FRANCIS (1946–   )
active Vermont

Francis Giles was born in Chicago. He is an editorial and commercial photographer. Currently living in Burlington, Vermont, Giles teaches photography at Goddard College and at the University of Vermont. He has a B.A. in photography and an M.A. in art history from Burlington College in Vermont. Giles has been a photojournalist for *The Washington Post* and the *Evanston* [Illinois] *Review.*

Giles' editorial photography began in 1975 while the photographer was living in Washington, DC. He worked primarily covering White House, Congressional and diplomatic events. As a free-lance photojournalist, he photographed in Israel, Egypt, Syria and Jordan. A Vietnam veteran, Giles covered veteran affairs and events in Washington for *The Post.*

He continues to do freelance editorial, documentary and portrait work including his own more personal images. He often photographs, with compassion, the plight of the elderly in this country. An advocate for the aging, he once wrote about one of his photo essays, "I feel they beg for words of feeling—explanations of these sort of illnesses [Alzheimer] and a plea for rationality in dealing with aging now!"

Giles has exhibited in galleries in Vermont, New York and New Jersey. He is listed in *Who's Who in American Colleges and Universities, 1969* and has received two grants for his photography: one from the Yaddo Foundation (1980) and the other from the Burlington Arts Council (1985).

SELECTED EXHIBITIONS
1987. "Seven Black Photographers: 1920–80, The Cooper Union, New York, New York
1987. "Transubstantiation" (series about growing old), Daily Planet Gallery, Burlington, Vermont
1987. "Portrait Retrospective 1970–87," Grand Central Gallery, Burlington, Vermont
1987. "Art in Vermont '87," Helen Day Art Center, Stowe, Vermont

See photographs page 273.

GIRAUX, LEISANT
active Brooklyn, New York, 1970s

GLEATON, TONY (1948–)
active Los Angeles and Mexico

Tony Gleaton, born in Detroit, Michigan, moved to Los Angeles at the age of eleven. Gleaton studied industrial design at the University of California, Los Angeles, and photography at the Art Center College of Design in Los Angeles.

Gleaton has worked as a fashion and dance photographer in New York City. Tired of big-city life in the early 1980s, he embarked on a project documenting the black cowboy in the West and Mexico entitled "Cowboys and Indians, A MultiEthnic Portrait."

Since 1985, Gleaton has been working on "La Raza Negra," a photo essay on the present-day descendants of survivors of a slave ship, transporting black slaves, wrecked in coastal waters south of the Bahia de Acapulco. (Between 1580 and 1750 more than 100,000 men and women were brought from Africa through Cuba to colonial Mexico by Spanish slave traders.)

SELECTED EXHIBITIONS

1987. "Sangre Pura" [Pure Blood], Mexico's African Legacy, William Grant Still Community Arts Center, Los Angeles, California

1987. "The West, A Multi-Ethnic Portrait," Los Angeles City Hall Bridge Gallery, Los Angeles, California

See photographs pages 274–275.

GLOSTER, DOROTHY
active New York City, 1970s

GORDON, DAVID A. (1954–)
active Buffalo, New York

Architectural, industrial and commercial photographer, Gordon is based in the Buffalo/ Niagara Falls area. He has a B.A. in architecture from Yale University and a M.F.A. in photography from the State University of New York at Buffalo. Gordon also teaches college-level photography classes. His personal work is primarily concerned with social issues in his community. Discussing his current project, "Hold," on black churches, Gordon states, "The camera provides me with a personally secure means of entrance to an experience. These photographs and the taking of them were essential in my quest to understand the demonstrative, spirit-filled worship that typifies the services of the Church of Our Lord Jesus Christ of the Apostolic Faith. The Buffalo member of this organization is the Refuge Temple of Christ. Most of the time spent on this four-year project was spent here.

"The photographs in the exhibition 'Hold' relate objective documentary information concerning the church people and their rituals. Further, I feel these images work in indicating the attachment the congregation has for their beliefs. The photographs also provide a revealing window of understanding to the culture from which these individuals come".

SELECTED EXHIBITIONS

1986. "Hold," Buscagila-Castellani Art Gallery, Niagara Falls, New York
1986. "Hold," CEPA Gallery, Buffalo, New York
1986. "Photography: A Regional Survey," Visual Studies Workshop, Rochester, New York
1986. "Point of View," Peopleart Gallery, Buffalo, New York
1986. "Cray, Gordon, and Pappas," Community Folk Art Gallery, Syracuse, New York
1986. "Western New York Exhibition", Albright-Knox Art Gallery, Buffalo, New York
1986. "Exchange Show," University of Oklahoma, Norman, Oklahoma

SELECTED BIBLIOGRAPHY

CEPA Quarterly, Summer 1986, Volume 1, Issue 4, Buffalo, New York.

See photographs page 276.

GRANNUM, HUGH P. (1940–)
active Detroit

Hugh Grannum, a photojournalist for the *Detroit Free Press* has been active in photography for the last twenty years. As a free-lance photographer in New York City in the late 1960s, he worked for the television program "Black Journal," the textbook publishers Harcourt, Brace and for the New Lafayette Theatre. In 1969, Grannum was hired as the photography director for the Free Southern Theatre to document the touring company's performances in the South.

Grannum studied photography and art at the Society of Arts and Crafts in Detroit, Michigan, and at New York City's Community College. A cinematographer and teacher, he has taught classes at Wayne County Community College (Michigan). An award-winning photographer, Grannum is a member of the National Association of Black Journalists, National Conference of Artists, National Press Photographers Association and Detroit Metro Photographers Association. His works have been published in the *Black Photographers Annual*, Vols. I and II, and in *Newsweek, Time, Sepia,* and *Black Enterprise* magazines.

Selected Exhibitions

1983. "Image and Imagination," Jazzonia Gallery, Detroit, Michigan

1980. Detroit Republican National Convention, Hart Plaza Ethnic Gallery, Michigan

1975. "Black Photographers Annual Touring Exhibition" (United States, Europe and Russia)

1975. Gallery 7, Detroit, Michigan

1971. "One Man Show," Studio Museum in Harlem, New York, New York

1971. "Black Arts Festival," Concept East Theatre, Detroit, Michigan

See photographs pages 277–279.

Grant, Joe
active New York City, 1970s

Grant, Milton B. (1944–   )
active New York City

Milton B. Grant was born in Jamaica, West Indies. He attended the School of Visual Arts in New York City and joined the staff of the United Nations in 1969. Since joining the Department of Public Information as a staff photographer, he has been on assignments in the Middle East, Africa, Central and South America, the Caribbean and Europe. His photographs include environmental and living conditions, effects of natural disasters, United Nations peace-keeping operations and development projects. At the United Nations headquarters, he has photographed heads of state and government as well as prominent artists and political leaders. His photographs have appeared in numerous publications worldwide. A member of the United Nations Camera Club, his photographs have been in exhibitions throughout the world.

Collections

The United Nations, New York, New York

The Schomburg Center for Research in Black Culture, The New York Public Library, New York, New York

See photographs pages 280–282.

Gray, George
active Compton, California, 1980s

GRAY, RONALD K.
active New York City, 1970s

GRAY, TED
active Chicago, 1970s

See photograph page 283.

GRAY, TODD (1954–)
active Los Angeles

Gray, a commercial and fine art photographer, is fascinated by the possibilities of abstract forms and shapes. He produces unconventional fashion photographs, which have been published in trade magazines and newspapers in New York and Los Angeles. Born in Los Angeles, Gray is primarily interested in his personal work in the exploration of the human form through the photographic medium. He combines text and images, creating ambiguous forms suggesting transformed reality. A graduate of the California Institute of the Arts, he received a B.F.A. in 1979.

COLLECTIONS

University of Parma, Parma, Italy

SELECTED EXHIBITIONS

1986. "Personal Icons," Los Angeles Center for Photographic Studies, Los Angeles, California
1985. "Outspeak," Los Angeles Center for Photographic Studies, Los Angeles, California
1984. "Photography: Large Scale New Work," Rex W. Wignall Museum Gallery, Loma, California
1984. "All California '84," Laguna Beach Museum of Art, California
1984. "Hard Werken, Hamde Isdrukwerk: Gebruikte Fotografie," Perspektief Gallerie, Rotterdam, The Netherlands
1983. "Contemporary Photoworks II," Albuquerque United Artists, Albuquerque, New Mexico
1982. "Pigazzini e Gray," It Diaframma, Milan, Italy
1977. "Three Points of View," Soho Cameraworks, Los Angeles, California

SELECTED BIBLIOGRAPHY

La Palma, Marina, "Reflecting Inner Worlds," *Artweek*, April 26, 1986.
Gray, Todd, "Icarus and Odysseus," *Spectacle*, No. 3, 1985.
Ohland, Gloria, "Black, White, and Gray," *LA Weekly*, August 9, 1984.

Muchnic, Suzanne, "Two Schools: Faculties of Life," *Los Angeles Times*, September 15, 1984.

"New Art in Los Angeles," *High Fashion* (Tokyo), July 1984.

Johnstone, Mark, "Questions of Scale," *Artweek*, April 7, 1984.

"70's Style Is Photo Exhibit Focus," *The New Mexico Sun*, January 16, 1983.

See photographs pages 284–286.

GREEN, ALEX
active Brooklyn, New York, 1970s

GREEN, JOHN
active Massachusetts, 1963–present

John Green received a B.S. from the University of Massachusetts at Amherst in 1977. As a teenager in Philadelphia, he became fascinated by nature. Green's photographs of nature have been widely published and exhibited for their artistic and scientific merit. He began to photograph birds while stationed in the U.S. Army in Alaska in 1963. He has been employed by the U.S. Forest Service. Green is a member of the Massachusetts Camera Naturalists, the Photographic Society of America, American Nature Study Society and the Massachusetts Environmental Education Society.

As a photographer, he has recorded natural history projects in the Everglades, Glacier National Park and across southern Canada.

SELECTED BIBLIOGRAPHY

Booth, Ed, "Photographs Give Nature Special Focus," *Richmond Times Dispatch*, April 20, 1986.

GREEN, WILLIAM
active New York City, 1980s

GREENE, STANLEY
active Paris, France, and San Francisco, 1970–present

Greene received a B.F.A. in 1978 and an M.F.A. in photography in 1980 from the San Francisco Arts Institute. He has studied photography with photojournalist W. Eugene Smith and in workshops in the early 1970s such as Imagework in Cambridge, Massachusetts, and the School of Visual Arts in New York City.

He has worked as a photojournalist for newspapers and magazines in the San Francisco area and acted as free-lance photographer for trade magazines in the music industry. In the mid-1980s Greene moved to Paris, France, working as a photojournalist and exhibition photographer. French photographer and curator Alain Dister wrote: "To be a black photographer today in America is, almost without exception, to find yourself cornered in a small ghetto, without any access to the official media. Very few escape this treatment. Stanley's problem was even worse. Not only did America refuse to accept him as anything but a black photographer, but in addition he felt attracted by something which is usually the reserved domain of middle-class white youths: rock and roll."

COLLECTIONS

Bay Area Music Archives, San Francisco, California
Bibliotheque Nationale, Paris, France
Camerawork Gallery, San Francisco, California

See photographs pages 287–289.

GREENE, TREVOR (1956–)
active New York City

Trevor Greene was born and raised in New York City. A self-taught photographer, Greene moved to California in 1980 to take photography classes at Long Beach Community College. His primary interest in photography since 1984 has been to document musicians and singers in the New York area. His portfolio consists of photographs of "rap" stars such as Whodini, Kurtis Blow, Run-DMC, and Dr. Jeckyll and Mr. Hyde.

Inspired by Roy DeCarava's jazz photographs, Greene began taking photographs using available light (without flash) at concerts, discos and night clubs. His photographs have appeared on Run-DMC's first album (Profile Records, 1984) and in trade publications such as *Black Beat, Right On, Rock and Soul,* and *Billboard,* among others. Commenting on his work, Greene states, "I thought it was really important to preserve what they [rappers] were doing. For a long time I was the only one on stage shooting."

COLLECTIONS

Schomburg Center for Research in Black Culture, The New York Public Library, New York, New York

GRIFFIN, WALTER
active Minneapolis, 1980s

GRIMES, JOHN
active Los Angeles, 1980s

GROSS, MICHAEL
active Washington, DC, 1980s

HAGGINS, ROBERT
active New York City, 1960s

HALE, KEITH N.
active Chicago, 1970s

HALE-HAMMOND, LYDIA
active New York City, 1970s

HALLETT, GEORGE (1942–)
active South Africa, England, France, The Netherlands

George Hallett was born in Cape Town, South Africa. His interest in photography started at the age of seventeen. He enjoyed going to movies and looking at picture magazines. He was hired by a studio to take photographs as he worked in other jobs such as a librarian, computer operator and factory worker. His early photographs were of the daily activities of the black people in Cape Town. In 1970, Hallett emigrated to London to learn more about the art of photography. He wanted to work as a photojournalist, an experience he would never have in South Africa.

Moving to London, he worked as a photojournalist for Times Educational Books. Then in Paris in the early 1970s, Hallett had the opportunity to exhibit his photographs, make films and teach photography and communication courses. He has also taught photojournalism classes in Zimbabwe.

Hallett's portrait work consists of images of African artists, musicians and writers living in exile in Europe and the United States. He has designed calendars and posters for SWAPO (SouthWest Africa's Peoples Organization of Namibia) and produced bookcovers for the Heinemann African Writer Series in London. Hallett stated in an interview with American journalist Kelly Mitchell Clark that "photography is a powerful tool to be used to record the history of our struggle." His aim "... is to make visible the invisible.

Images of black South Africans that are not in the hands of the people. The inability to present a positive image of our culture is the result of a deliberate attempt to deny us our voice."

COLLECTIONS

Schomburg Center for Research in Black Culture, The New York Public Library, New York, New York

SELECTED EXHIBITIONS

1984. "Art Against Apartheid," Exhibition of 4 Photographers, Schomburg Center for Research in Black Culture, The New York Public Library, New York, New York

1983. "14 Photographers," Schomburg Center for Research in Black Culture, The New York Public Library, New York, New York

1983. "George Hallett Photographic Images," Howard University, Gallery of Art, Washington, DC

1983. "Black Photographers: from South Africa to South Carolina," Otto Rene Castillo Center for Working Class Culture, New York, New York

1982. "Women In Southern Africa," Harare, Zimbabwe

1982. "George Hallett Photographic Images" (traveling exhibition, University of Illinois, Emory University, Michigan State University and Tuskegee Institute)

1981. "George Hallett," Ceret, Southern France

1976. S. Henie Museum of Modern Art (one-person show), Oslo, Norway

SELECTED BIBLIOGRAPHY

The South Africa Calendar, 1988 (text and photographs by George Hallett), distributed by the Holland Committee on Southern Africa, The Netherlands, 1987.

"George Hallett, Photographic Images" (exhibition brochure), Howard University Gallery of Art, Washington, DC, 1983.

Ola, Akinshiju C., "Images from Imagination," *The Guardian* (New York), December 7, 1983.

Hallett, George, and Matthew, James. *Images*, published in South Africa, 1980.

Hallett, George. *South African Photographs* (text by Cosmo Peterse), London: Hickey Press, 1974.

Black Photographers Annual, Vol. II, New York: Black Photographers Annual, Inc., 1974.

See photographs pages 290–292.

HAMILTON, ALEXANDER
active New York City, 1980s

HANSBERRY, GAIL ADELLE
active Washington, DC, 1970–present

Hansberry became interested in photographing as a teenager, while living in Cairo, Egypt. She studied art and art history at Howard University (B.A.) and Smith College (M.A.). Known as a printmaker and photographer, Hansberry has free-lanced for over fifteen years. Her clients include publishers and advertising agencies in New York City and Washington, DC. She has taught art history at North Carolina Central University and worked as a researcher in the Books Division of Time, Inc. and has exhibited her prints and photographs in numerous exhibitions. She continues to photograph on her own during her trips around the United States as an Escort Officer, contracted by the United States Department of State.

She has exhibited at the Howard University Museum, Washington, DC and at Diana Gallery, American Museum of Natural History, and in the Bank Street College of Education's exhibition "Growing Up on the West Side," all in New York City.

COLLECTIONS

Howard University, Washington, DC
The Library of Congress, Washington, DC
Smith College, Northampton, Massachusetts
I.B.M. Corporation, New York, New York
International Center of Photography, New York, New York
Boston University, Boston, Massachusetts
Harvard University, Cambridge, Massachusetts

See photographs pages 293–294.

HANSBERRY, MORRIS G., JR.
active Louisville, Kentucky, 1970s

HARDISON, INGE
active New York City, 1948–present

Hardison has been active in photography since the late 1940s. Harlem has been her focus as a photographer. She studied art at the Art Students' League in New York City and during the 1950s worked as a teacher, actress and commercial artist. Currently she is working primarily as a sculptor, casting busts of civil and human rights leaders such as Frederick Douglass, Sojourner Truth and Dr. Martin Luther King, Jr.

Selected Bibliography

Moutoussamy-Ashe, Jeanne. *Viewfinders: Black Women Photographers*, New York: Dodd, Mead & Company, 1986.

See photographs pages 295–298.

Harris, Charles "Teenie" (1908–)
active Pittsburgh

"Teenie" Harris' major contribution to photography is his extensive documentation of black Americans in Pittsburgh from the post-Depression period through the post-civil rights era. In 1931, Harris became a photojournalist for the national black news weekly, *The Pittsburgh Courier*. For over forty years, Harris photographed every black social event, church group, organization, restaurant and night club for the *Courier*. Rare photographs of the "Negro" baseball league; jazz musicians such as Duke Ellington, Count Basie, Cab Calloway, Lena Horne, Eartha Kitt and Billy Eckstine; and the famous, infamous and lesser-known people who lived in or frequented the Pittsburgh area are also in his collection.

Subjects of interest include street scenes, classrooms, weddings, funerals and family portraits. Harris, a self-taught photographer, worked for *Flash* magazine in the 1930s as a salesman. He was later hired by the *Courier* as a free-lance photographer. "Teenie" Harris was the first black photographer to join the Pittsburgh chapter of the Newspaper Guild. He retired from the *Courier* in 1975.

In 1986, the University of Pittsburgh's Black Studies Department acquired over 50,000 "Teenie" Harris negatives. Sociologist Rollo Turner of the Black Studies Department is presently documenting the collection. He describes it as the most complete documentation through photographs of a black community anywhere. The collection is housed at the University of Pittsburgh and is presently owned by Pittsburgh sculptor Dennis Morgan.

Exhibitions

1987. "At Bat: Blacks at Forbes Field," University of Pittsburgh, Pennsylvania
1987. "Children of the Crossroads," Mercy Hospital, Pittsburgh, Pennsylvania
1987. "Highlights of the Hill," Hill House Association, Pittsburgh, Pennsylvania
1987. "Black Soldiers," Wilkinsburgh Public Library, Wilkinsburgh, Pennsylvania
1987. "Black Politics in Pittsburgh," Allegheny County Courthouse Gallery, Pittsburgh, Pennsylvania
1987. "Black History in Music," Pittsburgh Black Action Corporation, Pittsburgh, Pennsylvania

Selected Bibliography

Turner, Rollo, "Charles 'Teenie' Harris," *Pennsylvania Ethnic Heritage Studies Center Bulletin*, 1987.

HARDISON

"One Shot Harris," *Pittsburgh News*, February 25, 1987.

Byrd, Jerry, "Heyday on the Hill," *The Pittsburgh Press Sunday Magazine*, March 1, 1987.

"Exposing Black History," *Pitt* magazine, March 1987.

"'Teenie' Harris Life in Pictures," *The New Pittsburgh Courier*, February 28, 1987.

"Pitt to Restore 40,000 Hill Photos," *The Pittsburgh Press*, October 17, 1986.

Klopher, Milt, "Pittsburgh Courier Photographer Depicts 40 Years of Living History," *The Pitt News*, University of Pittsburgh, Vol. 81, No. 10, September 22, 1986.

"Harris Photo Exhibit Lauded," *The New Pittsburgh Courier*, July 19, 1986.

HARRIS, DOUG
active New York City, 1963–present

Born in Portsmouth, Virginia, Harris grew up in North Carolina and New York City. A college student in the early 1960s, Harris volunteered in the New York office of the Student Non-Violent Coordinating Committee (SNCC). Encouraged to photograph SNCC activities, Harris was given a camera by SNCC members as he traveled with the Freedom Singers who were touring in Alabama, Mississippi and Tennessee.

As Harris began to photograph more frequently, he studied with famed photographer Richard Avedon who agreed to train SNCC photographers. As his vision developed, he began to document the voter registration project in Raleigh, North Carolina. He later photographed the movement activities in Mississippi in 1964.

In Selma (1964–68), Harris set up his darkroom and documented the voter registration drives he organized throughout the area. One of his photo essays on the civil rights movement appeared in *Camera* magazine in 1973.

Returning to New York in 1968, Harris began to study film. He was the photographer-in-residence at the New Lafayette Theatre in Harlem and worked as photographer for the Black Theatre Alliance in the early 1970s. Traveling often in Africa during this period, Harris also taught at the Packer Film Institute, City College of New York, which he helped establish. His work has been published in numerous books and magazine articles.

As a filmmaker, he made two films, *Speaking in Tongues* and *Nicodemus*. The former was funded by a German television station and profiled two musicians; the latter was funded by the Kansas Historical Society and traces a community founded by free blacks at the end of Reconstruction.

SELECTED EXHIBITIONS/BIBLIOGRAPHY

1980. "We'll Never Turn Back," (exhibition catalog) Smithsonian Institution, National Museum of History, Washington, DC

Black World, February, 1971, p. 48

See photograph page 299.

HARRIS, JOE
active New York City, 1980s

HARRIS, JOHN "TEX" (1917–1979)
active New York City

John Harris was born in Baltimore, Maryland. A free-lance photographer and columnist for New York's *Amsterdam News*, he instituted a weekly feature entitled "The Roving Photographer." Tex Harris photographed almost every social and political event in Harlem during his tenure at the *Amsterdam News*; he was considered by his colleagues as "the tireless" photographer. His photographs included images of Muhammad Ali, Joe Frazier, Louis Armstrong, Adam Clayton Powell, Jr., Nina Simone and Josephine Baker.

HARRIS, MICHAEL D.
active Kent, Ohio, 1970s

HARRIS, THOMAS (1962–   )
active New York City

After studying biology at Harvard University (B.S. in biology), Harris traveled extensively in Europe and in 1984 began to use photography to document black artists living in European cities such as Paris and Amsterdam. While living in Italy, he worked for *Vogue Italia* as an assistant and photographer.

Harris has embarked on a photographic essay entitled "Women in Churches." In his own words, "Even as a child I observed women bringing a human element to church; supplying this place of worship with a special intimacy which appealed to me. I found the women—strong stewardesses, devout Sunday school teachers, choir women filled with emotion, the missionary society—all beautiful, all intriguing. 'Women in Churches' is about the memories and associations of growing up as a young boy in church."

A filmmaker as well as a photographer, Harris has produced a documentary about ten black and Hispanic Harvard students who move into a poor black neighborhood to set up an enrichment program. He writes about his work: "I see photography and film as a way to make my views of people, relationships and the world accessible to a diverse and large populace." His carefully composed images have been exhibited in Paris, France, New York City and in Cambridge, Massachusetts. His work has been published in *Axis* (Japan), January 1987, *New Observations* (New York), October 1987 and in the *Schomburg Center Journal* (July 1987).

SELECTED BIBLIOGRAPHY

Bourne, Kay, "Harvard students record project life" *The Bay State Banner*, October 8, 1987.

See photograph page 300.

HARRISON, JAMES
active New York City, 1980–present

Harrison became interested in photography in his early teens and later studied commercial art at New York City Community College. A social worker (B.A. Sociology from Virginia Union) as well as a photographer, Harrison does reportage in a very personal manner. He writes ". . . my photography collection is an extension of myself. My portfolio has a very special meaning to me in that I was compelled spiritually to take the photographs. At the decisive moment each one dominated my whole being. In my work, I seek to capture the innate beauty in those intrinsic qualities that people of African ancestry possess that are so rarely seen, frequently ignored and are often overlooked. My ultimate goal is to help remove the veil of stereotypical imagery that covers and hides the natural beauty of Africans at home and abroad."

Harrison has photographed in Africa, South America and the Caribbean as well as in the streets of New York.

SELECTED BIBLIOGRAPHY

"African Legacy." 475 *The Interchurch Center Newsletter*, Volume XXX, Issue 2, February 1987.
Seidel, Mitchell, "Black Women Portrayed in a Variety of Images," *Sunday Star Ledger* (Newark), July 20, 1986.

SELECTED EXHIBITIONS

1987. "Honoring the Arts of Harlem," Harlem Urban Development Corporation, New York, New York
1987. "Sources: Photographs by James Harrison," The Interchurch Center, New York, New York
1986. "Women of Color: Defined and Redefined," Unicorn Gallery, Newark, New Jersey

See photographs pages 301–302.

HARSLEY, ALEX (1938–)
active New York City

Committed to photography as a profession as well as being a mentor/curator/educator for minority photographers, Harsley has been active in the field since 1959. During the early sixties, he studied photography, worked as a photographer's assistant, and free-lanced for black publications such as the Amsterdam News (New York). In the early seventies, Harsley started an organization called the Minority Photographers, Inc. He held workshops, organized exhibitions and reviewed work from photographers worldwide. In 1975, he opened the 4th Street Photo Gallery as part of Minority Photographers, Inc.

In addition, Harsley has acted as mentor to a number of photographers. He has also continued his personal work. Harsley states, "I'm a visual artist in search of truth. I work as a documentarian with a conceptual approach and more specifically in the esoterics."

SELECTED EXHIBITIONS

1988. "100 Years: A Tradition of Social and Political Art on the Lower East Side," P.P.O.W., New York, New York

1988. "Visual Search for Truth in Materialism," (solo show), 4th Street Photo Gallery, New York, New York

1987. "Fabrication" (man-made objects by the Waterside, solo show), 4th Street Photo Gallery, New York, New York

1987. "History of Jazz Photography" (group show), Charas Gallery, New York, New York

1987. "Photo Exhibit on Photo Journalism" (group show), Cellar Gallery, Nyack, New York

1986. "R&R" (images taken before or after professional shooting to relax by; solo show), 4th Street Photo Gallery, New York, New York

1985. "Parallels of Inspiration (solo show), Nassau Community College, Garden City, New York

1982. "Five Black Photographers," Downtown Cultural Center Gallery, BACA, Brooklyn, New York

1978. "Exhibition of Photographs" (solo show), Black History Museum, Nassau County Museum, Hempstead, New York.

SELECTED BIBLIOGRAPHY

Braff, Phyllis, "Pictures Work a Thousand Words" Sunday *New York Times*, April 14, 1985.

"East Village", *ICI NEW* (French magazine), April 1984.

Bey, Dawoud, "Image Problems" *American Arts*, July, 1984.

SWN Discoveries "Alex Harsley: Photography's Black Gnome", The *Soho Weekly News*, August 14, 1975.

See photographs pages 303–304.

HAYNES, RICHARD, JR. (1949–   )
active New York City

A staff photographer for publisher Holt, Rinehart and Winston/CBS Inc., Haynes has a strong consciousness of composition and form in his work. He has an M.F.A. in photography from Pratt Institute (New York). His work has been published in *American Heritage, Ebony Man* and *Reader's Digest*. He has also frequently photographed for corporate annual reports and advertisements. Haynes, born in James Island, South Carolina, has taught mural painting, costume design, stage design and puppetry classes in community centers in the New York area.

EXHIBITIONS

1986. "Women of Color: Defined and Redefined," Unicorn Gallery, Newark, New Jersey
1978. "Thesis Exhibition Show," Pratt Institute, New York, New York
1978. "Group Show," Focal Point Gallery, City Island, New York
1977. Herbert H. Lehman College, Bronx, New York
1974. Bronx Museum, Bronx, New York

See photographs pages 305–306.

HELITON, BOB
active Houston, 1980s

HENDERSON, ED
active Inglewood, California, 1980s

HENDERSON, LEROY W.
active New York City, 1965–present

Henderson began his career as a fine artist, with an emphasis in painting, drawing and printmaking. His interest in photography began as a child when he would pore over picture magazines such as *Life* and *Look*, from impressions received looking at old photographs with his grandmother's stereoscopic viewer and from the excitement he recalls from his first experience of seeing an image reflected on the ground glass of an old box camera. He bought his first camera, a Brownie Hawkeye, at the age of twelve. He often emulated the kinds of photographs contest winners published in his hometown newspaper—usually genre scenes with dramatic cloud formations.

Photography remained an interest during his formal art studies, but he never took photography classes while pursuing his B.A. and M.A. at Virginia State University and Pratt Institute. He later bought a 35mm camera and light meter and read extensively about photography in books and magazines. Henderson learned basic darkroom techniques in his spare time while in the U.S. Army. After leaving the army, he took additional courses in darkroom, color photography and photojournalism at the School of Visual Arts in New York.

After a brief career in teaching, he yielded to his growing interest in photography. He became especially interested in journalism and documenting events related to the social changes of the 1960s and 1970s (particularly as they related to the concerns of black Americans). His first assignment in 1967 was a photo essay on shoeshine boys in the Times Square area that accompanied an article by Piri Thomas, author of "Down These Mean Streets." Henderson became a regular contributing photographer for *Black Enterprise* magazine from its first issue in 1970 until 1983. He documented the most active years of the development of the Bedford-Stuyvesant Restoration Corporation, in Brooklyn from 1969 to 1985. He also worked for corporations photographing annual reports and activities, social agencies, advertising companies, public relations firms, picture agencies, and government agencies. His photographs have appeared in magazines such as *Der Spiegel* (Germany), *Panorama* (Italy), *Jet, Ebony Man, New York, Newsweek* and *Essence.*

Henderson has exhibited in museums, galleries and colleges in the United States and Europe. Awards for his photography include the CEBA Award of Distinction; Photo/Graphis, International; and the Art Director's Club Award. He has also worked on documentary films and television productions in Germany, Holland and the United States.

See photographs pages 307–308.

HENRY, LAURANCE   (1933–1978)
active Philadelphia

Laurance Henry, a Baptist minister and a photographer, was active during the civil rights movement. In the early 1960s, Henry photographed leaders in the black community of New York and Philadelphia. He documented protest marches in Philadelphia, Selma and Washington, DC. Prominent names found in his collection include Dr. Martin Luther King, Jr., Rev. Adam Clayton Powell, Jr., the Honorable Elijah Muhammad, Malcolm X, Dick Gregory, Ruby Dee, and Philadelphia radio personality Georgie Woods. He accompanied Malcolm X on his trip to Mecca, shortly before he was assassinated and photographed the last rites of the slain leader in 1965.

COLLECTIONS

Afro-American Historical and Cultural Museum, Philadelphia, Pennsylvania
Schomburg Center for Research in Black Culture, New York, New York

See photographs pages 309–311.

HERRING, MARK
active Phoenix, Arizona, 1970s

HICKS, CALVIN
active Los Angeles, 1980s

HIGGINS, CHESTER, JR. (1946–)
active New York City

Best known for his publications, *Black Women* and *Drums of Life*, Chester Higgins has an enormous archive of images of African-Americans and Africans during the post-civil rights/post-independence era of the 1960s. He began photographing while a student at Tuskegee Institute (B.S., Business Management, 1970). As a student at Tuskegee he published his first photographs of the South in *The Negro Digest*. In 1967, he bought his first camera, a Praktika. His early photographs were of his friends and other students at Tuskegee. Higgins, at this time, met the school photographer and noted Tuskegee studio photographer, P. H. Polk. He began to read photographic books and look at the works of Farm Security Administration photographers Dorothea Lange, Walker Evans, Arthur Rothstein and Gordon Parks.

Born in Alabama, Higgins published his first book *Student Unrest at Tuskegee Institute: A Chronology* in 1968. Often photographing the black community, Higgins employs a style that is both straightforward and compassionate.

In 1980, Higgins, also a lecturer, published his fourth book *Some Time Ago*, a photo essay of the history of blacks in American between 1850 and 1950.

In his own words, "What I find most interesting about photography is that the act of taking pictures is like that of a time machine. By capturing life as it was the moment the picture was taken, the camera preserves it and lets us 'reach back' and gain, albeit in a limited manner, a sense of a different time." A staff photographer for *The New York Times* since 1975, Higgins has photographed for many magazines, including *Look, Life, Time, Ebony, Essence, Encore* and *Black Enterprise*. He has also frequently photographed for authors in such books as Nikki Giovanni's *Gemini* and *Re-Creation* and Charles Hamilton's *Preacher Man*.

He is featured in a PBS-TV film entitled "An American Photographer: Chester Higgins, Jr." and has received numerous grants from the Ford Foundation, The Rockefeller Foundation and the National Endowment for the Arts, among others. Higgins is a member of the American Society of Magazine Photographers and the Rapho-Guillumette Pictures Agency, Inc. His works in progress include "Conversations with Myself," personal journals and other writings; "Diaspora," a photo essay on people of African descent throughout the world; "Things We Do," a socio-anthropological photo essay on the universality of human behavior. Higgins has exhibited at the National Portrait Gallery, the International Center of Photography, The Nigerian Museum, the Maison de la Negritude, Yale University and the Studio Museum in Harlem.

COLLECTIONS

The Museum of Modern Art, New York, New York
International Center of Photography, New York, New York
Tuskegee Institute University, Tuskegee, Alabama
Library of Congress, Washington, DC

SELECTED BIBLIOGRAPHY

Drane, Francesca, "Photographer's Quest: A Universal Human Vision," *New York's News-world*, February 26, 1981.

Sheppard, Nathaniel Jr., "Love Marks Higgins Photos of Blacks," *The New York Times*, June 14, 1974.

Emerson, Frank, "His Photo Subjects Are Black But the Message Is Universal, *New York Post*, June 20, 1974.

Coleman, A.D., "Warm and Gentle, but Incomplete," *The New York Times*, June 16, 1974.

"Photography: Chester Higgins, Jr.," *New York Age*, June 15, 1974

Fraser, C. Gerald, "Going Out Guide" *The New York Times*, June 3, 1974.

Langer, Don, "Camera Talk" *The New York Post*, May 30, 1974.

Coleman, A.D., "Black Women" by *The New York Times*, Jan. 17, 1971.

Higgins, Chester, and McDougall, Harold, "Men on Women" *Essence*, January 1971.

BOOKS BY CHESTER HIGGINS:

Higgins, Chester, and Combs, Orde, *Some Time Ago*, New York: Doubleday, 1980

Higgins, Chester, *Drums of Life*, New York: Anchor Press/Doubleday, 1974

Higgins, Chester, and McDougall, Harold. *Black Women*, New York: McCalls, 1970.

See photographs pages 312–315.

HILAIRE, MAX
active New York City, 1980s

HILL, MADELEINE
active New York City, 1970s

HINTON, ARNOLD
active New York City, 1970s

Hinton, Bill
active Westchester County, New York, 1980s

Hinton, Milton J. (1910–   )
active New York City

Hinton was born in Vicksburg, Mississippi. His connection with jazz musicians and composers and his own accomplishments as a jazz bassist made him the first well-known jazz musician/photographer. He received his first camera as a birthday present in 1935, an Argus C-3 35mm. At that time, he was playing with Cab Calloway's band. He began photographing his friends in candid poses in small towns, backstage and in their dressing rooms.

Hinton, who had been photographing his musician friends more as a record of their activities than as a commercial venture, photographed almost every night. Often he did not have the opportunity to process a roll of film, as he was constantly traveling. For more than thirty years, he saved unprocessed rolls of film, later to realize that he had a vast and most accurate record of jazz musicians and singers in performance and off stage. Hinton's photographs are of jazz greats he performed with including Cab Calloway, Erskine Tate, Art Tatum, Billie Holiday, Dizzy Gillespie, Lionel Hampton, among others. His fifty-year career as a musician has never overshadowed his photographic interest—rather it complemented it.

Milton Hinton also had a brief career as a free-lance photographer. His photographs have appeared in publications such as *Popular Photography* and *Downbeat*. His work has been in group exhibitions in Europe and the United States, among them shows at Rutgers University (Newark, New Jersey), The Floating Foundation of Photography (New York City), The Addison Gallery of American Art (Andover, Massachusetts) and the Rhode Island School of Design (Providence). His solo exhibitions have been at the West Las Vegas Library, (Las Vegas, Nevada); Northwestern University (Evanston, Illinois); Paul Cava Gallery (Philadelphia); the MidWest Museum of American Art (Elkhart, Indiana); and the Parsons School of Design (New York City).

Selected Bibliography

Hinton, Milt and Berger, David G., *Bass Line: The Stories and Photographs of Milt Hinton.* Philadelphia: Temple University Press, 1988.

Berger, David, "On the Road: 50 Years of Jazz Photographs by Milt Hinton" (exhibition brochure) Parsons School of Design, New York, New York, 1985.

The Christian Science Monitor, July 22, 1985.

A Century of Black Photographers: 1840–1960 (exhibition catalog), Rhode Island School of Design, 1983.

Diversions Magazine, May 1982.

See photographs pages 316–318.

HOLLAND, BOBBY
active Los Angeles, 1980s

See photograph page 319.

HOLLINS, LEON
active Los Angeles, 1980–present

Hollins is a free-lance photographer and computer analyst. He has worked as an editorial and sports photographer for the network stations, newspapers, trade magazines and the wire news services. His assignments include auto races, political conventions and the launchings of the Space Shuttle at Kennedy Space Center.

See photographs pages 320–321.

HOLT, JOHN
active Chicago, 1970s

HOOD, ZEBONIA
active Atlanta, 1970s

HOPKINS, STEPHEN L. (1946–   )
active New York City and Salvador, Bahia

Stephen L. Hopkins was born in Brooklyn, New York. He studied drawing, painting, photography and film at Cooper Union, New York (B.F.A., 1974). Hopkins has had various free-lance photographic assignments which include editorial and commercial, multimedia and video. He has worked on a number of documentary film and video projects and is the recipient of the Jessie H. Neal Award for Outstanding Journalism.

Hopkins assignments have been in Europe, Canada and South America. His work has been exhibited in galleries throughout the world. He is an affiliate of the Black Star Photo Agency, and some of his color work is in their collection. His most recent personal project is entitled "Project Afro Cabelo," a collaboration with Brazilian anthropologist/sociologist Ana Meire Aguiar. This photo documentation project explores and describes the women of Salvador, Bahia's retention of African culture through fashion and hairstyles.

See photographs pages 322–323.

HOWELL, BILL   (1944–1975)
active New York City

Born in Tennessee, Howell studied at the Philadelphia Museum College of Art. In the mid-1970s, Howell was a member of the artists group Weusi Nyumba Ya Sanaa. The group was noted for exhibiting works by black artists. He was also the artist in residence at the New Lafayette Theatre in Harlem during this time. Howell was a painter, photographer and collagist. His photographs were noted for the use of hand-coloring in selected areas enhancing surrealist studies of his images of Africa and the people of Harlem.

See photograph page 324.

HUDNALL, EARLIE, JR.   (1946–   )
active Houston, Texas

Earlie Hudnall is a staff photographer for Texas Southern University. He has a B.A. in Art Education from Texas Southern and is a free-lance photographer, graphic arts consultant and staff photographer for the *Houston Informer*. Hudnall has exhibited in museums and galleries throughout the United States. His work is included in private and public collections and has been published in the *Permanent Collection of Traditional African Art* catalogue published by Intercollegiate Press, Texas Southern University Library.

Hudnall has been working on a study of Houston's oldest neighborhoods for over ten years. His study is entitled "Images of the Wards" and captures the changing faces and facades of this distinguished community. In his own words, "I chose to use the camera as a tool to document different aspects of life—who we are, what we do, how we live, what our communities look like. These various patterns are all interwoven like a quilt into important patterns of history. A unique commonality exists between young and old because there is always a continuity between the past and the future. It is this commonality which I strive to depict in my work. The camera really does not matter; it is only a tool. What is important is the ability to transform an instance, a moment into a meaningful, expressive, and profound statement, some of which are personal, some of which have a symbolic and universal meaning. My photographs are mere archetypes of my childhood. They represent a literal transcription of actuality—the equivalent of what I saw or felt. The viewer must accept the image as his own and respond emotionally as well as aesthetically to the captured image."

EXHIBITIONS

1986. The Hale Woodruff Memorial Exhibition, "Emerging Artists from the Southwest," Studio Museum in Harlem, New York, New York
1986. "Architecture and Culture: The Fourth Ward," Diverse Works, Houston, Texas
1986. "America: Another Perspective," New York University, New York, New York

1985. "Sixteenth Annual Juried Photo Exhibition," Deutser Art Gallery, Jewish Community Center of Houston, Houston, Texas

1984. "Images of the Wards," Houston Public Library, Texas

1984. "African American Photographers of the Southwest, 1950–1984," Texas Southern University, Houston, Texas

1982. "Africa, America, and the Black Caribbean," Sutton's Black Heritage Gallery, Houston, Texas

1982. "Through the Eyes of Earlie Hudnall," M.D. Anderson Library, University of Houston, Houston, Texas

1981. Permanent Photography Exhibition, Kashmere Gardens Library, Commissioned by the Cultural Arts Council of Houston, Houston, Texas.

COLLECTIONS

Texas Southern University, Houston, Texas
Kashmere Gardens Library, Houston, Texas
Eliza Johnson Center for the Aged, Houston, Texas

SELECTED BIBLIOGRAPHY

"Emerging Artists from the Southwest" (exhibition catalogue), The Hale Woodruff Memorial Exhibition, The Studio Museum in Harlem, New York, 1986.

See photographs pages 325–327.

HUFF, LAWRENCE

active Georgia and California, 1980–present

Studying photography at the George Tice Photographic Workshop, the Maine Photographic Workshop and the Ansel Adams Workshop, Huff has earned a reputation as a fine art photographer. He explores the boundaries of the medium of photography and the idea of surrealism. Huff's life has been characterized "by his determined pursuit of the goals that he sets for himself." He has a sign on the door of his studio that says "Push Hard" and he does! When an injury ended his career as a world contender in competition karate, he began to focus on photography.

He has a masterful command of nineteenth- and twentieth-century photographic processes. He uses a large-format camera (8 × 10″) and uses the platinum process for printing his images. His imagery is formal. He has been developing a personal style that incorporates the qualities of classism and formalism and uses his well-developed ability to draw from inner resources. He is exploring what he calls "dark places"—those hidden and sensitive recesses of heart and soul.

Huff has received the 1986 State of Georgia artist grant and the Artist in Residence Fellowship at the Montalvo Center for Arts (California), among other awards.

COLLECTIONS

Atlanta Life Insurance Company, Atlanta, Georgia

Montalvo Center for the Arts, Saratoga, California

Polaroid Corporation, Cambridge, Massachusetts

AT&T Corporation, Atlanta, Georgia

St. Mary's Hospital Corporate Collection, Athens, Georgia

Dawson Gallery, Dedham, Massachusetts

Lamar Dodd Art Center, LaGrange, Georgia

SELECTED EXHIBITIONS

1987. Tisch School of the Arts, New York University, New York, New York

1987. Visual Arts Main Gallery, University of Georgia, Athens, Georgia

1987. Art Gallery, North Georgia College, Dahlonega, Georgia

1987. San Jose Art League, California

1986. California Works, Sacramento, California

1986. Photospiva 86, University of Nebraska-Lincoln, Lincoln, Nebraska

1985. Artist in Georgia: 1985, Georgia Museum of Art, Athens, Georgia

1985. Birmingham Biennial, Birmingham Museum of Art, Alabama

1985. The 5th Annual Afro-American Art Competition and Exhibition, Atlanta Life Insurance Company, Georgia.

SELECTED BIBLIOGRAPHY

The Photo Review, Vol. 9, No. 3, Summer 1986.

Birmingham (Alabama), Vol. 25, No. 9, August 1985.

The Best of Photography Annual 1983, published by Photographers Forum, Santa Barbara, California.

See photograph page 328.

HULL, ADONICA
active Los Angeles, 1980s

IFALADE, ADEOSHUN
active Chicago, 1980s

See photograph page 329.

JACKSON, BILL
active Greenville, Mississippi, 1970s

JACKSON, FRANK
active Los Angeles, 1980s

JACKSON, LEANDRE
active Philadelphia, 1980s

JACKSON, REGGIE
active New Haven, Connecticut, 1960s

JACKSON, REGINALD L.
active Boston 1965–present

Very active and well known internationally, Jackson graduated from Yale University, School of Art and Architecture (M.F.A., Photography) in 1970. A visual anthropologist, college professor and free-lance photographer, Jackson periodically exhibits, gives lectures and teaches workshops. He is recipient of numerous awards and fellowships, among them Ford Foundation, Smithsonian Research Fellowship and National Endowment for the Arts. Much of Reggie Jackson's work is anthropological in nature. He holds a Ph.D. in Visual Anthropology and is a member of the National Conference of Artists. Traveling throughout the Caribbean, Brazil and West Africa, Jackson's photographs explore the commonalities of the African diaspora.

COLLECTIONS

Hampshire College, Amherst, Massachusetts
Bishop College, Dallas, Texas
University of Massachusetts, Amherst, Massachusetts
Studio Museum in Harlem, New York, New York
Bowdoin College, Portland, Maine

SELECTED EXHIBITIONS

1986. "Perspectives: Nicaragua-Soviet Union: Children Are the Future," Museum of the National Center of Afro-American Artists, Boston, Massachusetts
1985. "Out of Africa," Massachusetts State House exhibit organized by the Smithsonian Institution, Anacostia Museum, Washington, DC
1985. Institute of Contemporary Art, Boston, Massachusetts
1984. "No Place to Be," Photographic Essay on the Homeless in the Commonwealth, State House Exhibit, Boston, Massachusetts

1983. Simmons College, Boston, Massachusetts
1982. Bowdoin College Museum of Art, Portland, Maine
1981. West Virginia State College, Charleston, West Virginia
1980. High Museum of Art, Atlanta, Georgia
1979. San Francisco Art Museum, San Francisco, California
1977. FESTAC, Lagos, Nigeria, West Africa
1973. Studio 777, Accra, Ghana, West Africa

See photographs pages 330–331.

JACKSON, VERA (1912–   )
active Los Angeles

Born in Wichita, Kansas, Vera Jackson is a writer, teacher and artist as well as a photographer. Her interest in photography began as a child. Her father, an amateur photographer, often photographed family outings and events.

She studied in a photography workshop in the late 1930s and began to take pictures of events and family friends soon after. She worked for a photographer in the Los Angeles area as a printer early in her career. She later met the editor of a black newspaper, *The California Eagle*, and was hired as the newspaper photographer. In that capacity she photographed the celebrities and sports figures who lived in and visited the Los Angeles area. In the 1940s, Jackson produced a large body of work as a photojournalist. Photographing social events, parties and political activities, Jackson became a familiar face in the society world. She left the *Eagle* to continue her education and received a B.A. and M.A. in Education. After completing her degree requirements, she taught for the Los Angeles City School system for a number of years. A world traveler, Jackson has exhibited her photographs in libraries and museums throughout the state of California.

SELECTED BIBLIOGRAPHY

Moutoussamy-Ashe, Jeanne. *Viewfinders: Black Women Photographers.* New York: Dodd, Mead and Co., 1986.

"The Tradition Continues: California Black Photographers" (exhibition catalogue), California Museum of Afro-American History and Culture, 1983.

JAMES, EARL
active New York City, 1970s

JEAN-BART, LESLIE
active New York City, 1970s

JEFFERSON, LOUISE
active New York City and Connecticut, 1958–present

A self-taught photographer, Louise Jefferson moved to New York City from her native Washington, DC, to study fine art at Hunter College and later graphic arts at Columbia University. Moving to New York, she lived in Harlem, acquainting herself with poets and writers such as Langston Hughes, Countee Cullen and Zora Neale Hurston and sculptor Augusta Savage. A calligrapher and illustrator, Jefferson has received widespread attention for her artistic activities.

In 1942, Jefferson was hired as the Art Director of Friendship Press (publishing agent of the National Council of Churches) where she worked until 1968. Jefferson was involved in every aspect of book production. Her interest in photography became more serious during her early years at Friendship. She took her most memorable photograph in Tuskegee, Alabama, of a crying young black boy on a step dressed in tattered clothes.

She was more active as a photographer in the 1950s. Jefferson's images include portraits and genre scenes. Her portraits are of friends who were also familiar faces to the general public such as Lena Horne, Dr. Charles Drew, Louis Armstrong, Ralph Bunch, and Martin Luther King, Jr.

Upon retiring in 1968, she began her free-lance career as a photographer, illustrator, researcher and writer. She moved from the city to a small town in Connecticut. In the 1960s, Jefferson traveled extensively. Her first trip to Africa was in 1960; she was struck by the beauty, the art and the history. Jefferson returned with the assistance of two Ford Foundation fellowships in subsequent years, photographing the people of East and West Africa and their arts.

Jefferson has done art and photographic work for such major publishing companies in New York as Doubleday and Viking. She has organized a number of exhibitions related to her research in black historical matters and experiences in Africa. In 1984 she received a Certificate of Recognition from the National Urban League, the Connecticut Historical Society Certificate of Achievement and the Operation Crossroads, Africa award. Her works have been exhibited at the Schomburg Center for Research in Black Culture, the Baltimore Museum of Art, the Oliver Wolcott Library (Connecticut), Austin Arts Center at Trinity College (Connecticut) and the CRT's Craftery Gallery (Hartford, Connecticut).

SELECTED BIBLIOGRAPHY

Moutoussamy-Ashe, Jeanne. *Viewfinders: Black Women Photographers*, New York: Dodd, Mead Inc., 1986.

"Connecticut Illustrator, Louise E. Jefferson" by Dr. James A. Miller (exhibition brochure), CRT's Craftery Gallery, Hartford, Connecticut, 1984.

"Louise Jefferson, A Renaissance Woman" by Joyce Peck, *The Register*, Litchfield, Connecticut, February 16, 1980.

Jefferson, Louise, *The Decorative Arts of Africa*. New York: Viking Press, 1973.

See photographs pages 332–333.

JEFFREY, JAMES
active Los Angeles, 1980s

JEFFRIES, MICHELLE M.
active Washington, DC, 1980s

JOHNSON, CHRIS (1948–)
active San Francisco

An exhibiting fine art photographer, Johnson emphasizes nontraditional portraiture. He studied photography with Ansel Adams and worked as his assistant at his Yosemite, California, workshop in the early 1970s. Johnson, born in Brooklyn, New York, also studied with Imogene Cunningham and Wynn Bullock. He is currently head of the photography department at the California College of Arts and Crafts in Oakland. Johnson's community activities in photography include his work with the San Francisco Camera Work Gallery, a major alternative non-profit organization specializing in the works of emerging artists. He is a past president and current board member of this organization.

Johnson has been widely exhibited, including one-man exhibitions at Focus Gallery (1983) and Southern Exposure Gallery (1987) in California. His style of work is large-format black and white fine art portraiture. He is currently working under a grant from the Polaroid Foundation, which affords him the opportunity to extend the boundaries of portraiture. His works are multi-image portraits/self-portraits on Polaroid SX-70 material that are enlarged to 15 x 15-inch Ektacolor prints. In his own words, "my work deals with complex, psychological and emotional projections onto women in my life. Recently I have been exploring a process of self-generated images whereby the portraits are created by an unconscious, intuitive ordering dynamic—the images are not planned, they are fluid, transparent and suggestive. These long exposures create an instant dreamlike psychodrama scenario."

SELECTED BIBLIOGRAPHY

Johnson, Chris. *The Practical Zone System*, Stoneham, Massachusetts: Focal Press, 1986.
"Hot Shots," *Darkroom Photography* magazine, December 1985.

See photograph page 334.

JOHNSON, EDDIE, JR.
active Newark, New Jersey, 1980s

JONES, BRENT M. (1945–   )
active Chicago

Brent Jones, a Chicago-based photojournalist, has written and photographed stories for such noted publications as *The Chicago Tribune, USA Today, Black Enterprise, Time, Newsweek,* and *Ebony.* His clients include: AT&T, British Airways, Illinois Bell, World Book Encyclopedia, and Hill and Knowlton.

In 1971, Jones covered the inauguration of President William R. Tolbert of Liberia. The photographs appeared in several publications and were used in a television documentary. Other special assignments include the coverage of the funeral of the Honorable Elijah Muhammad for *Ebony Magazine,* photo essays for the *Milwaukee Journal* on Milwaukee's school integration program and on the Englewood and Marquette Park communities in Chicago. He has provided photographs for five children's books including, *Basketball Basics* (Prentice-Hall, 1976); *I Love Grandma, The Babysitter, We Can't Afford It* and *I Know You Cheated,* all published in 1977 by Raintree.

Jones received the Public Arts Award, Columbia College, 1969; was selected to judge the Buckingham Art Festival, 1972; represented the United States at the Second World Black and African Festival of Arts and Culture in Lagos, Nigeria, 1977 and was featured artist in Black Aesthetic, Chicago Museum of Science and Industry, 1978.

SELECTED EXHIBITIONS

1987. Chicago Jazz Festival, Chicago, Illinois
1987. Black Chicago Press Photographers Show, Prairie Avenue Gallery, Chicago, Illinois
1976. The Black Male: From Cradle to the Grave, The Southside Community Art Center, Chicago, Illinois
1976. On the Job in Illinois: Then & Now, A Bicentennial Exhibition, Illinois Archives, Chicago, Illinois
1973. The Black Male, traveling exhibition for the National Publishers Convention, Nashville, Tennessee
1972. Black Arts Festival, Roosevelt University, Chicago, Illinois
1972. Liberia, Chicago Public Library, Chicago, Illinois
1970. One Person Show, Columbia College, Chicago, Illinois

See photographs pages 335–337.

JONES, BRIAN V. (1952–   )
active Washington, DC

Brian Jones studied journalism at Howard University (B.A.) and photography at Illinois Institute of Technology and the Institute of Design in Chicago (M.S.). At one time a photographer/reporter for weekly newspapers and trade magazines in the Washington, DC, area he turned to free-lance photography and teaching. In his personal work, Jones explores the overlapping of reality and abstraction found in both fashionable and deteriorating neighborhoods in Chicago and Washington, DC. "I try to create images that have some value for me. If the photograph I make is successful it will have, in some way, addressed a subject honestly, simply and with some degree of eloquence. The subject, whether it is an object, a person, a circumstance or a perception, is criticially important. However, if I fail to communicate that importance, I have done nothing."

In 1985 he was awarded a Merit for Outstanding Achievement, Black Creativity Juried Art Show at the Museum of Science and Industry in Chicago. Concerned with the printing and preservation of archival photographic collections, Jones has supervised the Photography Department at Moorland-Spingarn Research Center, Howard University in Washington, DC, since 1983.

SELECTED EXHIBITIONS

1983. "Hyde Park: A Sociological Document," The Institute of Design, Chicago, Illinois
1983. "Eight Varieties of Photographic Vision," University of Illinois at Chicago, Illinois
1983. Vandercook College of Music, Illinois
1982. "Editorial Photography," Institute of Design, Chicago, Illinois
1981. "The American Document," Institute of Design, Chicago, Illinois

SELECTED BIBLIOGRAPHY

The Journal of Negro Education (cover photograph), summer 1985.
The Journal of Negro Education (cover photograph), winter 1985.
The Journal of Negro Education (cover photograph), summer 1984.
The Psychology & Mental Health of Afro-American Women: A Selected Bibliography (cover photograph), Washington: Howard University, 1984.

See photographs pages 338–340.

JONES, JULIA
active Washington, DC, 1977–present

Julia Jones has for many years photographed day-to-day events in the Washington, DC, area. She is president of Sol, Inc., a photographic stock agency that holds 35mm color slides and black and white prints—images of national and local interest. Her interest in photography began at age seven. As she owned a Brownie, she photographed members of her family. She continued photographing during her teenage years and later bought a 35mm camera.

After studying photography at Howard University, Fine Arts Department, she was hired as the photographer for the Public Relations Office there. Her free-lance assignments included newspapers, corporations and small businesses in the District. Jones photographed Jesse Jackson's trip to Syria when he secured the release of Lt. Robert Goodman. She has photographed demonstrations and political events. Her portrait file consists of images of politicians, musicians, actresses and activists, including Ben Chavis, Jesse Jackson, Louis Farrakhan, Ossie Davis, Ruby Dee, Wynton Marsalis, Ntozake Shange, among others. Also an exhibiting photographer, Jones' work has been published in numerous periodicals.

SELECTED BIBLIOGRAPHY

"For Women Only: An Exhibition of Local Black Women Photographers," Howard University Museum, Howard University, Washington, DC (exhibition catalog), 1983.

See photographs page 341.

JONES, KENNETH GEORGE (1956–)
active Houston, Texas

Born in Birmingham, Alabama, Kenneth Jones studied photography and art at Texas Southern University and the Maryland Institute College of Art. While in the U.S. Air Force in 1976–78 in Italy, he worked as a staff photographer for military publications, which included covering activities such as military ceremonies, official portraits, sports events and surveillance photography. Also in Italy he had a number of free-lance assignments, which included portrait work, fashion and architectural photographs.

A photography teacher and photojournalist in the Washington, DC, area in the late 1970s, Jones covered the Camp David Peace Summit as well as Senate and Congressional activities. Jones started working for a photographic company in 1980 and moved to Houston, Texas, in 1983. His personal work explores contemporary black cowboys. Since 1985, he has been documenting the life of these men in the Southwest, on the rodeo circuit and on the ranches and farms in Texas. "Through my work, I am attempting to go beyond this misconception surrounding the role of black men in the American West. My interest is to capture in photographs some of the spirit, intensity, and pride of a culture which is fundamental to the development of the Southwest, but which never receives enough media or academic attention. My goal is to illustrate a lifestyle which in many cases has been handed down through generations. I have an obligation to myself and to the descendants of these talented and daring men and women who keep the spirit of Afro-American cowboys alive and vibrant. Still obscure but proud, these men continue to ride the forgotten black rodeo circuits of the Southwest. Cowboys are real and very often black."

JONES, MARVIN T.
active Washington, DC, 1975–present

Marvin Jones is president of his own commercial photography firm in Washington, DC. Jones, born in Cofield, North Carolina, studied photography at Columbia College in

Chicago, where he received a B.F.A. in 1976. He moved to Washington, DC, that same year and has worked as a medical, commercial and studio photographer there for a number of years. His personal work includes documenting historical sites such as the Citadelle in northern Haiti. Photographs from the Citadelle project have been exhibited at the galleries of the Organization of American States, Howard University, and the California Afro-American Museum in Los Angeles.

Jones has also photographed in Peru, Ecquador, Venezuela, Colombia and Havana, Cuba. He has studied French and Spanish at the University of the District of Columbia and in 1980 studied photojournalism at the University of Missouri in Sedalia, Missouri. Jones's clients include Howard University, General Electric and C&P Telephone, among others. He is a member of the American Society of Magazine photographers and the International Association of Business Communicators.

See photographs page 342.

JONES, MIKE
active Los Angeles, 1980s

JONES, ORLANDO P.
active Sacramento, California, 1980s

KARP, LEAH JAYNES
active Philadelphia, 1975–present

Leah Karp's work encompasses many types of nonsilver photographic processes and found objects creating symbolic forms reminiscent of material culture found in twentieth-century homes and churches. A fine art photographer, Karp studied at the Tyler School of Art, Temple University (M.F.A.,B.F.A.) in Philadelphia. She teaches photography in workshops, art centers and colleges in the area.

COLLECTIONS

High Museum, Atlanta, Georgia
Portland Museum, Portland, Maine
Bellevue Museum of Art, Bellevue, Washington

SELECTED EXHIBITIONS

1986. "Leah Jaynes Karp," The Museum of Contemporary Photography, Chicago, Illinois
1985. "Contemporary Issues for Black Artists," The Upstairs Gallery, Tryon, North Carolina
1984. "Subjective Vision," High Museum of Art, Atlanta, Georgia

1983. "Handmade Cameras: Contemporary Images," Tyler School of Art, Temple University, Philadelphia, Pennsylvania

1981. "Machine Messages," Goucher College, Baltimore, Maryland

1980. "New Photographics/80," Ellensburg, Washington

1979. "Uniquely Photographic," Honolulu Academy of Art, Honolulu, Hawaii

1977. "A Woman's Show," H.E.R.A., Wakefield, Rhode Island

1976. "Bicentennial Show," William Penn Museum, Harrisburg, Pennsylvania

See photographs page 343.

KELLOGG, IRENE C.
active Washington, DC, 1980s

KELLY, BILL
active New York City, 1980s

KELLY, KARL
active Los Angeles, 1980s

KHAREM, OMAR
active Chicago 1970s–present

See photograph page 344.

KING, ALEXANDER, JR. (1916–1986)
active Brooklyn, New York

Alexander King was an active community leader and photographer in Brooklyn. Originally interested in a career in engineering, he studied at the City College of New York. His interest in photography developed while studying at CCNY. In 1950, he opened a studio on Fulton Street in Brooklyn with three friends—George Bing, Everett Reese and Leonard Fitchett and named it Bing Studios; it was later renamed King Photographers. His photographs chronicle Brooklyn neighborhood life from the mid-1950s to the 1970s. They include portraits of families, men, women and children, and political and religious leaders of the area.

SELECTED BIBLIOGRAPHY

"Obituary: Alex King Dies," New York *Amsterdam News*, January 25, 1986.

KING, ED
active New York, 1970–present

KING, LUCIUS (1947–   )
active Miami, Florida

Born and educated in Florida, King is a free-lance photographer interested in documenting the changing communities in Miami and south Florida. He has taught art, graphics and photography in Dade County Schools and at the Dade Community College Outreach Program. A member of the Kuumba Artist Association, King has exhibited his photographs at the Miami Public Library, University of Alabama, University of Miami, Florida Atlantic University, Free Southern Theatre and the African Cultural Center of Jacksonville, Florida.

See photographs page 345.

LACHATANERE, ROMULO (1906–1952)
active New York City, Puerto Rico, Cuba

A self-taught ethnologist and photographer, Romulo Lachatanere y Crombet was born in Santiago de Cuba. He immigrated to the United States in 1939. He authored two books and several articles on the religious beliefs of Afro-Cubans. The books, *Oh Mio! Yemaya* (1938) and *Manual de Santeria* (1942), were highly praised by Fernando Ortiz, the then-preeminent authority on Afro-Cuban culture and its continuities with African culture. In addition to these ethnological works, Lachatanere wrote numerous articles and news reports on the conditions of Puerto Rican migrants in the United States, race relations in Cuba and related subjects.

During the last years of his life, Lachatanere became deeply interested in photography as a documentary resource. He was concerned with documenting Puerto Ricans and African-Americans in East Harlem and Brooklyn. A vacation trip to Puerto Rico in March 1952 provided him the opportunity to photograph the life of Puerto Rican workers, their families and also to gather materials for a study of African influences on the culture of Puerto Rico. On the return flight back to the United States, the airplane crashed, killing Lachatanere and most of the other passengers and crew members.

Some of the photographs shown in this volume were taken during that ill-fated trip. Fortunately, he mailed the film to his wife, Sara, who turned it over to Jack Lessinger, a colleague in the photographic section of the Council of the Arts, Sciences and Professions. Lessinger developed the film and organized an exhibition of the photographs at a memorial service held one month after the photographer's death. Lachatanere was also a member of the Photo League, which was established during the thirties as a political/social organization that viewed photography as a tool for class struggle.

COLLECTIONS

Schomburg Center for Research in Black Culture, The New York Public Library, New
York, New York
PhotoFind Gallery, New York, New York

SELECTED BIBLIOGRAPHY

Lachatanere, Romulo, *Oh, Mio Yemaya!* Manzanillo, Cuba: Editorial "El Arte", 1938.
Lachatanere, Romulo, *Manual de Santeria*. La Habana, Cuba: Editorial Caribe, 1942.

See photographs pages 346–348.

LANGE, TED
active Los Angeles, 1980s

LARKIN, ALLIE SHARON
active Los Angeles, 1980s

LARKINS, GEORGE R. (1953–)
active San Diego, California

Born in Tallahassee, Florida, Larkins became interested in photography at the age of seven.
His father, an amateur photographer, taught him the rudiments of the craft. Later moving
to the Los Angeles area, Larkins photographed in the major cities of the United States.
Continuing the study of photography on his own, he studied business at Florida A&M
University and opened his studio in 1981.

See photograph page 349.

LA SALLE, ARCHY
active Boston, 1980s

A graduate of the Massachusetts College of Art (B.F.A. in photography), LaSalle is a
teacher, photojournalist and free-lance architectural photographer. In 1980 he went to
Cuba to work on a photodocumentation project on Cuban architecture and artwork.
While in Cuba, he also photographed children from other socialist countries, such as
Angola, Ethiopia, Nicaragua and Vietnam, who received their educational training in
Cuba.

As a lecturer, LaSalle has given talks on topics such as "How to Survive as An Artist" and "Arts and Marxism." In 1981, he was commissioned to photograph the Mobile, Alabama, Mardi Gras Association members activities, including their parades and processions.

COLLECTIONS

Museum of Fine Arts, Boston, Massachusetts

Museum of Fine Arts, Havana, Cuba

Museum of National Center for Afro-American Arts, Boston, Massachusetts

Museum of Modern Art, New York, New York

Massachusetts State House, Boston, Massachusetts

EXHIBITIONS

1983. "Jamaican Reds," Gallery at the Piano Factory, Boston, Massachusetts

1981. "Neon Lights," New England School of Photography, Boston, Massachusetts

1980. Massachusetts College of Art, C-10 Gallery, Boston, Massachusetts

See photographs pages 350–351.

LAVALAIS, ABE C. (1948–   )
active New York City

Lavalais, who received his first camera at the age of eleven, had been taking photographs of his family since the age of nine. His mother was an amateur photographer, who enjoyed photographing her seven children in Alexandria, Louisiana. During his stint in the U.S. Army, Lavalais continued to take photographs wherever he was stationed—Germany, Vietnam, Alaska or Colorado. After leaving the army he moved to Los Angeles and studied photography at the Art Center of Design. He received a B.F.A. in 1977 and did free-lance photography for recording studios whose clients included Nancy Wilson, Dionne Warwick and Florence LaRue. An immediate success, his photographs appeared in trade publications and in magazines such as *Black Enterprise, Black Stars* and *Sepia*.

Returning to Louisiana in 1979, he continued to do portraiture and also worked in advertising photography. That same year, he won the coveted New Orleans Advertising Club's Gold Medal for his work, the first black photographer in Louisiana to win the award.

Moving to New York City in 1981, he opened a studio and became successful almost immediately in advertising and editorial photography. His clients include *Essence, Rolling Stone* and *Billboard* magazines; in the record industry—Atlantic, RCA and Cotillion Records.

LAWSON, JEFF
active Dayton, Ohio, 1970s

LAYSON, CECIL
active Atlanta, 1970s

LEACH, NATHAN
active Ohio, 1980s

LEE, DAVID C.
active Brooklyn, New York, 1980s

LEE, JOYCE
active New York City, 1980s

LEE, RON
active Atlanta, 1970–present

LEE, SA'LONGO J.R.
active Los Angeles, 1970–present

Lee's career in photography began in the mid-1970s. He has worked as a free-lance photographer and photojournalist as well as an audiovisual video technician and a photography instructor.

This West-Coast-based photographer is noted for his fine art photographic prints and often exhibits in the Los Angeles area. His photographic work ranges from portraiture to commercial. A dance and theater photographer, he has documented productions in Atlanta, Georgia, and Miami, Florida, as well as companies in Los Angeles.

SELECTED EXHIBITIONS

1987. "A Day in the Life of Santa Barbara's Invisible Culture," The Art Corner Gallery of Standard Brands, Santa Barbara, California

1985. Black Gallery (group show), Los Angeles, California
1984. "Peace and Justice," University of Southern California, Los Angeles, California
1983. "Departures" (one-person show), Phoenix Art and Theatre Gallery, Atlanta, Georgia
1982. "Random Samplings," (one-person show), Art Gallery, Atlanta Junior College, Atlanta, Georgia

See photograph page 352.

LEWIS, CARL E. "DJINN" (1951–   )
active Dallas, Texas

A native of New York City, Lewis is one of the few black photographers using laser technology in creating his imagery. He gives photography and computer graphic classes in workshops around the country including the Tucson Museum of Art School, University of Wisconsin and the New School for Social Research. His laser images are creative abstractions of natural environments and environments created by the artist. His photographic images blend high technology and fine art; his work transforms static forms into changes that imply movement, energy and three-dimensional form. As stated in the exhibition press release for "Seeds," "Synthesizing ideas and images of a disparate sort into a unified creative body, Lewis makes a cultural/technological statement of significant proportions." Lewis has been a consultant for a number of years on laser-generated art for theatrical productions as well as for publishing companies.

COLLECTIONS

University of Wisconsin, Madison, Wisconsin
Schomburg Center for Research in Black Culture, The New York Public Library, New York, New York
Cathedral Choir School of Saint John the Divine, New York, New York
San Antonio Museum of Art, San Antonio, Texas
Nieman-Marcus, Houston, Texas

SELECTED EXHIBITIONS

1987. "Photographic Imagery of Carl Lewis," Paul Mellon Arts Center, Wallingford, Connecticut
1986. "Seeds," The Cathedral School, New York, New York
1985. "Art for a Sunday Afternoon," D-Art Visual Art Center, Dallas, Texas
1984. Paul Mellon Arts Center (solo show), Wallingford, Connecticut

See photograph page 353.

LEWIS, HARVEY JAMES   (1878–1968)
active McDonald, Pennsylvania

Initially interested in painting, Lewis began his photographic career in 1896. Born in Unionville, Virginia, he moved to Pittsburgh in 1901. He opened a studio and over the years produced a large body of work depicting events in western Pennsylvania. His clients were working class and both black and white. His images of the changing community through two world wars, the Depression and a recession are an extraordinary record of this photographer's life's work.

SELECTED BIBLIOGRAPHY

The Photographs of Harvey James Lewis (1878–1968) The Lewis Studio, McDonald, Pennsylvania (exhibition brochure), Chicago: Black Woman Collaborative, Inc, 1981.

A *Century of Black Photographers: 1840–1960*, (exhibition catalog), Providence: Rhode Island School of Design, 1983.

LEWIS, MATTHEW   (1930–   )
active Washington, DC

A photojournalist for *The Washington Post*, Lewis studied photography at the New York Institute of Photography. He began his photojournalism career in the 1950s and is the grandson of Harvey James Lewis, the pioneering studio photographer from McDonald, Pennsylvania. In 1975, he won the coveted Pulitzer Prize for his portrait studies of Washingtonians. A photographer during the civil rights movement in Washington, Lewis has also won the White House News Photographers Association first prize in 1968 and 1971.

SELECTED BIBLIOGRAPHY

A *Century of Black Photographers: 1840–1960*, (exhibition catalogue), Providence: The Rhode Island School of Design, 1983.

"Selected by Jurors for the Pulitzer Prize for 1975," *The New York Times*, May 6, 1975.

LEWIS, ROY
active Washington, DC, and Chicago, 1960–present

Roy Lewis has been a photographer, advocate for the arts, lecturer and cinematographer for over twenty years. He grew up in Mississippi and moved to Chicago in 1956. He started working for *Ebony* and *Jet* magazines during this time, but he did very little photography. During the early 1960s, Lewis began working as a photojournalist for black periodicals covering cultural activities, the civil rights protest marches, social events and entertainers in the Chicago area. Trained by photographers Ted Williams and Lacey Crawford, Lewis developed a documentary style of photography. During this time he also photographed public and controversial figures such as Dr. Martin Luther King, Jr., the Honorable Elijah Muhammad, Nikki Giovanni, Sonia Sanchez and "Little" Stevie Wonder, as well as Dick Gregory, Duke Ellington, Gwendolyn Brooks, Stokely Carmichael, Miles Davis, Alice Walker and the Jackson Five with the young Michael Jackson.

Lewis moved to Washington, DC, in 1973 and continued a successful free-lance career. He also teaches and lectures in the DC area. His work has appeared in the local press as well as in national periodicals. As a filmmaker his credits include "WATTSTAX," "Save the Children," "Fight of the Century" (Muhammad Ali and George Former title bout in Zaire) and "Nation of Common Sense" (a documentary about Muslims in America). His works have appeared in exhibitions in Chicago, Washington, DC, New York and Mississippi.

See photographs pages 354–356.

LIGHT, LARRY
active Hollywood, California, 1980s

LLOYD, BOB
active Spokane, Washington, 1980s

LOGAN, FERN (1945–)
active New York City

Logan quit her job in the corporate world in 1982 to pursue her long-standing interest in photography and graphic art. In 1974, she studied with Paul Caponigro at the Apeiron Workshop—this was the turning point in her determination to pursue her interest in photography. Logan studied at the State University of New York and Pratt Institute in the early 1970s.

Influenced by Paul Caponigro, her vision concentrates on graces of nature, architecture and country living. In 1983 she began a photodocumentation project on black artists, the "Artist Portrait Series." Her portraits of painters, sculptors and photographers include Gordon Parks, Bo Walker and Romare Bearden. The portrait series was supported and funded by individuals as well as government agencies. It initially focused on visual artists, however Logan has expanded it to include performing artists as well.

Logan's interest in nonsilver processes developed in 1985. She took classes at the International Center of Photography with Bea Nettles and began to expand her photographic interest. She incorporates old family photographs with recent images taken by her, experiments with hand coloring and produces gum-bichormate prints. Logan has taught classes at the International Center of Photography and operates a photography and design studio in New York.

EXHIBITIONS

1986. "Vision and Re-Vision," The Gallery at the Adam Clayton Powell State Office Building, New York, New York

1985. "Fern Logan–Recent Photographs," Cinque Gallery, New York, New York

1985. "The Artist Portrait Series," Gallery 62, The National Urban League, New York, New York

1984. "Affirmations of Life," Kenkeleba House Gallery, New York, New York

1984. "Faces and Quiet Places," 4th Street Photo Gallery, New York, New York

1983. "14 Photographers," Schomburg Center for Research in Black Culture, New York, New York

SELECTED BIBLIOGRAPHY

Moutoussamy-Ashe, Jeanne. *Viewfinders: Black Women Photographers*, New York: Dodd, Mead & Co., 1986.

"'About the Artist: Fern Logan" by Norman Schreiber (exhibition catalog) "The Artist Portrait Series," National Urban League, New York, New York (article reprinted from *Popular Photography*, 1985).

See photographs pages 357–359.

LUCAS, BOB
active Los Angeles, 1980s

LYNCH, EDIE
active New York 1970–present

Lynch trained and worked in the theater, then became interested in photography. She spent six years studying with Lee Strasberg, Bill Hickey and Lloyd Richards. She worked as a producer, director and composer. Her first film, "Lost Control," deals with drug addiction and rehabilitation. A second film, "Mister Magic," a documentary about young people in Mexico, received critical acclaim in Mexico.

As a photographer, she has exhibited at the Museum of the City of New York, New York University and the Equitable Insurance Gallery and has been commissioned to do portrait studies of business and political leaders. She is the author and photographer of a book on children in Jamaica entitled *With Glory I So Humbly Stand*. A reviewer states, "These studies are unusual. They are portraits of ordinary country Jamaicans without tourist gloss or enticement, in uniformly arresting black and white photographs, so that one wonders in what, exactly, consists the 'superiority' of color in any photographic medium."

SELECTED BIBLIOGRAPHY

Lynch, Edie. *With Glory I So Humbly Stand*, New York: Vantage Press, 1982.
Dawes, Neville, "With Glory I So Humbly Stand" *The Daily Gleaner*, April 12, 1982.

See photographs page 360.

MADISON, JULIETTE
active Cleveland, Ohio, 1970s

MAGUBANE, PETER (1932-   )
active South Africa and New York City

Born in Johannesburg, South Africa, Peter Magubane began his career as a photographer on *Drum* magazine in 1956. In 1965, he became a staff member of the *Rand Daily Mail*, a Johannesburg newspaper. His experiences over twenty years as the only major black South African news photographer—including arrests, solitary confinement, banishment—are noted in his first book, *Magubane's South Africa*. Since the publication of that book, he has completed photographic assignments in various parts of the world for such magazines as *Time* and *Geo* and has worked in television news. His second book, *Soweto*, was published in 1978 with an introductory text by Marshall Lee. He has also had a number of exhibitions in the United States, Europe, South America and the Far East.

Magubane's first significant photographic experience occurred when he covered the ANC Congress in Bloemfontein in 1955. Magubane also photographed the Sharpeville massacre funeral services and the Zeerust trials, which he covered for *Drum* magazine. No photographers were allowed into Zeerust to cover the trials. He went in dressed as a farm laborer with a concealed camera in half a loaf of bread. He later used an empty milk carton with a cable release going through the straw. *Drum* was the only magazine that had pictures of the trials as a result of his ingenuity.

Magubane spent 586 days in solitary confinement, six additional months in jail and was banned professionally and personally for five years. He was never convicted of a crime. The banning order was lifted in 1975.

Magubane's work is unique in that it combines realism, pathos and graphic abstraction in describing communities united and divided in South Africa. In 1976 Magubane was awarded the Enterprising Journalism Award and the Nicholas Tomalin Award by *The*

London Sunday Times. His concern and commitment continues. Magubane lives and works in New York and South Africa. He continues to document the atrocities of apartheid.

SELECTED EXHIBITIONS

1986. "On Freedom: The Art of Photojournalism," The Studio Museum in Harlem, New York, New York

1985. "Art Against Apartheid Photography Exhibition," The Schomburg Center for Research in Black Culture, The New York Public Library, New York, New York

1982. "Photographs from South Africa," The Photographer's Gallery, London, England

1978. "Magubane's South Africa," International Center of Photography, New York, New York

1978. "Black Child," Johannesburg, South Africa

SELECTED BIBLIOGRAPHY

"The Focus of Somalia's Pain" by Earl Caldwell, *New York Daily News*, December 17, 1982.

"Number One Black Photographer in South Africa," *Sepia*, October, 1980.

Magubane, Peter. *Magubane's South Africa*, New York: Alfred A. Knopf, 1978.

———. *Soweto*, New York: Alfred A. Knopf, 1978.

———. *Black As I Am*, with poetry by Zinzi Mandela, Los Angeles: Alfred A. Knopf, 1978.

Fraser, C. Gerald, "A Black Photojournalist Depicts Apartheid Life, *The New York Times*, May 14, 1978.

"Magubane's South Africa," *Essence*, July 1978.

"South African Photographer Honored," *Christian Science Monitor*, February 24, 1977.

MANNAS, JIMMIE (1941–   )
active New York City

Jimmie Mannas has been an active filmmaker and photographer for over twenty years. Presently he is coordinator of New Images, a film co-op that produced its first film, "A Time to Read," in 1967. Mannas' photographic career began in the early 1960s. As members of the Kamoinge Workshop, he and his colleagues began to discuss the art of photography, set up workshops and exhibit their works. He studied photography and film at the New York Institute of Photography, the School of Visual Arts and at the New York University School of Film and Television. In the mid-1960s, Mannas set up and directed photography workshops in Brooklyn, Manhattan and the South Bronx.

In 1971, Mannas moved to Guyana, South America, where he served as film advisor to the country's Ministry of Information and Culture. Living in Guyana for four years, he produced films and photographed the country. After moving back to the United States, he lectured in colleges and universities and continued to show and make such films as *Aggro-*

Seizeman (a first all-Guyanese feature film), *The Folks*, and *Head and Heart* (*Tom Feelings*), among others.

His photographs have been published in *The Black Photographers Annual, Saturday Review, The New York Times, Camera, Life* and *Saturday Review* magazines. Mannas has received many filmmaking awards including the American Film Institute Fellowship, the Martin Luther King Filmmaking Scholarship, the National Endowment for the Arts Filmmakers Grant and the Black Filmmakers Hall of Fame award (first place in the documentary category).

Active in video productions, he has directed and produced "The Plight of Vietnam Black Vets" (1984), "Black Veterans for Social Justice" (1983) and "Mind Builders" (1983). He has also acted as consultant to WCBS-TV's "The Cities," WNEW-TV's "Black News" and to the Museum of Broadcasting, Brooklyn Museum and the Bedford-Stuyvesant Restoration Corporation. Mannas has exhibited his still photographs in a number of galleries and museums such as the Studio Museum in Harlem, Bishops College in Guyana and Amherst College in Massachusetts, among others.

SELECTED EXHIBITIONS

"Black Photographers Annual Exhibition," San Francisco Museum of Art, San Francisco, California

Brooklyn Muse, (group exhibition), Brooklyn, New York

"Kamoinge Workshop," Countee Cullen Library, New York, New York

See photograph page 361.

MARTIN, CHARLES
active New York City, 1980s

MARTIN, GEORGE
active Flushing, New York, 1970s

MARTIN, LOUISE   (1915–   )
active Houston, Texas

Martin, who received her first camera from her mother at the age of eleven, is one of the few black women who became interested in photography at an early age. In the beginning, she photographed her friends at school. As a high school student, she became the unofficial school photographer.

Born in Brenham, Texas, Martin moved to Chicago in the 1930s to study photography. In Chicago, she attended the Art Institute and the American School of Photography, eventually receiving a degree in photography from Denver University in Colorado. Returning to Houston, Martin opened a portrait studio in 1946. Her studio was a popular one; she photographed the black community events in and around the Houston area. During the 1950s she joined photographic organizations such as the Southwestern Photographers Convention, Texas Professional Photographers, Professional Photographers of America and the Business and Professional Women's Association.

As a stringer for two black Houston newspapers, The *Forward Times* and *The Informer*, she provided photographs of the last rites of civil rights leader Dr. Martin Luther King, Jr., in 1968. In 1973, she founded the Louise Martin School of Photography, which held classes in all aspects of photography. The school remained active for three years. She has received over twenty-five awards for her exceptional photographic career.

SELECTED EXHIBITIONS

1984. "Louise Martin: An Exhibition," Houston Public Library, Houston, Texas

SELECTED BIBLIOGRAPHY

Moutoussamy-Ashe, Jeanne. *Viewfinders: Black Women Photographers*, New York: Dodd-Mead, 1986.
"Louise Martin: Giving It Her Best Shots," *Houston Post*, February 12, 1984.
"Houston's Lady Photographer," *Houston Informer*, February 16, 1965.
"Houston's Leading Black Woman," *Houston Chronicle*, June 12, 1969.

MASSIE, RICHARD
active New York, 1970s–present

See photograph page 362.

MATHIS, MICKEY
active New York City, 1970–present

Mickey Mathis lives and works in New York City. He studied photography with noted photographers Bruce Davidson and Arthur Rothstein. He attended photographic workshops at the International Center of Photography in New York and at the National Geographic Workshop in Washington, DC. Mathis is a free-lance photographer and has worked for the *Village Voice* and United Press International. His work has also been published in *Camera 35*, *Essence* and *Ebony* magazines. Mathis has taught photography at Bedford Hills Women's Prison and at the Harlem Minisink School.

Mathis lectured at the International Center of Photography at its Dialogue and Lecture Series for the exhibition "The New Harlem on My Mind." Reviews and articles regarding his work have appeared in the *Washington Review,* the *Chicago Tribune* and *Popular Photography* magazine. His photographs have appeared in the *Black Photographers Annual.*

SELECTED EXHIBITIONS

1986. "America: Another Perspective," New York University, New York, New York
Corcoran Gallery of Art, Washington, DC
Studio Museum in Harlem, New York, New York
Cultural Arts Project Gallery, Baltimore, Maryland

See photographs page 363.

MAYDEN, JOHN CLARK
active Baltimore, 1970s

MAYNARD, CARROLL T. (1899–1982)
active Chicago

The popular Maynard Studios were owned and operated by Mr. and Mrs. Carroll Treas Van Maynard. Before moving to Chicago in 1925, Carroll Maynard worked in several photographic studios in Philadelphia and Pittsburgh, Pennsylvania. At his own studio, Maynard advertised a customer could "Get Photos that Please—Downtown Quality at Popular Prices."

The Maynard School of Photography was opened in 1947. Carroll Maynard taught classes in professional photographic techniques. The Maynards' photographs were often published in the *Chicago Defender, Ebony* and *Bronzeville* magazines. One of Carroll Maynard's photographs was exhibited in 1942 at the annual meeting of the Photographers Association of America.

SELECTED BIBLIOGRAPHY

"A Century of Black Photographers: 1840–1960" (exhibition catalog), Museum of Art, Rhode Island School of Design, 1983.
Moutoussamy-Ashe, Jeanne. *Viewfinders: Black Women Photographers,* New York: Dodd-Mead, 1986.

MAYNARD, JOSEPH
active New York City, 1980s

McCLEAN

McCORMICK, CHANDRA
active New Orleans, 1980s

McGHEE, REGINALD
active Atlanta, 1970s

McKENZIE, JENNIE
active London, England, 1980s

McLAMORE, LAMONTE
active Encino, California, 1980s

McNEILL, RHASHIDAH ELAINE
active New York City, 1980s

MELVIN, RODGERS
active Los Angeles, 1980s

MEN'ARD, KENNETH
active Los Angeles, 1980s

MIDDLEBROOK WILLIE R.
active Compton, California, 1980s

MILES, BERTRAND (1928–)
active New York City

Bertrand Miles, the son of a fisherman, has been active in photography since 1945. Born on a houseboat on Lake Mary, Mississippi, he bought his first camera at the age of fifteen, after using his mother's box camera. His early photographs are of his friends at school and family members. Miles' first professional assignment was to photograph his high school prom.

In 1939, Miles moved to Chicago where he met studio photographer Carl Adair and began working in the Adair studio as his assistant. Adair moved to Atlanta and Miles became his partner for one year. Miles moved back to Chicago and was hired as a free-lance photographer and later worked for *Ebony* and *Jet* magazines. He moved to the New York office in 1952 and worked until he was fired in 1954. Within six months he was working for *Collier* magazine and free-lancing for *Life* magazine. In 1956 Cornell Capa and Yale Joel, staff photographers at *Life* informed Miles of a staff position in *Life*'s photographic department. He was subsequently hired and worked as an assistant to the *Life* photographers.

Interested in returning to studio photography and fascinated with advertising work, Miles free-lanced with the advertising agencies on Madison Avenue. His experiences in photography expanded. In 1963 he photographed the March on Washington for personal explorations. His photographs of Dr. Martin Luther King, Jr., Lena Horne, A. Philip Randolph, Whitney Young, Sammy Davis, Jr. and Adam Clayton Powell, Jr., among others were published in periodicals. Later working as Nelson Rockefeller's personal photographer during his 1968 presidential campaign, Miles captured the lifestyles of famous and lesser-known Americans, both black and white. By 1969 Miles had stopped making still photographs, concentrating on filmmaking instead. Hired as a cameraman for CBS and working closely with Walter Cronkite, he covered some of the more explosive news events in this country such as the Attica prison riot and the student unrest on Cornell University's campus in the 1970s.

See photographs pages 364–367.

MILLER, JON
active Los Angeles, 1980s

MINGO, GEORGE
active New York City, 1980s

MITCHELL, WILLIAM H.
active Los Angeles, 1980s

MONTOUTE, MARLENE
active New York 1980–present

Marlene Montoute studied photography at the School of Visual Arts in New York City where she received her B.F.A. An activist in the arts and an exhibiting photographer, Ms. Montoute has exhibited her work at the School of Visual Arts' 21st Street Gallery, Cinque Gallery, the First Women's Bank, Nassau Community College's Firehouse Gallery, the 4th Street Photo Gallery and at the Les Muses des Femme/Manhattan Healing Arts Center.

Montoute's work has been published in *Exhibitions: School of Visual Arts Catalog* and in *Gap Tooth Girlfriends: The Third Act, An Anthology*. Her photographic career has incorporated many aspects of photography. She writes, "my work enables me to reveal the most intimate and immediate concerns of the artist's world. As photography has become an advanced vehicle of artistic expression, it has permeated the vision of modern art. My canvas is painted through the lens of the camera."

MOREHEAD, HOWARD
active Los Angeles, 1940–present

Howard Morehead, a prolific photographer, during his long and active career has organized beauty contests, photographic organizations, produced film documentaries and became a television news cameraman. Born in Topeka, Kansas, Morehead began his career in photography in the early 1940s. As a free-lance photographer he worked for a number of black publications such as the *Los Angeles Sentinel, Jet* and *Ebony* magazines.

Morehead has traveled throughout the world photographing news events, celebrities and sports figures. His photographs of Billie Holiday, Paul Robeson and actress Jayne Kennedy are poignant studies rather than straightforward documents.

SELECTED BIBLIOGRAPHY

"The Tradition Continues: California Black Photographers" (exhibition catalog), Los Angeles: California Museum of Afro-American History and Culture, 1983.

See photographs pages 368–370.

MORGAN, ALLEN
active New York City, 1970s

MORGAN, MICHELLE
active Washington, DC, 1980s

MORIAS, K. A.
active New York City, 1970s

MORRIS, DENNIS
active London, England, 1980s

MORRIS, LENNY
active New York City, 1970s

MOSLEY, JOHN W. (1907–1969)
active Philadelphia

Born in Lumberton, North Carolina, in 1907, Mosley became interested in photography in his early twenties. Moving to Philadelphia in the 1930s, Mosley is best recognized as a chronicler of black society in the Philadelphia area. Noted for photographing four to five events a day, Mosley was a dedicated and hard-working photographer. He covered virtually every sporting event between 1936 and 1967, whether a boxing match, a relay race, basketball or football game.

Mosley's portrait work is characterized by Dr. Richard Beard of Temple University as empathetic to the sitter. "Mosley seems to have known instinctively how to frame a shot, how to catch people in their environment so that place and face seemingly interact. His subjects characteristically reveal dignity [and] strength. . . ." John W. Mosley's photographs of organizations, sports figures and celebrities such as Wilt Chamberlain, W. C. Handy, Langston Hughes, Marian Anderson, Duke Ellington and national leaders such as Richard Nixon and Paul Robeson have been donated to the Charles L. Blockson Afro-American Collection at Temple University, Philadelphia, Pennsylvania.

COLLECTIONS

Charles L. Blockson Afro-American Collection, Temple University, Philadelphia, Pennsylvania

SELECTED BIBLIOGRAPHY

Colombo, Paolo, and Beard, Richard, "John W. Mosley: Photographs 1937–67" (exhibition brochure). Philadelphia: Temple University, Tyler School of Art, 1987.

See photographs pages 371–373.

MOSLEY, LEIGH
active Washington, DC, 1980s

MOUTON, GIRARD, III
active New Orleans, 1980s

MOUTOUSSAMY-ASHE, JEANNE (1951–   )
active New York City

Jeanne Moutoussamy-Ashe was born in Chicago and lives and works in the New York metropolitan area. She earned a B.F.A. in photography in 1975 from Cooper Union (New York). She has done free-lance work for *Ebony* and *World Tennis* and for such corporations as Philip Morris and IBM. Moutoussamy-Ashe has also worked with NBC-television and the Associated Press. She is a former contributing editor for *Self* magazine and has worked as photo commentator for television's "PM Magazine."

Moutoussamy-Ashe has lectured widely on her photography throughout the United States. She is one of the few contemporary photographers who have been successful in publishing books about their work. Concerned about human rights, Moutoussamy-Ashe traveled to South Africa, documenting her subjects' way of living under apartheid. Moutoussamy-Ashe is noted for her photographs of the people of Dafuskie Island in South Carolina. She has recently completed a pioneering research and publication project on the contributions of black women photographers in the United States. The book, entitled *Viewfinders: Black Women Photographers*, has received laudatory attention by sociologists, historians and photographers.

COLLECTIONS

Schomburg Center for Research in Black Culture, The New York Public Library, New
    York, New York
The Studio Museum in Harlem, New York, New York
The Columbia Museum of Art and Science, Columbia, South Carolina

SELECTED EXHIBITIONS

1986. "America: Another Perspective," New York University, New York, New York
1985. "Three Photographers," Black Gallery, Los Angeles, California
1984. "Art Against Apartheid: 3 Perspectives," Schomburg Center for Research in Black
    Culture, The New York Public Library, New York, New York
1983. "Daufuskie Island: A Photographic Essay," Sutton's Black Heritage Gallery, Houston,
    Texas
1982. "Image and Imagination," Jazzonia Gallery, Detroit, Michigan

1981. "Products of the Seventies," Cooper Union, Houghton Gallery, New York, New York

1980. "Still Photographs," Chicago Public Library Cultural Center, Chicago, Illinois

1979. "Official Portraits: Photographs of the Carter Administration," National Portrait Gallery, Washington, DC

1978. "Black Photographers Annual, Traveling Exhibition" (travel to the Soviet Union)

SELECTED BIBLIOGRAPHY

Moutoussamy-Ashe, Jeanne. *Viewfinders: Black Women Photographers, 1839–1985*, New York: Dodd, Mead and Company, 1986.

Reynolds, Pamela, "The Black Experience in Pictures," *The Boston Globe*, April 12, 1986.

Moutoussamy-Ashe, Jeanne, *Daufuskie Island: A Photography Essay*. Columbia, South Carolina: University of South Carolina Press, 1982 (foreword by Alex Haley).

Sepia, December 1981.

Jet, May 8, 1980.

Champions and Challengers Series, *Tracy Austin, Bjorn Borg, Franco Harris, Reggie Jackson*, EMC Publishers, 1977.

Ashe, Arthur. *Getting Started in Tennis*, photographs by Jeanne Moutoussamy, New York: Atheneum, 1977.

Black Photographers Annual, Volumes II & IV, Brooklyn, New York: Another View, Inc., 1972, 1975.

See photographs pages 374–375.

MUHAMMAD, OZIER (1950–   )
active New York and Chicago

During a fifteen-year career, *New York Newsday* photographer Ozier Muhammad has had thousands of his photographs published all over the world. He received the prestigious Pulitzer Prize for International Reporting in 1985 for a photographic essay entitled, "Africa: The Desperate Continent."

Ozier Muhammad studied photography and journalism at Columbia College in Chicago and received a B.F.A. in photography in 1972. Later that same year, he joined the staff of *Ebony* magazine where he and other staff photographers documented the black experience worldwide.

From the early 1970s through the mid-1980s, Muhammad's cameras were focused on every type of subject, from the streets of Chicago to the awesome suffering of the famine victims in Ethiopia. Muhammad worked for the *Charlotte Observer* (North Carolina) before accepting a position as staff photographer for *Newsday*.

Ozier Muhammad, the grandson of the Honorable Elijah Muhammad, the founder of the Nation of Islam, also photographed the first Ali–Frazer title bout. He has done varied photo essays; included among them are: "The Nation of Islam," a "Profile of

Jamaica," coverage of the 1974 Pan-African Congress in Dar-es-Salaam, Tanzania, and the Second World Black and African Festival of Arts and Culture in Lagos, Nigeria, in 1977.

Muhammad covers every conceivable fast-breaking news story and event for *Newsday*. His unique ability to capture human suffering and emotions translated through body gestures has yielded him many accolades, among them the Jesse Merton White Award for International Photography, the National Association of Black Journalists Print Award for International Reporting, the George Polk Award for News Photography, the First Place General News Award from the New York Press Photographers Association, the John S. Knight Journalism Fellowship and the Neiman Fellowship at Harvard University.

Combined with his experiences and knowledge of what it takes to be a successful photographer, Ozier Muhammad's vision concentrates on the graces of humanity. He writes, "Throughout my career as a photojournalist, I've always tried to make personal images that evoke the way I feel about myself, people and the community we/I live in. My first love has always been art photography, it's my training. I've tried to incorporate (as great photojournalists have always tried to do) a high level of the aesthetic of photography in my photojournalism. Sometimes I am successful. . . . My interest in the art of photography nurtures my successful moments as a photojournalist—it's most definitely a symbiotic duality."

Muhammad credits his uncle, Herbert Muhammad, for piquing his interest in photography. His uncle was a studio photographer in Chicago and a photographer for the newspaper *Muhammad Speaks*. Ozier Muhammad bought his first camera at the age of sixteen. Being the grandson of Elijah Muhammad, he was accustomed to seeing his private world photographed by photojournalists such as Gordon Parks and Magnum photographer Eve Arnold. With his first camera, he began photographing the streets of Chicago, meeting other photographers like Bobby Senstacke and Billy Abernathy.

COLLECTIONS

R. J. Reynolds Foundation, Winston-Salem, North Carolina
The Southside Community Art Center, Chicago, Illinois
Columbia College, Chicago, Illinois
The Berman Gallery at the University of Chicago, Illinois

SELECTED EXHIBITIONS

1986. "On Freedom: The Art of Photojournalism," The Studio Museum in Harlem, New York, New York
1986. "Two Schools: Chicago and New York," Kenkeleba Gallery, New York, New York
1983. "Ozier Muhammad," Air Gallery, New York, New York
1979. "Perspectives," R. J. Reynolds Foundation, Winston-Salem, North Carolina
1972. "Chicagophoto 1" (photographs by Chicago photographers), John Hancock Center, Chicago, Illinois

SELECTED BIBLIOGRAPHY

Hatch-Billops Collection, Inc., edited by Leo Hamalian and James V. Hatch, *Art and Influence, 1986*. Interview with Hershel Johnson, May 19, 1985.

"On Freedom: The Art of Photojournalism" (exhibition catalog), Studio Museum in Harlem, New York, 1986.

"Ozier Muhammad Awarded Fellowship," *The New York Times*, May 13, 1986.

"Kup's Column," *Chicago Sun-Times*, April 26, 1985.

Time-Life Photography Annual, 1973.

The Black Photographers Annual, Volume II, 1972.

See photographs pages 376–379.

MURPHY, ROGER
active Atlanta, 1970s

MURRAY, RONALD
active Los Angeles, 1970s

MUSSA, MANSA K.
active Newark, New Jersey and New York City, 1974–present

Mussa first exhibited his work in 1974 at the Newark Museum under the Mayor's Teen Arts Festival. A self-taught photographer, he is best known for his collection of black concert dance photographs. He has studied Media Arts at Jersey City State College and has worked as a graphic designer for over ten years. His works have been published in local newspapers such as the *Newark Star-Ledger*, *New Jersey Afro-American* and the *Village Voice*. His documentary work includes two extensive projects: "Cuba, Si! See, Cuba!" and "Newark: A Day In The City." He not only contributed to the Newark project as a photographer, he was the organizer and curator along with Newark-based photographer, Eddie Johnson, Jr.

See photograph page 380.

MUTLAQ, AL HAKIM
active New York City, 1980–present

Mutlaq is a free-lance photographer based in New York's Harlem community. He is noted for his photographs of celebrities who frequent the Apollo Theatre and is the staff photographer for *National Scene* magazine. He is also the official photographer for the Nigerian Consulate and the National Council for Culture and Art. His works have been published in *Rock and Roll*, *Class International* and *Essence* magazines. He has taken portraits of Nancy Wilson, Sugar Ray Leonard, Bill Cosby, Rev. Jesse Jackson and Stevie Wonder, among others.

See photographs page 381.

NANCE, MARILYN (1953–   )
active New York City

Marilyn Nance is a photojournalist based in New York City. A 1987 recipient of a New York State Council on the Arts Individual Artists Grant Program, she has photographed the black Indians of New Orleans, Appalachian folk musicians, the funeral of an Akan priest and an African village in South Carolina. She is currently organizing an exhibit of her photographs on the religious and spiritual expressions of African Americans.

Nance was the staff photographer for the North American Zone of FESTAC 77, the African arts and cultural festival held in Lagos, Nigeria. Nance's work has been published in New York's *Village Voice*, *Essence*, *St. Louis* magazine and *the Black Photographers Annual*, Volumes III and IV, among others.

Nance's photograph of a father holding his son received critical acclaim and received the 1985 and 1986 CEBA Award of Excellence for its use in an Anheuser Busch corporate ad and calendar. Nance is the associate producer of "Voices of the Gods," a film on two ancient African religions that are practiced today in the United States, and has been artist-in-residence at the Goddard-Riverside Community Center in New York and at Lightwork (Syracuse, New York) and has won the Leica Medal of Excellence.

She studied graphic design and photography at Pratt Institute and journalism at New York University.

COLLECTIONS

Schomburg Center for Research in Black Culture, The New York Public Library, New York, New York

SELECTED EXHIBITIONS

1987. "Her Story, Her Space, Her Moments," Rotunda Gallery, Brooklyn, New York

1986. "Africa in the Americas," Caribbean Cultural Center, New York, New York

1986. "Reflections of Self," Fordham University, New York, New York

1986. "America: Another Perspective," New York University, New York

1986. One-woman show, Goddard-Riverside Community Center, New York, New York

1985. "From Alabama to Zambia," DC 37 Gallery, New York, New York

1984. "Alternative Visions," Mercer County Community College, Trenton, New Jersey

1983. "Five Black Photographers," BACA Downtown Cultural Center, Brooklyn, New York

SELECTED BIBLIOGRAPHY

Wallace, Michelle, "The Harlem I Love," *The Village Voice*, October 6, 1985.

Strickland-Abuwi, Lula, "Marilyn Nance: An Eye on the Ordinary," *Daily Challenge* Weekend Edition, April 12, 1987.

See photographs pages 382–383.

NARIN, PRINCE
active Los Angeles, 1980s

NEILSON, LARRY
active Hollis, New York, 1980s

NGE
active New York City, 1970–present

A jazz photographer, Nge studied painting and drawing at the Huguenot School of Art, Pratt Institute and the Brooklyn Museum School of Art. He spent a number of years in Europe as a painter and worked in the conservation department at the Guggenheim Museum (New York City). His slide and print collection is extensive, containing over 500 titles, among them Art Blakey, Betty Carter, Miles Davis, Dizzy Gillespie, Milt Jackson, Eddie Palmieri and Archie Shepp. He has exhibited his jazz photographs in galleries in the New York area.

See photographs page 384.

NORFUS, RANDY O.
active Cleveland Heights, Ohio, 1980s

NORMAN, SKIP (WILBERT R.)
active Jackson, Mississippi and Columbus, Ohio, 1970–present

Skip Norman is a photographer, filmmaker and ethnographer who is presently an assistant professor in the Department of Radio, Television and Film at the University of Southern Mississippi. Over the past eighteen years, he has produced seven films depicting various aspects of African American life and photographed fifteen films of such diverse types as documentary, dramatic, educational, experimental, instructional, political and promotional. Emphasizing the *cinema verite* approach of filmmaking, six of them were filmed in West Berlin, Germany, and nine in various parts of America. He received an interdisciplinary Ph.D. combining anthropology and sociology with photography and cinema from the Ohio State University in 1984. He is interested in the visual study of culture.

His photo essay of a black man in Ohio entitled "Jim Towns" is a story about a man who works as a custodian to survive although he is an accomplished artist. His art interest is unknown to the "outside" world, however, and the essay is a poignant and sympathetic portrayal of this man's story. His film credits as cinematographer include "Wilmington-10," ". . . But Then, She's Betty Carter," and "The Migrant Family," among others. Norman has received numerous awards and has exhibited at Silver Image Gallery in Ohio, Milestone Gallery in Washington, DC, and the Colorfax Gallery, also in Washington, DC.

OGBURN, OGGI
active Washington, DC, 1980s

OLIVER, CLIFFORD
active Syracuse, New York, 1980s

OLIVER, DEXTER
active Washington, DC, 1980s

OLMSTEAD, DWOYID
active Pittsburgh, 1940s

See photograph page 385.

OUTLAW, HARMON NELSON
active Los Angeles, 1980s

PARKER, CHRISTOPHER
active Hollywood, California, 1980s

PASLEY, JAMES B.
active St. Louis, 1970s

PATRICK, REG
active Chicago, 1957–present

Patrick studied photography in workshops, independently and at the San Francisco Art Institute. He became interested in the medium in the mid-1950s and states "My approach is basically to follow my sensitivities; to focus on imagery that is a reflection of our responses to ourselves and others. I strive to promote the best of our being, our spirit and the miracle of our existence. That the moment conveys a humanistic value from the perspective of my ethnic and human heritage, and contributes to our caring and connecting with ourselves, each other and our Creator–these are the qualities by which I hope my work is measured."

See photographs pages 386–387.

PAYNE, YVONNE
active Washington, DC, 1980s

PECK, BILL
active New York City, 1970s

PERONNEAU, BILL
active Philadelphia, 1970–present

Fine art photographer Bill Peronneau has been a photography instructor at Drexel University, the Philadelphia College of Art and the Abington Art Center (Abington, Pennsylvania). Also a free-lance photographer and photojournalist, Peronneau has worked for a number of city dailies and magazines.

Peronneau has also curated "The James Van Der Zee Retrospective" at the Delaware Art Museum. He has been published in *Essence*, the *National Leader* and *Time* magazine. Special honors awarded him include "Discover of the Year" in the 1977 *Time-Life Annual* and a 1978 Rockefeller Foundation grant for research on photographer James Van Der Zee.

His imagery explores forms found in nature, expanding their recognizability. Experimenting with natural and artificial light, he gives his subjects a new sensibility, whether they be a flower petal or a nude. In his own words, "art is original, personal, emotional and spontaneous. To stimulate basic responses, be they beautiful, exhilarating or sensual is a truly wonderful experience. People should be able to view an image and record the experience as pleasurable or view an image and enjoy a momentary respite from the day-to-day struggle to survive. This is what I must achieve in order to continue working in this medium."

Titles of his portfolios include "Still Life"; "Nudes II"; "Seascapes"; "Buildings"; "Nudes."

COLLECTIONS

Library of Congress, Washington, DC
Free Library of Philadelphia, Philadelphia, Pennsylvania
Brooklyn Museum, New York, New York
Pereirra Collection, Lisbon, Portugal
The National Gallery of New Zealand, Wellington, New Zealand
Lehigh University, Bethlehem, Pennsylvania

SELECTED EXHIBITIONS

1983. "14 Photographers," Schomburg Center for Research in Black Culture, The New York Public Library, New York, New York
1982. "Black Photographers I," The Afro American Historical and Cultural Museum, Philadelphia, Pennsylvania
1981. "Philadelphians," The Photography Gallery, Philadelphia, Pennsylvania
1981. Foto Gallery (one-person exhibit), Philadelphia, Pennsylvania
1981. Art Alliance of Philadelphia (one-person exhibit), Pennsylvania
1980. "Pennsylvania Photographers," The Governor's Mansion, Harrisburg, Pennsylvania
1978. "The Nude in Photography," Photopia Gallery, Philadelphia, Pennsylvania

See photographs page 388.

PHILLIPS, BERTRAND D.
active Chicago, 1970s

PHILLIPS, RONNIE
active Hollywood, California, 1980s

PHIPPS, PATRICIA
active New York City, 1970s

PINDERHUGHES, JOHN (1946–   )
active New York City

Pinderhughes is one of a small group of vigorously active photographers whose work is viewed by two separate audiences—those in the commercial world and those in the art world. A hard-working and dedicated photographer, Pinderhughes moves back and forth between the two worlds with ease. His poetic compositions manage to meet the individual yet diverse needs of both art directors and gallery curators as well as to satisfy their separate audiences.

Pinderhughes was born in Washington, DC. His early years were spent there, in Tuskegee, Alabama, and in Montclair, New Jersey where he graduated from high school. He originally aspired to be a painter/graphic artist, but instead attended Howard University where he majored in marketing. He became interested in photography during the summer of 1966 while working in Ethiopia with Operation Crossroads Africa. After that summer, he returned to America, determined to become a photographer. Pinderhughes began by photographing student life on the Howard University campus. As a result of this project he co-produced a book: *Centennial Plus One: A Photographic and Narrative Account of the Black Student Revolution: 1964–1968*.

After leaving Howard University, Pinderhughes worked for publishing firms in New York City. It was at this time that he became interested in commercial photography. He also took classes in film production with WNET Black Journal Film and Television Workshop (1972). His assignments have included national ads, posters, album covers, magazine illustrations and annual reports. He has received many awards from the World Institute of Black Communications (CEBA) as well as the Art Directors Club Award of Excellence and the Clio Award.

Pinderhughes' fine art photography is not an appendage of his commercial work but a separate sphere of activity. While most of his commercial work is in color, black and white and soft color are his choices for his personal images. He does not attempt to make explicit social statements in this—he is drawn to beaches, the sea, family and extended family ties, and objects found in kitchens and bathrooms. His images explore tonal variation, pattern and textural design, light and delineated line. The periodic shift in his subject matter attests to his continued experimentation with new ideas.

COLLECTIONS

The DeMenil Foundation, Houston, Texas

The Schomburg Center for Research in Black Culture, The New York Public Library, New York, New York

The Studio Museum in Harlem, New York, New York

Howard University, Washington, DC

The Afro-American Museum of Detroit, Detroit, Michigan

The Allen Memorial Art Museum, Oberlin, Ohio

EXHIBITIONS

1987. The Port Washington Library (one-person show), Port Washington, New York

1986. "Two Schools: New York and Chicago," Kenkeleba House Gallery, New York, New York

1986. "America: Another Perspective," New York University, New York, New York

1984. Gallery 62 (one-person show), The National Urban League, New York, New York

1983. "Contemporary Afro-American Photography," Oberlin College, Oberlin, Ohio

1979. "The Black Photographer," The San Francisco Museum of Modern Art, San Francisco, California

1976. "Light Textures Three," Just Above Midtown Gallery, New York, New York

SELECTED BIBLIOGRAPHY

"The Versatile Sweetpotatoe," *The New York Times*, January 6, 1988.

"Flash Is Back in Style," *Popular Photography*, December, 1985.

"When It's His Turn to Cook," *Essence*, November, 1984.

Willis-Thomas, Deborah, "John Pinderhughes" (exhibition catalog), New York: The National Urban League, Gallery 62, 1984.

"The World of Commercial Photographers," *Black Enterprise*, 1982.

See photographs pages 389–390.

PONTIFLET, TED
active Oakland, California and New York City, 1962–present

Pontiflet studied sculpture and painting at the California College of Arts and Crafts (B.F.A.) and received a M.F.A. from Yale University School of Art and Architecture. In the mid-'60s he left this country to live in Ghana, West Africa. In West Africa, he began to write and photograph while living as "an apolitical, self-imposed exiled artist." Pontiflet maintains two residences, one in New York and one in Oakland. He teaches courses in African-American art and art in Africa in colleges on both coasts. As an author he published a children's book entitled *Poochie* (Dial Press, Ltd., 1978). He has traveled extensively in West Africa and Europe and has a remarkable collection of photographs and writings from this experience. Pontiflet has exhibited in numerous galleries and libraries in the United States, among them the Grand Oak Gallery, Oakland Public Library (both in Oakland, California) and the Smithsonian Institution in Washington, DC.

See photograph page 391.

POPE, CARL ROBERT
active Indianapolis, 1980s

PROVIDENCE, WAYNE (1948–)
active New York City

Wayne Providence attended the School of Visual Arts (B.F.A.) and Hunter College (M.F.A.) in photography. Providence (a poet and a free-lance photographer) creates works that have a painterly quality. He states about his work, "the ability and perspective of the photographic image unveils many mysteries and secrets, beyond what the eye sees. My work addresses these mysteries and secrets in a collective expression that is based on the photographic image, coming from points where the real and the surreal interweave and emanate. . . ."

Providence's photographs have been featured in a number of books published by poets in New York. Most recently, his photograph entitled "Dangerously Suite" was published on a record album by Hamiet Bluitt (Black Saint Record Co.). He has taught photography and poetry workshops in New York to teenagers and young adults.

SELECTED EXHIBITIONS

1985. Hunter College Art Gallery, New York, New York

1984. Union Theological Center, New York, New York

1983. Allen Memorial Art Museum, Oberlin College, Ohio

1983. Schomburg Center for Research in Black Culture, New York Public Library, New York, New York

1982. Jazzonia Gallery, Detroit, Michigan

1981. The Studio Museum in Harlem, New York, New York

1980. El Group Morivivi Galeria, New York, New York

See photographs page 392.

RAGLAND, PHILLDA (1940–)
active United States, Africa, Europe

In 1969 Ragland was production manager and photographer for the Filmstrips and Photography section of the Commission on Ecumenical Mission and Relations of the United Presbyterian Church overseas department. She was responsible for photographing all social and economic projects sponsored by the church. During the high point of the civil rights movement, Ragland photographed the activities of the leaders and community groups who marched and protested in cities such as Washington, DC. She also organized an exhibition of photographs from her collection of photographs of children entitled "Kids Next Door."

SELECTED BIBLIOGRAPHY

Moutoussamy-Ashe, Jeanne. *Viewfinders: Black Women Photographers*, New York: Dodd, Mead & Co., 1986.

"Phillda Ragland Is Globe-hopping Fotog for United Presbyterian Church," *Ebony*, March, 1969.

RAMSESS, ARKILI-CASUNDRIA
active Los Angeles, 1980s

RANDALL, HERBERT
active New York City, 1970s

REED, CORNELIUS
active Brooklyn, New York, 1970s

REED, ELI
active New York City, 1980s

ROBERTS, RONALD
active New York City, 1970s

ROBINSON, GEORGE L.
active New York City, 1970s

ROBINSON, HERB
active New York City, 1970s

ROBINSON, ROBERT (1939–   )
active Philadelphia

Born in Philadelphia, Robinson describes himself as a self-taught photographer—self-taught through his exposure to outstanding art and commercial photographers in the Philadelphia area. He further credits his self-education to his exhaustive study of technical manuals and practical experimentation.

He began his career in the early seventies working as a darkroom assistant in a stock photography agency in Philadelphia. Later he began teaching photography at the Fleisher Art Memorial in the city and at the Haystack Mountain School of Crafts in Maine. From

1976 to 1979, he was the staff photographer for the Philadelphia College of Art. Late in 1979 he decided to free-lance and developed a wide range of clients in the Philadelphia business community. Also a staff photographer for the Afro-American Historical and Cultural Museum in Philadelphia, he photographed events and consulted on photography exhibits.

Robinson's personal projects include photographing the black rodeo circuit in the United States, which he started in 1981.

SELECTED EXHIBITIONS

"Eleven Philadelphia Photographers," Fleisher Art Gallery, Philadelphia, Pennsylvania
"Faces at Fleisher," Fleisher Art Gallery, Philadelphia, Pennsylvania

See photographs page 393.

ROBINSON, RUDOLPH   (d. 1987)
active Boston, 1958–1987

Over the past four decades, Robinson has received numerous awards not only for photography but also for art, furniture design and graphic design. Since 1982, he has been a faculty member of the Massachusetts College of Art, and since 1978 he has been an artist-in-residence at Northeastern University.

Studying art in Philadelphia early in his career, he later studied at the Institute of Art in Tours, France, at the Kunstschule, in Wiesbaden, West Germany and at the Fogg Art Museum.

Robinson has received awards from the Atlanta Life Insurance Company and the Philadelphia Museum of Art as well as the City of Philadelphia Gold Key. Several of his photographs have been published in the Boston area.

SELECTED EXHIBITIONS

1985. Museum of the National Center for Afro-American Artists, Boston, Massachusetts
1983. Harriet Tubman House, Boston, Massachusetts
1983. Boston Museum of Fine Arts Afro-American Commission, Boston, Massachusetts
1978. Afro American Center, Tufts University, Boston, Massachusetts
1965. Powelton Village Arts Festival, Philadelphia, Pennsylvania
1959. Friends Neighborhood Guild Art Gallery, Philadelphia, Pennsylvania

See photograph page 394.

ROGERS, ODETTA
active Boston, 1980s

RYAN, CYRIL (1946–   )
active Montreal, Canada

Ryan has been interested in photography since the mid-1960s. He attended photographic workshops at the International Center of Photography, Visual Studies Workshop and Sun Valley Center for the Arts and Humanities, among others. Ryan graduated from Concordia University (B.A. in Communication Arts) and is a M.A. candidate at Concordia.

A free-lance photojournalist and fine art photographer, Ryan teaches photography and film at Concordia. He has created strongly realized reportage images, and his work has been published and reviewed in photographic journals such as *Ovo* and *The Black Photographers Annual*, Volume II.

COLLECTIONS

The Art Bank of the Canada Council, Ottawa
Still Photography Division, National Film Board of Canada
Public Archives Canada, Ottawa
Bibliotheque Nationale du Quebec, Quebec, Canada

SELECTED EXHIBITIONS

1983. Yajima Gallery (10th anniversary show), Montreal, Canada
1979. The Workshop, Loyola Campus, Concordia University, Montreal, Canada
1979. Peter Whyte Gallery, Banff, Alberta, Canada
1977. "13 Canadian Photographers," Madison Art Center, Madison, Wisconsin
1976. "21 Canadian Photographers," National Film Board of Canada, Ottawa, Ontario, Canada
1975. The Studio Museum in Harlem, New York, New York
1972. Vanier Library Exhibition Center, Loyola College, Montreal, Canada

See photographs pages 395–396.

SADDLER, VERONICA
active New York City, 1980s

SAFFO, GLENN
active New York City, 1980s

SALTER, JEFFREY A.
active Newark, New Jersey, 1980–present

Salter received his formal training by studying photojournalism at Syracuse University. He worked as a photographer during his five-year tour of duty with the United States Navy in the early 1980s. There he won numerous awards, such as the "Photographer of the Year" competition. His assignments have taken him all over the world.

Returning to civilian life in 1985, he joined *The Record*, New Jersey's largest evening newspaper, as a photojournalist. In 1986, he completed a photographic portrait of the city of Newark (New Jersey). Salter spent two weeks recording hundreds of city life images for a comprehensive visual study of Newark.

SANTOS, JUMA
active New York City, 1965–present

A self-taught photographer, Santos is interested in documenting African and African-American communities. He states, "I look to Africa and the African-influenced world for my inspiration. I use the camera as a tool to document and capture those compositional manifestations; colors, forms, moments, moods, movements, shapes and structures which speak to my sense of aesthetics." His present body of work represents his interest in photographing the "drama and compositional manifestation that takes place in traditional African performances, rituals, ceremonies and festivals".

See photograph page 397.

SAUNDERS, LLOYD E.
active Chicago, 1950s

SAUNDERS, RICHARD (1922–1987)
active United States and Africa

Saunders was an award-winning photojournalist throughout his forty-year career. He first became interested in photography as a young boy growing up in Bermuda. A local photographer whom Saunders followed around gave him some old equipment to experiment with. At the age of eight, he and his family moved to the United States, and he put his early training to use while still in school. Saunders' family returned to Bermuda at the outbreak of World War II, and he worked as a photographer with the police department.

During the 1940s, Saunders returned to the United States and received formal training in photography at Brooklyn College and the New School for Social Research in New York City. In the mid-1940s, through his friendship with Gordon Parks, Saunders got a job as a photographic technician in a lab, and this work enabled him to study the skillful techniques of some of America's leading photojournalists at *Life*.

In 1951, Saunders was selected by the former chief of the Farm Security Administration Photo Division, Roy Stryker, to join a team of top photojournalists in Pittsburgh for the purpose of depicting the city's transition from a decaying steel mill town to a growing modern city. Saunders spent nearly two years, taking four to five thousand photographs of the Hill district, a predominately black community. Also a resident in the district, he documented virtually all facets of the Hill, and his work became a significant part of the documentation project.

For the next eleven years, he received assignments from top publications such as *Ladies Home Journal, Fortune, Ebony* and *Look*, among others. In 1964, an assignment from the United States Information Agency (USIA) in Washington, DC, sent him to Latin America to document the Alliance for Progress, an economic development program sponsored by the U.S. government. During this period, he received a number of assignments from the USIA. In 1967, he accepted a staff position with *Topic*, USIA's magazine for Africa, and for the next six years he was based in Tunis. He traveled throughout Africa photographing events, leaders and people.

He was transferred in 1972 to the magazine's editorial office in Washington, DC, and continued to travel and photograph for *Topic*. His assignments included a trip to Nigeria to cover FESTAC, the Second World Black and African Festival of Arts and Culture.

For nearly twenty years, until his retirement in 1986, Saunders' work in Africa focused on economic and agricultural development. Unique to his style was his emphasis on people, especially young children. In addition to the publication of his photographs in *Topic*, he has exhibited his work in group and one-person shows.

SELECTED BIBLIOGRAPHY

Bardagjy, Andres M., "An African Portfolio: Photographs by Richard Saunders," United States Information Agency (undated).

Washington, Elsie B., "An American at Festac," *Topic*, No. 107 (undated).

Saunders, Richard, "Beyond 'Roots': Searching for the Past in Mali," *Topic*, No. 112 (undated).

"Women of Africa: A Vital Force in Development", *Topic*, No. 92, (undated).

"The Supreme Court of the United States: Symbol of America's Dedication to Rule by Law" (photographs by Richard Saunders), *Topic*, No. 121 (undated).

Ebony, May, 1959.

A Century of Black Photographers: 1840–1960 (exhibition catalog), Providence: Museum of Art, Rhode Island School of Design, 1983.

See photographs pages 398–399.

SCALES, JEFFREY CHARLES (1954–   )
active New York City

Scales, a free-lance photojournalist, photographs the ordinary scenes of everyday life in New York City. He is very selective and imposes his vision by isolating his subjects from the background, thus manipulating the viewer's thoughts about the subject. Born in San Francisco, Scales began taking photographs at the age of eleven when his father gave him his first Leica. He was first published in the *Black Panther* newspaper when he was fourteen. His early influences were post cards that photographer Bill Dane sent to his family throughout the early 1970s.

Scales studied at the San Francisco Art Institute and has lectured at the School of Visual Arts and at the University of Southern California at Los Angeles. His personal work involves documentary projects on black communities in the United States. They include "Traditional Black Blues Bars, Musicians and Music in Chicago" and "Black Teen Gangs in South Los Angeles," among others. He states about his Harlem series, "In these photographs I have focused on Harlem of the 1980s. I try to make images that allude to the reality of being Black in the America of the 80s. Perhaps to even help us to see ourselves more clearly. That is, as clearly as I can affect the medium of photography. My work does not take or direct the observer. Instead the photographs are descriptions of my perceptions of ordinary places and people—in the complexities of living. I do not pretend to understand them, each person. In fact, the discoveries are most often within myself, observing these documents of my own sights."

Scales' photographs have been published in *Paris Photo, Essence, New York Magazine, Los Angeles Times Sunday Magazine, Time* and *Black Enterprise*, among others.

SELECTED EXHIBITIONS

1987. "Harlem," The Hampshire College Gallery of Photography, Amherst, Massachusetts
1986. "Harlem," Midtown "Y" Gallery, New York, New York
1984. "Central American Refugees," Los Angeles Photographers Association, California
1979. "Portraits," Camerawork, San Francisco, California
1970. "Photographs of the Black Panther Party and Student Unrest in the SF Bay Area," University of California at Berkeley, California

See photographs pages 400–402.

SCOTT, WILLIAM J. (1915–   )
active Washington, DC

Born in Massachusetts, Scott studied photography at the Camera School of the Camera Club of the Boston Young Men's Christian Union and Massachusetts Institute of Technology Extension Course Program in Photography. Moving to Washington, DC in the late

1930s, Scott worked as staff photographer for the Washington Afro-American (1937–1945), studio photographer for Scurlock Studios, Washington, DC (1945–1975) and staff photographer for Moorland-Spingarn Research Center, Howard University, Washington, DC. (1975–1983).

See photograph page 403.

SCURLOCK, GEORGE H. (1919–   )
active Washington, DC

A son of Addison N. Scurlock, George began work in his father's photography studio in 1954. The Scurlock Studio, one of the most noted photography studios in Washington, DC, opened in 1911 and documented the activities on the Howard University campus and the social, political and cultural events in the DC area.

SELECTED BIBLIOGRAPHY

A Century of Black Photographers: 1840–1960 (exhibition catalog), Providence: Museum of Art, Rhode Island School of Design, 1983.

The Scurlock Family Photographers: Twentieth Century Black Life and Leaders: 1900–1981 (exhibition catalog), Chicago: Black Woman Collaborative, 1981.

The Historic Photographs of Addison N. Scurlock (exhibition catalog), Washington, DC: Corcoran Gallery of Art, 1976.

See photographs pages 404–405.

SCURLOCK, ROBERT S. (1916–   )
active Washington, DC

Robert, also a son of Addison N. Scurlock, was taught photography by his father. As a studio and editorial photographer, his work has been published in *Ebony* and *Our World* magazines. In 1948, he established the Capitol School of Photography. Seeing the need for specialized photography services for business and government agencies, Scurlock started the Custom Craft Studio, Inc. He is also president of the Scurlock Studio.

SELECTED BIBLIOGRAPHY

A Century of Black Photographers: 1840–1960 (exhibition catalog), Providence: Museum of Art, Rhode Island School of Design, 1983.

The Scurlock Family Photographers: Twentieth Century Black Life and Leaders: 1900–1981 (exhibition catalog), Chicago: Black Woman Collaborative, 1981.

The Historic Photographs of Addison N. Scurlock (exhibition catalog), Washington, DC: Corcoran Gallery of Art, 1976.

See photographs pages 406–407.

SENGSTACKE, ROBERT (1943–)
active New York City and Chicago

Robert Sengstacke became acquainted with photography at the age of fourteen when his father gave him an inexpensive box camera. His personal work began at sixteen when he bought a larger camera and an enlarger. Setting up a portrait studio in his basement, he photographed his high school classmates and worked part-time as a free-lance photographer for his father's newspaper, *The Chicago Defender.*

After high school, he moved to Los Angeles to attend the University of Southern California and continued photographing through his college years. He returned to Chicago and took free-lance assignments in the area. In 1966, he became the staff photographer for the Nation of Islam's newspaper, *Muhammad Speaks.* On assignment for *Muhammad Speaks,* he photographed every aspect of the Nation of Islam, from personal encounters to public and social events.

A hard-working and socially committed photographer, Sengstacke documented the struggles, achievements and tragedies of the civil rights movement. Included among his files are the activities of the Rev. Martin Luther King, Jr., Rev. Jesse Jackson, the Student Non-Violent Coordinating Committee and black political conventions and organizations.

Sengstacke collaborated with other black photographers in Chicago in documenting the black community. Recounting that experience, he states, "We saw ourselves as graphic-historians, conveyors of love, combating what we felt were negative photographic images of blacks in the major American press. Whether we achieved recognition or not, we knew that someday people would look back and want to know what the black photographer had to say about his experience. So we had a job of documenting the black experience through eyes of love, pride and strength."

During this creative period, Sengstacke artfully composed his subjects with a sense of naturalism, whether they were standing at a podium or working in a mechanic's shop. Art historian David Driskell wrote in an exhibition catalog of Robert Sengstacke's work: "The visual record which Bobby has given black and white America through his photography in these turbulent decades will add memorable pages to the history and culture of a young nation still groping with the problems and pains of becoming a Free Society."

Sengstacke has exhibited widely and has had his photographs published in *Life, Ebony, Downbeat* and *Look* magazines.

SELECTED EXHIBITIONS/BIBLIOGRAPHY

1986. "Two Schools: New York and Chicago: Contemporary African-American Photography of the 60's and 70's" (exhibition catalogue), Kenkeleba House, New York, New York

1986. "Tradition and Conflict: Images of a Turbulent Decade, 1963–1973," The Studio Museum in Harlem, New York, New York

1986. "On Freedom: The Art of Photojournalism," The Studio Museum in Harlem, New York, New York

1980. "A Romance of Freedom: Bobby Sengstacke, Photographer," Traveling exhibition and catalogue, organized by the Tri-State Defender Publishing Co., Inc. Memphis, Tennessee

"Photo Bob Sengstacke Lets Camera Do Talking" by Mel Tapley, *New York Amsterdam News*, October 25, 1986

See photographs pages 408–411.

SHACKELTON, CHERYL (1958–   )
active New York City

A photographer, mixed media artist and conservator, Shackelton became interested in photography at Sarah Lawrence College where she studied art and the humanities. She entered Pratt Institute's graduate photography program and interned with the Studio Museum in Harlem's James Van Der Zee Photograph Collection, which led to her interest in preserving black material culture.

Currently, she is exploring the use of mixed media including photographs, found objects, video and sound in her art. In her own words she states, "The sense of photography being a two-dimensional experience is too limiting. My artistic voice strives to include a wide spectrum of ideas and experiences, all present in one piece of art. . . . My vision of the world is complex, and the information conveyed via a photograph must have more movement, more elements in order to manifest the entire picture. I seek to expand and include in my photography everything that contributes to creating a realistic and multi-dimensional portrait."

Shackelton, Preservation Administrator at the Schomburg Center for Research in Black Culture, graduated (M.L.S.) from Columbia University. She has curated a number of exhibitions including "Women of Color: Defined and Redefined" in Newark, New Jersey, and "Tap Shoes, Toe Shoes and Feet: Black Dance in America" at the Schomburg Center.

SELECTED EXHIBITIONS

1987. "Harlem on the Hudson," Harlem Urban Development Corporation, New York, New York

1987. "Self-Portrait," Castillo Gallery, New York, New York

1985. "Reflections of Self: Women Photographers," Fordham University, New York, New York

1984. "My Lady's Bureau: Photograms," Columbia University, New York, New York

See photograph page 412.

SHAMIS, BOB
active New York City, 1970s

SHERMAN, ED (1945–)
active New York City

Ed Sherman's photographic style embraces a full gradation of tone and controlled perspective. In his approach to photography there is no use of mechanical intrusion or tricks. His experience as a professional photographic laboratory technician with some of New York's leading labs has contributed to his reserve of technical skill.

Sherman has been art director of Benin Gallery in Harlem since 1976. His experience with this community art gallery, which features the works of African American artists, has added to the presentation skills he uses for the showcase of his own works. His continuing "Harlem on Parade" series of photographs is a sensitive interpretation of ordinary folks and their environments. His memorable images of musicians and artists also form a creditable and artistic recordation.

Since 1968, after serving a tour of duty as a photographer in the United States Marine Corps, Sherman focused his camera on the struggle and compassion of the "Black Family." His images have been exhibited at "FESTAC 77" National Theatre Exhibition Gallery, Lagos, Nigeria; Brooklyn College, New York; Howard University Fine Arts Gallery, Washington, D.C., Manhattan Arts & Trades Enterprises Exhibition, Germany; Marina City Club Penthouse, Los Angeles, California; and Bishop College, Dallas, Texas, to mention just a few.

Whether Sherman is using the documentary idiom or portrait technique, his images give us an intimate and honest account of the social, cultural and artistic life of the African American community.

In 1981 Sherman started another facet of his media pursuit. He served an internship with Community Film Workshop Council, Inc. in broadcast journalism. Training and working as a video cameraman/editor, he gained proficiency in his new creative efforts. Since then he has held an Eng camerman/editor position with N.B.C. affiliate station WNYT-TV in Albany, New York, covering general news and sports. He is currently a freelance media specialist in New York City, videotaping industrial productions.

SELECTED EXHIBITIONS

1988. "Who's Uptown: Harlem '87," Schomburg Center for Research in Black Culture, The New York Public Library, New York, New York

1987. "Focusing on 2000," The Black Gallery, Los Angeles, California

1987. "NYNCA Coast-to-Coast," NCA 29th Annual Convention Art Exhibition, California Museum of Science and Industry, Los Angeles, California

1987. "Artists and Images," City University of New York, New York, New York

1986. "Two Schools: Chicago and New York" (contemporary African American photography of the 60s and 70s), Kenkeleba House Gallery, New York, New York

1986. "Silver Shadows," Benin Gallery, New York, New York

1984. "Cultural Bridges," The National Conference of Artists Annual Exhibition, Center for the Arts, Mount Vernon, New York

1983. "Kugawa Ngono" (The Sharing Time), Cork Gallery, Avery Fisher Hall, Lincoln Center Plaza, New York, New York

1982. "Cross Section '82," Harlem State Office Building, Art Gallery, New York, New York

1981. "11 African American Artists," Baruch College, New York, New York

1981. "Vantage Points," Benin Gallery, New York, New York

1972. "Black Family" (interpretations by four black artists), Brooklyn College, New York, New York

See photographs page 413.

SIMMONS, ELLEN QUEEN VICTORIA
active Elizabethtown, North Carolina, 1980s

SIMMONS, HOWARD
active Chicago, 1980s

SIMMONS, RON
active Brooklyn, New York, 1980s

SIMPSON, COREEN (1942–   )
active New York City

Coreen Simpson's career is a kaleidoscopic series of art experiences. As a photographer, collagist, jewelry maker and writer, Simpson has successfully and creatively achieved unusual freedom and new heights in her work. She is a pioneer in photographing Harlem at night. One of her photo essays entitled "Uptown Saturday Night," is the sort of project that has not been done since the early 1930s and 1940s by such photographers as Weegee, Aaron Siskind, Roy DeCarava and Morgan and Marvin Smith.

Earlier in her career Simpson printed on mural-size paper and painted on her photographs with oils, acrylics, sparkles and fingernail polish, which took her imagery beyond the photographic form. Simpson is a photographer who takes chances with the medium and with her subjects. Her most recent documentation project entitled "B-Boys" or "Break Boys" is made up of enlarged portraits of young black and Latin boys and girls from the eighties "rap music" phenomenon. Simpson's portraits stress pride and dignity, whether of a cook in a Harlem restaurant or a transvestite in a local night club. As photo historian Rodger Birt states, "There is a strong humanist impulse in Simpson's photography. The transvestites, punk rockers, and "B-Boys" are not exotic specimens to Simpson. She sees her photographs as vehicles to the viewer's reaching a wider social understanding, windows opened up on the varying mores of human communities. Like Weegee and Diane Arbus, Simpson reminds the viewer of a common humanity into whose fabric all of us are inextricably bound."

An award-winning photographer, Simpson has received numerous grants, fellowships and commissions including the New York Foundation for the Arts Grant (1987); Light-work-Artist in Residence, Syracuse University, New York; official photographer for Rev. Jesse Jackson's Rainbow Coalition eight-nation African tour, among others. Her works have appeared in such publications as *Vogue*, The *Village Voice*, *Essence* and *Black Enterprise*.

COLLECTIONS

International Center of Photography, New York, New York
Oberlin College, Oberlin, Ohio
The Studio Museum in Harlem, New York, New York
Detroit State Council for the Arts, Detroit, Michigan
The Schomburg Center for Research in Black Culture, New York Public Library, New
        York, New York
Hatch-Billops Collection, New York, New York
Atlanta University, Atlanta, Georgia

SELECTED EXHIBITIONS

1987. "Eye of the Storm," E. M. Donohue Gallery, New York, New York
1987. "Curators Choice III," Bronx Museum of the Arts, New York, New York
1987. "Eye of the Storm," Sugizaki Gallery, Sedi, Japan
1986. "A Decade of En Foco: Documentation of the Hispanic Photographic Movement,
        Bronx Museum, Bronx, New York
1986. "Black Visions 86," Tweed Gallery at City Hall, New York, New York
1985. "Artists and Influences," Interview Series, Hatch Billops Collection, New York, New
        York
1984. "Affirmations of Life," Kenkeleba House Gallery, New York, New York
1980. "Nitebirds," Gallery 62 National Urban League, New York, New York
1979. "Encounters," Studio Museum in Harlem, New York, New York

SELECTED BIBLIOGRAPHY

Birt, Rodger, "Coreen Simpson: An Interpretation," Black American Literature Forum,
        Volume 21, Number 3, Indiana State University, Fall 1987.
Moutoussamy-Ashe, Jeanne. *Viewfinders: Black Women Photographers*, New York: Dodd,
        Mead & Co., 1986

Jones, Jacqueline. *Labor of Love, Labor of Sorrow*. New York: Basic Books/Harper and Row, 1986.

Laurie, Allison. *The Language of Clothes*. New York: Random House, 1981.

Schoener, Allon. *Harlem on My Mind* (re-release), New York: Delta-Dell, 1979.

See photographs pages 414–416.

SIMPSON, LORNA (1960–)
active New York City

Lorna Simpson has a M.F.A. in Visual Arts from the University of California, San Diego and a B.F.A. in photography from the School of Visual Arts (New York). She has worked in fine arts institutions as a consultant and administrator. Simpson's personal work makes statements about her community, whether the streets of California or New York. Her emphasis is on body language. Concerning Simpson's large works, gallery curator Kellie Jones observes, ". . . photographers are generally brought up on the enlarged images of the movies, TV close-ups, and Disneyland's overscale fantasies. Their [exhibiting photographers] aesthetic has been influenced and informed by the disco/club culture, where oversize video screens parade huge fragmentary imagery . . . for them it [large scale] is the natural form that their photographic language takes."

Simpson's photographs are usually 60″ x 40″, black and white. Written statements accompany the imagery. In her own words, "the juxtaposition of image and text in [this] series provides the viewer with multiple readings by stringing together several interpretations of a particular event and by butting segments of text so that they overlap more than one image." Her work has been published in *Get the Message*, an anthology edited by Lucy Lippard (1984), and in *Heresies* (1982), and has been reviewed in the magazine *American Arts*, among others.

SELECTED EXHIBITIONS

1987. "Large as Life: Contemporary Photography," Jamaica Arts Center, New York, New York

1986. "America: Another Perspective," New York University, New York, New York

1985. "Gestures/Reenactments," Alternative Gallery, San Diego, California

1984. "Contemporary Afro-American Photography," Allen Art Museum, Oberlin College, Oberlin, Ohio

1985. "Dropped Lines," Seneca Falls Gallery, San Diego, California

1982. "Heresies Annual Show," Frank Marino Gallery, New York, New York

1982. "Image and Imagination," Jazzonia Gallery, Detroit, Michigan

See photograph page 417.

SLAUGHTER, CHARLES
active Riverside, California, 1980s

SLEET, MONETA J. JR.   (1926–   )
active United States and Africa

Sleet was born in Owensboro, Kentucky. His career as a photographer began when his parents gave him a box camera as a child. Sleet studied business at Kentucky State College and continued his interest in photography. After graduating, he was invited to set up the photography department at Maryland State College in 1948. He later studied at New York University, where he obtained an M.A. in journalism in 1950.

Early in his career, Sleet worked for the *Amsterdam News* (New York) and *Our World*, a popular black picture magazine. *Our World* ceased publication in 1955, and Sleet joined the Johnson Publishing Company's *Ebony* magazine. His major contribution to photojournalism is his extensive documentation of the marches, meetings and rallies of the civil rights movement. In 1969, Moneta Sleet became the first black American to win a Pulitzer Prize in photography for his photograph of Coretta Scott King consoling her daughter at the funeral of Martin Luther King, Jr.

Sleet's long career as a photojournalist has taken him all over the Americas, Africa and Europe. "You try to develop the sensitivity and the 'eye' to see that very special mood of the moment. You develop the discipline to block out everything but you, the camera and the subject and you develop the tenacity to stick with it, to have patience. The picture will happen—that very special picture will happen." He has photographed heads of state, celebrities, and ordinary men, women and children while on assignment. His portraiture and reportage possess a warmth that reveals a patient understanding of the individual circumstances of the people who have passed before his camera. In the end, empathy with his subject—anonymous or renowned—is the dominant quality in all his work. "It is important," he explains "to have a support system to be a successful photojournalist. It's not an easy life so it's important to have a family who understands. I have been very fortunate."

SELECTED EXHIBITION/BIBLIOGRAPHY

1986. "Moneta Sleet, Jr.—Pulitzer Prize Photojournalist," The New York Public Library, New York, New York (traveling exhibition organized by Philip Morris Companies, Inc., and Johnson Publishing Company, Inc.) exhibition brochure text written by Julia Van Haaften and Deborah Willis.

"Image Maker: The Artistry of Moneta Sleet, Jr.," *Ebony*, January, 1987.

"The Vision of Moneta Sleet in Show" by C. Gerald Fraser, *New York Times*, October 19, 1986.

"Moneta Sleet, Jr., of *Jet/Ebony* and Jazz Photographer Chuck Stewart Receive Awards at the International Black Photographers," *Jet*, March 5, 1981.

"Jet's Moneta Sleet, Jr., Honored by Honeywell," *Jet*, December 11, 1975.
Ebony, August, 1971.
Ebony, June, 1969.
Ebony, February, 1969.
"Europe on a Budget," *Ebony*, May, 1962.

See photographs pages 418–420.

Sligh, Clarissa T.
active New York City, 1970–present

Sligh's career has encompassed diverse types of work and life experiences, including finance, computer science, art history, photography, film, painting and mixed media. She was born in Washington, DC, and has studied at Howard University (B.F.A.), Hampton Institute (B.S.), the University of Pennsylvania (M.B.A.), and attended workshops at the International Center of Photography, the Skowhegan School of Art (Maine) and the Collective for Living Cinema Workshops.

Sligh's work is personal and consists of old photographs of herself and family members, recent images taken by her and text written by her. She states "My work is semi-autobiographical. It is a journey in search of self-identity. Beginning with a photograph that already exists, I shoot, reassemble and reshoot to combine the photograph and the word to address the mind more than the eyes. The viewer becomes a participant in restaging the event." Sligh uses nineteenth-century processes such as cyanotypes, gum bichromate prints and Van Dyke prints and is recently making images with three-color photo silkscreen prints.

Sligh is a member of the Women's Caucus for Art, Friends of Photography and Franklin Furnace. She has produced multi-media presentations, photographed outdoor events and festivals and is developing a photographic journal of the Wall Street area.

Selected Exhibitions

1987. One-person show, C.E.P.A., Satellite Space, Buffalo, New York

1987. "With Her Body in Mind," Hera Gallery, Wakefield, Rhode Island

1987. "herstory," Castillo Gallery, New York, New York

1986. "Life Stories," Minneapolis College of Art and Design Gallery, Minneapolis, Minnesota

1986. "America: Another Perspective," New York University, Photo Center Gallery, New York, New York

1986. "Violations," Moonmade Space, New York, New York

1985. "Artists as Filmmakers Series," A.I.R. Gallery, New York, New York

1984. "ID," P.S. 1 Gallery, Long Island City, New York

1982. "Dangerous Work," Parsons School of Design Gallery, New York, New York

SELECTED BIBLIOGRAPHY

C.E.P.A. Quarterly, Volume 2, Issue 2, Winter, 1987.

Trend, David, "Black and White Photography," *Afterimage*, 13:10, May 16, 1986.

Raven, Arlene, "Not a Pretty Picture: Can Violent Art Heal?" *Village Voice*, June 17, 1986.

Heresies, Issue 20, 1985.

"Artists Focus," *Women's Quarterly Review*, Fall 1984.

"Art and Ego," *Pan Arts Magazine*, Issue 1984.

See photographs pages 421–423.

SMITH, BEUFORD (1939–   )
active New York City

Born in Cincinnati, Ohio, Smith became interested in photography in the early 1960s after seeing photographs by Roy DeCarava in the book *Sweet Flypaper of Life*. Moving to New York, he met other black photographers who were interested in working together and forming a group. The group, called the Kamoinge Workshop, of which he became a member in 1965, was, Smith feels, the most important phase of his early creative development.

Smith became a free-lance photographer in 1966 and a cinematographer in 1968. In an interview in *Ten:8* magazine, Val Wilmer states, "Beuford Smith is one of the outstanding documentary photographers whose art grew out of what has been called the 'cauldron of the sixties.' His concerns are diverse, his vision humane and thoughtful. . . ."

Smith has taught photography courses in workshops and on college campuses. He worked with Shawn Walker, Vance Allen, Ray Francis and Joe Crawford in publishing the first issue of *The Black Photographers Annual* in 1973. Smith is founder of the Cesaire Photo Agency and has free-lanced for a number of years. His photographs have been published in *Camera* magazine, *The Black Photographers Annual* and *Candid Photography* magazine. During the 1970s he exhibited at the Countee Cullen Library, Studio Museum in Harlem, and the Addison Gallery of Art in Andover, Massachusetts, among others. Most recently, in 1986 and 1987, his photographs were exhibited at the Kenkeleba House Gallery in the show "Two Schools: Chicago and New York" and at the Port Washington Public Library in New York—"Beuford Smith: Photographs."

COLLECTIONS

Schomburg Center for Research in Black Culture, The New York Public Library, New York, New York

Museum of Modern Art, New York, New York

SELECTED BIBLIOGRAPHY

Wilmer, Val, "Beuford Smith: In the Humane Tradition," *Ten:8*, quarterly photographic magazine No. 24, issue entitled "Evidence: New Light on Afro-American Images."

See photographs pages 424–426.

SMITH, GEORGE W. (1904–1986)
active Buffalo, New York

Born in Little Rock, Arkansas, George W. Smith became a photographer in the mid-1940s. He moved from St. Louis, Missouri, where he spent his young adult years, to Buffalo, New York. In the early years he studied photography at night and was hired later as a free-lance photographer for the two major black Buffalo newspapers—*The Buffalo Criterion* and *The Buffalo Challenger*. He photographed many of the social events sponsored by black organizations and church groups in the Buffalo area.

Smith operated the Cleartone Studio in Buffalo for over forty years. He had a large collection of prints and negatives, most of which was lost after Smith became ill and unable to preserve it. In 1984 he arranged to have a portion of his collection preserved on microfilm, which is housed at the Center for Local Afro-American History and Research in Buffalo.

SMITH, JAMYL OBOONG (1954–   )
active New York City

Originally a pre-med student, Smith became interested in photography while at Hunter College. His early influence is credited to his father, an amateur photographer in Ohio. He credits his sister, Ming Smith, for providing later guidance and inspiration. His personal work explores the concept of pictorialism in photography—but through the eyes of a twentieth-century photographer. He is a free-lance commercial photographer and his work includes fashion and advertising photography.

Smith has traveled throughout the Americas, Europe and Africa photographing. His portraiture is reminiscent of the soft-focus effect often seen in the nineteenth century. A self-taught photographer, Smith apprenticed with commercial photographer Anthony Barboza. His works have been used on recording albums and published in magazines and newspapers.

See photographs pages 427–429.

SMITH, JEFFREY (1948–   )
active San Francisco

Jeffrey Smith is a photographer and a filmmaker. He began photographing as a result of his early association with Robert Sengstacke, former staff photographer for the *Chicago Daily Defender*. After completing his undergraduate studies at the Art Institute of Chicago, he moved to California. In 1972, he began his graduate study in photography at the California College of Arts and Crafts. His most recent shows include his representation in the exhibition the "Tradition Continues: California Black Photographers" at the Afro-American Museum of History and Culture in Los Angeles. His free-lance projects include documenting New Wave and Latin bands, making portraits of employees of a predominately gay Folsom Street restaurant and photographing ceremonies.

He states of his style, "I work in the fine art/documentary style of photography in the tradition of Eugene Smith, Roy DeCarava, Robert Sengstacke and Billy Abernathy. My primary concern with photography is to explore and relate my personal experience of black culture with an emphasis on people-oriented, social commentary."

SELECTED EXHIBITIONS

1986. "America: Another Perspective," New York University, New York, New York
1985. Black Gallery, San Francisco, California
1974. "Sequences," California College of Arts and Crafts, Oakland, California

SMITH, MING
active New York City, 1970–present

Ming Smith was born in Detroit, Michigan. She attended Howard University, Washington, DC (B.S.). In the early 1970s, she was a member of the Kamoinge Workshop, a group of black photographers interested in discussing photography and exhibiting the works of black photographers. A free-lance photographer living in New York, Smith has also traveled and photographed in Europe for a number of years. Her photographs have been used on a number of jazz albums and have been shown in group and solo exhibitions.

Deba P. Patnaik described Smith's work in the exhibition catalog for *Contemporary Afro-American Photography* at the Allen Memorial Art Museum, Oberlin College, ". . . Ming Smith treats the cityscape from an entirely different point of view. In her refreshingly original use of color, she transmits a poetic sense of activity, busyness, light and drama in the city. . . ."

Smith's photographs of children in Africa are straightforward documents, soft and whimsical. As a social documentarian she views her subjects from a surrealist point of view. She has been the recipient of National Endowment for the Arts and CAPS grants in photography, and her work has been published in *The Black Photographers Annual*, Volume III.

COLLECTIONS

Schomburg Center for Research in Black Culture, The New York Public Library, New York, New York

The Museum of Modern Art, New York, New York

SELECTED EXHIBITIONS

1983. Contemporary Afro-American Photography, Allen Memorial Art Museum, Oberlin College, Oberlin, Ohio

1983. "14 Photographers," Schomburg Center for Research in Black Culture, The New York Public Library, New York, New York

1980. "Self-Portrait," Studio Museum in Harlem, New York, New York

See photographs pages 430–432.

SMITH, TONI
active Washington, DC, 1980s

SMITH, VERNON
active New York City, 1980s

SORRELL, MAURICE
active Washington, DC, 1980s

SPENCER PYNE, CHARLYNN
active Washington, DC, 1980s

SPROW, OTIS (1949–   )
active Detroit

Originally trained as a mechanical engineer at Cornell University (B.S and M.S.), Sprow became interested in photography during the early 1970s. He was born in Baltimore, Maryland, and has taught photography classes at such workshops as the Lake Superior PhotoWorkshops in Ontario, Canada.

Sprow is interested in the technical applications of photography and has written many articles on the zone system, developing black and white film and darkroom techniques. Basically self-taught, Sprow shoots with a large-format camera, and his imagery is very formal. He has lectured on such topics as "Nature Photography," "An Introduction to the Zone System," and "Concerning Art/Concerning Photography," among others. He acted as technical consultant to Stan Osolinki's book *A Guide to Taking Better Outdoor Pictures*, (Prentice-Hall). His photographs have appeared in such publications as *Darkroom Techniques, Petersen's Photographic, Photoworks, Colorlines* and *Facts* magazine.

COLLECTIONS

Baltimore Museum of Art, Baltimore, Maryland
The J. B. Speed Art Museum, Louisville, Kentucky
The Detroit Institute of Arts, Detroit, Michigan
Weiss Corporation Collection, Northville, Michigan
The K-Mart Corporate Collection, Troy, Michigan

SELECTED EXHIBITIONS

1983. Photographic Impressions Gallery, Highlands, North Carolina
1983. Baltimore Museum of Art, Baltimore, Maryland
1983. Detroit Public Library, Michigan
1983. Jazzonia Gallery, Detroit, Michigan
1982. Tamarack Craftsmen Gallery, Omena, Michigan
1982. Eloquent Light Gallery, Rochester, Michigan
1981. Exposures Gallery, Libertyville, Illinois
1980. Fine Arts Gallery of Dearborn, Michigan
1977. Colorfax Galleries, Washington, DC

SELECTED BIBLIOGRAPHY

Eisenberg, Mel, "Interview with Otis W. Sprow" *Metro Photo News*, Volume 1, No. 2, August 1983.

Sprow, Otis, "Introduction to the Zone System Photography" *Darkroom Techniques*, Vol. 4. No. 4, July/August, 1983.

Miro, Marsha, "The Viewer Can Create a New World" *Detroit Free Press*, July 15, 1983

Manty, Dorothy, "Otis Sprow" *Photoworks*, July/September, 1983.

Acosta, Dan, "Still Life on the Funny Farm" *Health Care News*, July 6, 1983.

See photographs pages 433–435.

STARKLEY, NORRIS
active Los Angeles, 1980s

STEVENS, JEMMIE
active Miami, Florida, 1980s

STEWART, CHUCK (1927–   )
active New York City

Chuck Stewart studied photography at Ohio University and moved to New York City after he graduated. While still in school, he and a fellow student photographed for corporations and celebrities. Stewart free-lanced also for magazines and newspapers such as *Our World* and began photographing jazz musicians and vocalists on stage and in his studio. Stewart is best known as a jazz photographer. He has been a mentor and teacher to a number of photographers. He photographed such musicians as Dizzy Gillespie, John Coltrane, and Billie Holiday. His photographs were used for album covers, publicity stills and illustrations for books and articles on a particular musician.

Stewart photographed virtually every musician active between 1950 and 1980; his coverage includes blues, bebop, fusion, salsa, popular and balladeers. His style is lively, exciting and serious. He is able to capture the mood and spirit of the performer, whether in performance or in the studio. His photographs create a sense of rhythm not only because of his subjects but because of what is actually going on in the frame. He incorporates instruments, microphones and reflections, creating patterns from his lights and props. Stewart has a tremendous archive of photographs describing the last forty years in music. His work has been published in books and has been exhibited in group and solo exhibitions.

SELECTED BIBLIOGRAPHY

Stewart, Charles, and Harrison, Paul Carter, *Jazz Files* Boston: New York Graphic Society Books, Little, Brown and Company, 1985.

See photographs pages 436–438.

STEWART, FRANK (1949–   )
active New York City

A graduate of Cooper Union (B.F.A. in photography), Stewart is a fine art photographer and a photojournalist as well as a curator. His camera focuses on Harlem and its people, young and old; proud and shy; rich and poor. He photographs the familiar, often overlooked by the untrained eye. He has taught photography at the State University of New York in Purchase and at The Studio Museum in Harlem and has trained a number of photographers in New York. Stewart was born in Nashville, Tennessee, and spent his formative years in Chicago, where he met a number of active black photographers who were documenting their community.

Stewart's photographs have been published in *The Black Photographers Annual, Life, The New York Times,* among others. In 1984, he was one of ten photographers to be commissioned by the Los Angeles Olympics Committee. He has also worked for corporations in the New York area photographing their events and annual reports and has lectured and exhibited widely. He has received grants for his work, including the Creative Artists Public Service Program in New York and two National Endowment of the Arts awards. Most recently he was responsible for curating and organizing the exhibition "Two Schools: Chicago and New York," on contemporary Afro-American photography. He also wrote an essay for the catalog describing the activities of the black photographers in both cities.

In 1987, Stewart was Artist in Residence at Kenkeleba House in New York City. He has worked on numerous film projects, including *Two Centuries of Black Art in America* (Pyramid Productions), and *Romare Bearden* (Third World Cinema), and is associate director of Contemporary American Artists Series, Inc., a non-profit historical film company that documents living Afro-American artists.

COLLECTIONS

Schomburg Center for Research in Black Culture, The New York Public Library, New York, New York

The Studio Museum in Harlem, New York, New York

SELECTED EXHIBITIONS

1986. "Two Schools: Chicago and New York," Kenkeleba House Gallery, New York, New York

1983. "Contemporary Afro-American Photography," Allen Memorial Art Museum, Oberlin College, Oberlin, Ohio

1980. "Jules Allen/Beuford Smith/Frank Stewart," Gallery 62, National Urban League, New York, New York

1980. "Still Photographs," Chicago Public Library, Chicago, Illinois

1979. "Black Eyes/Light," Studio Museum in Harlem, New York, New York

1979. "Harlem on My Mind 68–78," International Center of Photography, New York, New York

1977. "Impressions of Cuba," Parsons School of Design, New York, New York

1977. "Black Photographers Annual," Corcoran Gallery, Washington, DC

See photographs pages 439–440.

STEWART, JO MOORE
active Iowa, 1970s

STOKES, CELESTE P.
active Toluca Lake, California, 1980s

STRANGE, AL C.
active Los Angeles, 1980s

STRAW, GERALD
active Bronx, New York, 1980s

SUNDAY, ELISABETH
active Oakland, California, 1980–present

Sunday became interested in photography as a teenager; her first photographs were of her family and friends. Later she traveled to Europe to photograph—intending to stay for two years, Sunday stayed four. While overseas she traveled, photographing in Africa as well as various countries in Europe. Her photographs are a visual journal of her experiences while abroad. Her images are not just straightforward documents of the subject; they are lucid, full of texture and form. She is interested in extending the boundaries of traditional photographs: ". . . to move inside the liquid lines and prismatic diffractions in search of the anima of human existence. This is the goal to which I have devoted myself. I have tried, through my use of elongations and swirling backgrounds, to capture the ambivalence and paradox, the magical and pragmatic elements of life's symmetry and dissonance."

Sunday has produced limited-edition portfolios entitled "Transitions," "Africa" and "Southwest Native Plants." She has taught workshops in France, Switzerland and in California.

COLLECTIONS

The San Francisco Museum of Modern Art, San Francisco, California
Bibliotheque Nationale de Paris, Paris, France
F.R.A.C. Foundation, Lyon, France
San Francisco Arts Commission, San Francisco, California

SELECTED EXHIBITIONS

1987. Reese Bullen Gallery, Humboldt State University, Arcata, California
1987. Le Bibliotheque Nationale de Paris, Paris, France
1987. "New American Photographs," Fogg Art Museum, Harvard University, Cambridge, Massachusetts

1986. Journées Internationales de la Photo et de L'Audio-Visuel, France
1985. Nikon Foto Galerie, Zurich, Switzerland
1985. "Flower Show," Detroit Institute of Arts, Detroit, Michigan
1983. Galerie Paule Pia, Anvers, Belgium

See photographs page 441.

SUTTON, ISAAC
active Chicago, 1970s

SUMMERS, DWIGHT
active Washington, DC, 1980s

SYKES, LAWRENCE (1931–)
active Providence, Rhode Island

Born in Decatur, Alabama, Sykes is best known for his photographs of the black American in the south. Sykes has produced numerous photo essays on this subject. As a professor of art at Rhode Island College, he has had the opportunity to travel to the Carribean, Africa and South America photographing the African diaspora. He has exhibited widely and in 1975 was a visiting lecturer in graphic design at the University of Science and Technology, Kumasi, Ghana.

Sykes has a M.S. from Pratt Institute, (New York) and a B.S. from Morgan State University (MD). He is noted for his sensitive studies that explore the effects of light and shadow on both rural and urban landscapes. His works have been published in publications as well as used for bookjackets.

SELECTED EXHIBITIONS
1981. The Rhode Island Black Heritage Society, Providence, Rhode Island (solo exhibition)
1979. American International College, Springfield, Massachusetts (solo exhibition)
1977. Museum of the Center of Afro-American Artists, Boston, Massachusetts (solo exhibition)
1977. University of Minnesota, St. Paul, Coffman Gallery
1976. Gallery of Art, Morgan State University, Baltimore, Maryland
1975. Howard University, Washington, DC
1974. Studio Museum in Harlem, New York, New York
1969. Photographer's Place, Providence, Rhode Island

SELECTED BIBLIOGRAPHY

"The Palenque Rehabilitation Project," photo essay, Esso-Care Report, printed Dominican Republic, March 1980.

"Chant of Saints," University of Illinois Press, 1979.

"The Massachusetts Review, Autumn, 1977.

"Sykes Photographs at Morgan" by Yvonne Owens Everett, *Baltimore Sun*, October 3, 1976.

See photographs pages 442–443.

TALAMON, BRUCE W. (1949–)
active Los Angeles

Born in Los Angeles, Talamon has been active in photography since 1972. Initially, he considered becoming a lawyer, but then became interested in the field of documentary photography. He wrote: "As a black American I thought it important to continue the tradition that black photographers James Van Der Zee and P. H. Polk began earlier in this century. Those pictures are the visual corollary to the tales that West African griots hand down to succeeding generations. They contribute to the collective memory of our people."

Talamon divides his time between special documentary projects (Jesse Jackson's Presidential campaigns for *Time* in 1984 and 1988, an ongoing photo history of the Monterey Jazz Festival and participation in Collins Publishing's *A Day in the Life of America*) and the film industry, where he works as a still photographer. He most recently completed the poster and publicity stills for the film *Beverly Hills Cop II*.

See photographs pages 444–445.

TAYLOR, THERON
active Denver, Colorado

TAYLOR, WILLARD
active Washington, DC, 1970s

THOMAS, DONALD
active Pittsburgh, 1970s

THOMAS, JON
active New York City, 1970–present

Thomas received a B.F.A. in visual communications at Ohio State University and a M.F.A. in film and television from New York University. A free-lance photographer and writer, he has had his works published in magazines such as *Essence, Elan* and *Oui*. Clients of his advertising photographs include radio stations, CBS Records and Clairol, among others.

For a number of years, Thomas has been working on a project of photographing middle-class black women. He has produced greeting cards and a portfolio on the theme. His portraits are sensual and comedic. He states, "My images are a visualization of women going through a transitional phase in a culture that is going through a similar transition. They are middle-class black women—many realizing for the first time what their real needs are—sometimes creating, sometimes adapting, and at times failing to surmount their problems in a culture being consumed by change."

COLLECTIONS

Schomburg Center for Research in Black Culture, The New York Public Library, New York, New York

Zoma Gallery, New York, New York

SELECTED EXHIBITIONS/BIBLIOGRAPHY

1984. "Jon Thomas-Photographs," Gallery 62 National Urban League, New York, New York.

1983. "14 Photographers," Schomburg Center for Research in Black Culture, The New York Public Library, New York, New York.

"Through the Eyes of a Lensman," New York *Daily News*, February 28, 1982.

TOMLIN, ELAINE
active United States, 1960–present

Photojournalist Elaine Tomlin became active during the civil rights movement. As the official photographer for the Southern Christian Leadership Conference (SCLC), she photographed the demonstrations, marchers, riots and the plight of the poor throughout the United States. Her photographs have been published in such publications as *Ebony, Jet* and *Life*.

She has also worked as a scientific photographer and art photographer. Tomlin taught basic photography and photojournalism at the Atlanta Institute of Photography in the mid-1970s. She received the Photographer of the Year award from the Atlanta Media Women and has received other citations for her activities. One of her most memorable photographic stories is her coverage of Charleston police arresting and beating a young black woman in 1968.

SELECTED EXHIBITIONS/BIBLIOGRAPHY

Moutoussamy-Ashe, Jeanne. *Viewfinders: Black Women Photographers*, New York: Dodd, Mead, 1986.

We'll Never Turn Back (exhibition catalog), Washington, DC: Smithsonian Institution, National Museum of History, 1980.

TROTMAN, ALBERT
active Queens, New York, 1980s

TUCKER, JEROME
active Brooklyn, New York, 1980s

TUCKER, ROGER
active Newark, New Jersey, 1980s

TURNER BOND, SANDRA
active Washington, DC, 1980s

TYTUS, RICHARD
active Hollywood, California, 1980s

UNDERWOOD, OLEAUN D., III
active Tucson, Arizona, 1980s

VALENTINE, DONALD R.
active Hillcrest Heights, Maryland, 1980s

VANN, DOUG
active New York City, 1980s

VANN, ERIC G.
active Wheaton, Illinois, 1980s

VAN SERTIMA, JACQUELINE LA VETTA
active New York City, 1977–present

Van Sertima studied photography and sociology at Hunter College (B.A.) in New York. She is a fine art photographer—photographing her subjects with black and white film, then hand tinting with oil paints. She is noted for the vibrant colors she uses to intensify her subjects, which include street vendors, family members, children and the elderly.

She has exhibited in New York and Los Angeles and has received awards for her photography.

SELECTED EXHIBITIONS/BIBLIOGRAPHY

"Jacqueline LaVetta Patten/Coreen Simpson: Photographs," Gallery 62, National Urban League (exhibition catalog), New York, New York, 1980

"The Expressive Sensations of Colour," New York University Contemporary Arts Gallery, New York, New York, 1981

See photographs pages 446–447.

VEREEN, DIXIE
active Washington, DC, 1980s

WALKER, CHRISTIAN
active Atlanta, 1970–present

WALKER, SHAWN
active New York City, 1960–present

Walker's uncle, a photographer, introduced him to the medium. From age five through sixteen, he photographed family, friends and his neighborhood. Raised in Harlem, Walker began to take his photographing seriously at twenty-one. In 1961, he began to talk with other photographers who had just formed the Kamoinge Workshop including Lou Draper, Al Fennar, Ray Francis, and Herb Robinson, among others.

During the 1960s, Walker photographed in the streets of Harlem. He exhibited in shows organized by the Kamoinge group in libraries and galleries in the area. Walker continued to be an advocate for the black photographer, documenting the community in which he lived and taught. In the seventies he traveled to Nigeria, Cuba and Guyana to photograph. He continues to exhibit his work. In a recent article he wrote "The Period 1962–72 was the most intense time of shooting for me. It was a period where a lot of cultural, social and political change took place in Harlem and I found myself at the center of a lot of it. I consider this time to be a monumental, historical period. . . ."

Walker is a cinematographer, commercial photographer and teacher. He has a B.F.A. in photography from Empire State College and has taken film classes at the Third World Newsreel and the Free School of New York. He has taught in community centers, colleges and art institutions over the last twenty years. Walker has received grants for his photographic essays. His work has been published in newspapers and magazines such as *Essence* and *National Alliance*.

COLLECTIONS

Museum of Modern Art, New York, New York

The Studio Museum in Harlem, New York, New York

Schomburg Center for Research in Black Culture, The New York Public Library, New York, New York

New Jersey State Museum, Trenton, New Jersey

SELECTED EXHIBITIONS

1987. Institute for Art and Urban Resources, New York, New York

1986. New Jersey State Museum, Trenton, New Jersey

1986. Queensborough Community College, Queens, New York

1986. Cafe Americano, New York, New York

1985. Picker Art Gallery, Hamilton, New York

1984. Chicago Public Library, Chicago, Illinois

1983. Allen Memorial Art Museum, Oberlin, Ohio

1982. Jazzonia Gallery, Detroit, Michigan

SELECTED BIBLIOGRAPHY

Walker, Shawn, "Preserving our History: The Kamoinge Workshop and Beyond," *Ten-8* (quarterly photographic magazine), No. 24 Issue: *Evidence of New Light on Afro American Images*, 1987.

"Shawn Walker," *Nueva Luz*, a photographic journal, Spring 1987.

"Shawn Walker, Photographer," *Photo Newsletter*, James Van Der Zee Institute, Vol. 2, Issue 2, March–April 1973.

See photographs pages 448–449.

WALLACE, WILLIAM ONIKWA
active Chicago, 1968–present

Wallace became interested in photography at the age of thirteen. In 1962 he was introduced to motion picture production and studied in workshops and colleges such as NET Black Journal Film Workshop and Kennedy King College in Chicago. Wallace has worked as a staff photographer for the *Chicago Daily Defender* and the *Tri State Defender* in Memphis, Tennessee. For the past twelve years he has combined his talents as a photographer and filmmaker, working as an independent television and film producer and editor.

His film credits are numerous, among them *Catch the Spirit* and *Images of Life, Visions of Hope* (1986, United Methodist Communication, Nashville, Tennessee); "The Brotherhood Experience of Mound Bayou", WDIA Radio, Memphis, Tennessee; and *The Last Affair*, Chelex Productions, Chicago, Ill. His awards and citations include the Martin Luther King Award (National Association of Black Journalists) for "The Brotherhood Experience of Mound Bayou", Certificate of Merit for a public affairs story entitled, "Robert's Story" and "Best News Photograph" certificate presented by the National Newspaper Publishers Association in 1973.

See photographs page 450.

WATSON-MAURO, SHARON (1949–   )
active Pittsburgh

Watson-Mauro studied photography at the Philadelphia College of Art and received a B.F.A. in 1976. She began photographing at the age of six when she received a camera from her father, an amateur photographer. Her early photographs were of family members and friends. She studied with Barbara Blondeau, Ray K. Metzker, Ron Walker and Anne Tucker. She was inspired by their teachings and began to develop her own photographic style.

She is a studio photographer and stylist. Her personal work is autobiographical and uses non-silver photographic processes.

See photograph page 451.

WATTS, LEWIS
active Berkeley, California, 1980s

WEEMS, CARRIE MAE
active San Francisco, 1972–present

Carrie Mae Weems is a photographer, folklorist and video artist. She has a B.F.A. in art and design from the California Institute of the Arts and an M.F.A. from the University of California, San Diego, and has done additional graduate study at the University of California, Berkeley. She has taught photography at the International Children's School in Los Angeles and is currently teaching at Hampshire College in Amherst, Massachusetts. A Smithsonian Fellow, she has exhibited in group and solo exhibitions in New York, Tennessee and California. Her work has been published in *Essence, Blatant* and *Image*, among others. Weems has received grants for her work from the National Endowment of the Arts and the California Arts Council. An advocate for the arts, she has organized exhibitions, conferences and meetings relating to photography, black photographers and women photographers.

Weems' photographs are personal and universal, she creates fiction and biography. They are whimsical and serious. In her own words she states: "I'm feeling extremely colored now days, and I'm happy about my 'condition.' For much too long, I've placed great emphasis on things European and Western. Often at the expense of overlooking the value of Afro-American culture, I've used European aesthetics and standards as a starting point for creating my own work. So this notion of 'feeling colored' has to do with drawing upon Afro-American culture as a foundation for creating art.

"My photographs have to do with my concerns as a black photographer, indeed a black person, who bottom line believes my folks have a 'right' to be shown, represented and dealt with by those amongst them, but one of their 'own kind.'

"My primary emphasis is to deal with Afro-American culture, to speak from my own place, my own experience, and to show Afro-Americans in a way not often seen or photographed by those from outside the culture. I believe that there is an Afro-American aesthetic working its way through Afro-American culture."

SELECTED EXHIBITIONS

1986. "America: Another Perspective," New York University, New York, New York
1984. "Family Pictures and Stories," Multi-Cultural Gallery, San Diego, California
1983. "Dropped Lines," Center for Women's Studies and Services, San Diego, California
1983. "4 West Coast Photographers," Vanderbilt University Art Gallery, Nashville, Tennessee
1981. "Women in Photography," Cityscape Photo Gallery, Pasadena, California
1980. "Contemporary Black Photographers," San Francisco, California

See photographs pages 452–453.

WERTS, ERNEST
active Detroit, 1970s

WEST, DOLORES
active Memphis, Tennessee, 1980s

WEST, EDWARD
active Albuquerque, New Mexico, 1980s

WEST, LEONARD D.
active Memphis, Tennessee, 1980s

WHITE, E. LEE
active New York City, 1970s

WHITE, JOHN
active Chicago, 1970–present

A photojournalist for the *Chicago Sun-Times*, White won the coveted Pulitzer Prize in photography in 1982.

SELECTED BIBLIOGRAPHY
Hesterman, Vicki, "Pulitzer Roundup in Ohio," *News Photographer*, May 1987.

WHITE, JUDITH C.
active New York City, 1970s

WHITE, WENDEL A. (1956–   )
active New York and New Jersey

White received a B.F.A. in photography from the School of Visual Arts in New York and an M.F.A. in photography from the University of Texas at Austin. He is a photography instructor at Stockton State College in New Jersey and is an exhibiting photographer and a photographic archival consultant. His work is included in the International Center of Photography's *The Encyclopedia of Photography* (Crown Publishers, 1983). White's personal work describes the urban landscape. He states, "Photography is a process which allows me to pursue my desire for expression and exploration of ideas. Photographing is a way for me to satisfy my curiosity about how things work physically and philosophically. Occasionally I will make a photograph that discloses more about its contents than a simple description of its surface. Beyond the photographic transposition of the subject, there is a quality present in such a photograph that makes it more than just a reproduction of that specific subject.

A recent development in my work concerns the photographing of a place where an ambiguous sign or symbol has been created and possibly altered. These photographs point up the capacity of a sign or symbol to convey emotional content which becomes most apparent when the subject is presented in an objective way. The photographs that I am producing are concurrently investigations of the world and reflections of the photographer."

COLLECTIONS

Atlanta Life Insurance Company, Georgia

Carver Museum, Austin, Texas

Erie Art Center, Erie, Pennsylvania

The Chase Manhattan Bank, New York, New York

Schomburg Center for Research in Black Culture, New York Public Library, New York, New York

SELECTED EXHIBITIONS

1987. "The Industrial Landscape," Stockton State College, Art Gallery, Stockton, New Jersey

1985. "Fifth Annual Art Exhibition," Atlanta Life Insurance Company, Atlanta, Georgia

1984. Midtown Y Gallery (solo exhibition), New York, New York

1984. "Mental Block," Danceteria, New York, New York

1984. "1984: Social Commentary and the Photographer," Moody Atrium Gallery, St. Edwards University, Austin, Texas

1983. "14 Photographers," Schomburg Center for Research in Black Culture, The New York Public Library, New York, New York

1983. "Photoworks II," A.U.A., Albuquerque, New Mexico

1982. "New Visions," Patrick Gallery, Austin, Texas

1982. "Celebrations," Gallery 104, Austin, Texas

SELECTED BIBLIOGRAPHY

"An American Landscape," *Bomb Magazine*, No. XI, 1985.

"Two Photographic Viewpoints" (exhibition catalogue), Austin, Texas: Carver Museum, 1983.

"14 Photographers" (exhibition catalogue), New York: Schomburg Center for Research in Black Culture, 1983.

"Asses," edited by Tom Houston, New York: Avocation Publisher, Inc., 1977.

See photographs pages 454–455.

WHITNEY, FITZGERALD
active Los Angeles, 1944–present

Whitney attended the School of Modern Photography in New York after his stint in the U.S. Army. After graduating in 1948, he worked as a staff photographer for the Hotel Theresa in New York, photographing the celebrities and sports figures who frequented Harlem during that time.

Whitney moved to Los Angeles in 1954 and became a free-lance photojournalist; in the 1960s he became the first black staff photographer at the *Los Angeles Times*. An award-winning photographer, Whitney covers events political and social, tragic as well as light-hearted for the *Times*.

SELECTED EXHIBITIONS/BIBLIOGRAPHY

"The Tradition Continues: California Black Photographers," California Museum of Afro-American History and Culture, Los Angeles, 1983.

WICKHAM, REGINALD
active Teaneck, New Jersey, 1980s

WILKINSON, CARLTON F.
active Nashville, Tennessee, 1980s

WILLIAMS, BUD
active New York City, 1980s

WILLIAMS, DANIEL S.
active Ohio, 1965–present

Williams studied painting and photography at Brooklyn College. His professors were Walter Rosenblum, Philip Pearlstein and James Ernst. Williams graduated with a B.A. in 1965. After one year of graduate-level painting at Brooklyn College, he was awarded a teaching fellowship at the University of Oregon and studied photography with Bernard Freemesser. Williams' photographic studies included workshops with Brett Weston, Ansel Adams, Imogene Cunningham and W. Eugene Smith. After earning his M.A. in photography in 1969, he began teaching photography at Ohio University where he is presently chairman of the photography department and associate professor of art. Williams has exhibited widely and his photographs are in private and public collections.

For a number of years, Williams has been traveling across the country photographing Emancipation, or "Juneteenth" Day celebrations. (News of the Proclamation did not reach some states until the "teen" days of June.) He states, "The content of my photographs have to do with celebrations held in observance of the Emancipation Proclamation of January 1, 1863. They [the celebrations] reached their peak by the turn of the century, and today, the tradition has all but died out. There are just a few places that still have an official observance. As an artist, I feel a need to preserve a little of what remains of an important Afro-American tradition. In my works I am trying to express my interactions with the people I have met, show them asserting their humanity among themselves, and contrast the ways in which each region has come to celebrate the Emancipation Proclamation."

Williams has lectured and held workshops in a number of art institutions across the country including the Smithsonian Institution, the University of Nebraska and the Center for Photographic Studies in Louisville, Kentucky. He has received an Ohio Arts Council grant, an Ohio University Research Grant and the Ruttenberg Fellowship, among other honors.

COLLECTIONS

Museum of Modern Art, New York, New York
Metropolitan Museum of Art, New York, New York
Studio Museum in Harlem, New York, New York
James Madison University, Harrisonville, Virginia
Murray State University, Murray, Kentucky

SELECTED EXHIBITIONS

1986. "America: Another Perspective," New York University, New York, New York
1986. Eye Gallery (solo exhibition), San Francisco, California
1985. Lightfantastic Gallery (solo exhibition), Michigan State University
1985. "Photo Flow," University of Texas, Arlington, Texas
1983. Lloyd Gallery, Spokane, Washington
1982. Columbia College, Chicago, Illinois
1982. "Photospiva," Joplin, Ohio

SELECTED BIBLIOGRAPHY

Popular Photography, November 1977, p. 52.
"Contemporary Icons," *The Georgia Review*, Vol. XXXI, No. 4, Winter 1977, University of
     Georgia Press.
Lewis, Samella, and Waddy, Ruth G., *Black Artists on Art*, Vol. I. Los Angeles: Contemporary Crafts, 1969.
Art Week, November 1975.
Black Photographers Annual, Vol I. 1972, Vol III, 1974, New York.
American Poetry Review, Vol. 6, No. 1, 1977.

WILLIAMS, ELIZABETH "TEX"
active Houston, 1970s

WILLIAMS, LUCY
active Washington, DC, 1980s

WILLIAMS, PAT WARD (1948–   )
active Baltimore, Maryland, and Washington, DC

Born in Philadelphia, Williams studied psychology at Cheyney State University and photography at Moore College of Art (B.F.A.) and Maryland Institute College of Art (M.F.A.–photography). Williams moved to Baltimore to initiate the photography program at the Baltimore School for the Arts (a high school for artistically talented students) and is currently teaching at the College of Notre Dame of Maryland in Baltimore and Bowie State College in Bowie, Maryland.

Williams' personal work investigates segmented imagery dealing with race, memory and family. Most of the works are responses to history, collective and/or personal. She states, "my photographic visions are not created in the camera but after the exposure is made. The expressive quality of non-silver process (cyanotype and Van Dyke prints) coupled with the technique of assemblage offer me the widest variety of devices with which to re-see the image rendered by the camera. Through these options, I can more clearly see the 'my' part in my work. I feel less detached and more a part of its creation. I believe these choices of technical manipulations have made me less of a conduit for visual facts and more of a personal voice."

Williams has received many accolades for her art including a Ford Foundation grant, Baltimore City Individual Artists Grant and Best News Photography award also given by the National Newspaper Publishers Association. She is one of the official photographers for the North Avenue Centennial Project, which is a year-long documentary project honoring the one hundredth anniversary of Baltimore's historic streets. Williams is a member of the Society for Photographic Education, the College Art Association and the Board of Trustees for the Maryland Art Place Gallery in Baltimore.

SELECTED EXHIBITIONS

1988. "Autobiography: In Her Own Image", INTAR Gallery, New York, New York

1988. "Windows and Portals," Gromley Gallery, College of Notre Dame of Maryland, Baltimore, Maryland

1987. "Race and Representation." Hunter College, New York, New York

1987. "Artspace '87, Rooms with Views" (installation), Baltimore, Maryland

1987. "Image/Identity: Self Portraits of Maryland Artists, Maryland Art Place, Baltimore, Maryland

1987. "Eighth Annual National Exhibition," J. B. Speed Museum, Louisville, Kentucky (First Place Purchase Prize).

1987. "Humor, Wit and Whimsy," Artists Today touring exhibit, Montpelier Cultural Arts Center, Laurel, Maryland

1983. "Black Woman: Power and Image," Antioch University, Philadelphia, Pennsylvania

1982. "Photo Credit to Read: Pat Ward Williams," Temple University, Philadelphia, Pennsylvania

See photographs pages 456–457.

WILLIAMS, SAM
active Brooklyn, New York, 1980s

WILLIAMS, SHEDRICH
active Portland, Oregon, 1970s

WILLIAMS, TED
active Chicago, 1960s

WILLIAMS, WILLIAM EARLE (1950–   )
active Haverford, Pennsylvania

Williams, a graduate of Hamilton College (New York) and Yale School of Art (M.F.A.), is an associate professor of Fine Arts at Haverford College in Pennsylvania. His M.F.A. thesis topic, "Flash Portraiture of People in Dark Places," has been an ongoing project for him. He has exhibited his photographs throughout the country and has researched his topic by attending social and political events and photographing the rich and the working classes in private and public places.

Also a curator and writer, Williams has received grants for his own photography and the exhibitions he has organized from the Ford Foundation, Pennsylvania Council on the Arts and Massachusetts Council for the Arts, among others. Williams has reviewed manuscripts and articles written about photography for editors and authors. He has lectured on photographers and photography at art institutions and conferences throughout the country.

K. Porter Aichele wrote in the exhibition catalog *William Earle Williams: Party Photographs*: "Five years ago William Earle Williams began photographing people at parties. The subject has proved to be a fruitful one. Although his party pictures portray a range of types in a variety of settings, Williams disavows the roles of social critic and cultural historian. His choice of subject matter was motivated by the possibility of establishing correspondences between the abstract configurations of photography and what he has called patterns of ritual behavior. In his most recent party pictures the confluence of form and content is skillfully and subtly realized."

COLLECTIONS

Philadelphia Museum of Art, Philadelphia, Pennsylvania
Lehigh University, Bethlehem, Pennsylvania
Metropolitan Museum of Art, New York, New York
Baltimore Museum of Art, Baltimore, Maryland
University of Maryland, Baltimore, Maryland
Brooklyn Museum, Brooklyn, New York
Allentown Art Museum, Allentown, Pennsylvania

SELECTED EXHIBITIONS

1986. Albin O. Kuhn Library, University of Baltimore (solo exhibition), Baltimore, Maryland
1985. Comfort Gallery, (solo exhibition), Haverford, Pennsylvania
1987. Allentown Art Museum, Allentown, Pennsylvania
1985. The Print Club of Philadelphia, Pennsylvania
1984. Feisher Art Memorial, Philadelphia, Pennsylvania
1983. Mid-Town Y Gallery, New York, New York
1980. Butler Institute of American Art, Youngstown, Ohio
1980. Herbert Acherman Gallery, Cleveland, Ohio

SELECTED EXHIBITIONS CURATED FOR HAVERFORD COLLEGE, HAVERFORD, PENNSYLVANIA

1987. "Lewis Hine, Jacob Riis: Photographic Humanists"
1986. "Edward Curtis, Doris Ulmann, The Last Photographs"
1985. "Larry Fink: A Mid-Career Retrospective"
1984. "Walker Evans: Photographs of African Art"
1984. "Masterworks of Photography from the Collection"
1982. "Lisette Model, Diane Arbus and Weegee Photographs"
1980. "A Tribute to James Van Der Zee"

SELECTED BIBLIOGRAPHY

Who's Who in American Art, 1987 (listed).
"Documentary Revival," Southwell, William, *Lens on Campus,* Feb/Mar, 1986.
Aichele, K. Porter, "William Earle Williams: Party Photographs", Comfort Gallery, Haverford College, Haverford, Pennsylvania.

Philadelphia Photo Review, Summer 1982.
Philadelphia Magazine, February, 1982.

See photographs page 458.

WILLIS, ALPHONSO
active Philadelphia, 1950s

See photograph page 459.

WILLIS, DEBORAH   (1948–   )
active New York City

Willis is a free-lance curator and photographer and head of the prints and photographic collections at the Schomburg Center for Research in Black Culture. She received a B.F.A. in photography from the Philadelphia College of Art, an M.F.A. from Pratt Institute (New York) and M.A. in Museum Studies from the City University of New York.

Willis' personal work records ceremonies and rituals in black family lives, such as funerals, weddings, celebrations and family reunions. She is interested in preserving family history through photographs and documenting the role that family photographs play in preserving material culture.

An exhibiting photographer, she has written critical essays on photographers and has done extensive research on black photographers from the turn of the century to the present. Willis is the author of *Black Photographers 1840–1940: An Illustrated Bio-Bibliography* (Garland, 1985) as well as the present volume. She has curated a number of historical and contemporary exhibitions throughout the United States and has lectured on the history of photography.

See photographs page 460.

WILLOCKS, CURTIS   (1950–   )
active New York City

Willocks is a commercial and fine art photographer. He studied photography at Lewis College (Illinois), the New School for Social Research and the Fashion Institute of Technology (New York). His photographs have been published in the *Village Voice*, the *Burlington Free Press* and *People* magazine.

Willocks states about his work, "I feel that I am an observer who records moments in time with my camera. Everyone has a different vision. I try to make my images contain the personality, the fire, that I see in the subject. To be an effective photographer, you have to be well-rounded. You can't shy away from things that you think are out of your realm. You have to get out there, you have to explore. I've been recording images for a long time. Some of it is emotional. Some of it makes you think. And, some of it makes you wonder!"

COLLECTIONS

Schomburg Center for Research in Black Culture, New York Public Library, New York, New York

SELECTED EXHIBITIONS

1986. "Honoring the Arts of Harlem," Harlem Urban Development Corporation, New York, New York
1986. African American Museum, Hempstead, New York
1986. Federal Plaza Building, New York, New York
1983. Fashion Institute of Technology, New York, New York

See photographs pages 461–462.

WILSON, CAROL R.
active Washington, DC, 1980s

WILSON, G. MARSHALL
active New York City, 1950s–present

WILSON, GILBERTO
active Philadelphia and New York City, 1975–present

Wilson is a graduate of Temple University, Tyler School of Art (Pennsylvania) and Cooper Union (New York). He has an M.F.A. in photography/printmaking, and his interest is in recording the Africa diaspora's religion and music.

He has taught photography and has been an artist-in-residence at the Brandywine Graphic Workshop in Philadelphia. He is a printmaker and his photo essays include images of children in the Caribbean and storefront churches. His storefront churches essay is a sensitive portrayal of small church services in New York. Using natural lighting, he captures the mood, movement and experiences of the minister and the congregation.

COLLECTIONS

Schomburg Center for Research in Black Culture, New York Public Library, New York, New York

SELECTED EXHIBITIONS

1986. "Honoring the Arts of Harlem" Harlem Urban Development Corporation, New
York, New York
1985. Allen Lane Art Center, Philadelphia, Pennyslvania
1985. Gallery Tyler School, Rome, Italy
1983. Race Street Gallery, Grand Rapids, Michigan
1982. Kenkeleba House Gallery, New York, New York
1982. Afro-American Cultural and Historical Museum, Philadelphia, Pennsylvania
1980. St. Eustatius Historical Museum, St. Eustatius Netherlands, Antillies
1980. Cayman Gallery, New York, New York.

SELECTED BIBLIOGRAPHY

Rudolph, Jill, "Black Arts Festival Tries to Unite Cultures," *The Dickinsonian*, March 6, 1986.
"Students Hold Annual Black Arts Festival," *Dickenson Today*, March 1986.
Calascibetta, Lucia, "Exhibit Combines Cultures," *The Press*, Atlantic City, New Jersey,
February 17, 1986.
Beyer, Rita, "Silkscreens of West Indies at ALAC," *Chestnut Hill Local* (Pennsylvania),
January 17, 1985.
Brinkley, Ora, "Medical Wives Give Student Art Seminar," *The Philadelphia Tribune*,
February 7, 1984.
Grundberg, Andy, "The Power to Convince Has Faded" *The New York Times*, July 17, 1983.

See photographs pages 463–464.

WILSON, JIM
active Detroit, 1980s

WILSON, SULE GREG (1957–   )
active New York City

An archivist by profession, Wilson uses various media to document the black experience in the Americas including photography, video, dance, music and poetry. He uses photography to explore "the persistence of Nature's forms, despite Man's intrusions, and the true persons hidden behind the stage personas of performing artists."

Born in Washington, DC, Wilson attended Oberlin College and New York University. Basically self-taught in photography, he has a B.F.A. in television production and an M.A. in archives management and history. He is a professional dancer and has photographed and documented on videotape Afro-Cuban, African-American, Afro-Brazilian and African dance companies in performance in New York City. His videos are in the collections of the Performing Arts Research Library at Lincoln Center, New York Public Library. Wilson also lectures on dance, archives and photography throughout the northeastern United States.

COLLECTIONS

Schomburg Center for Research in Black Culture, New York Public Library, New York, New York

SELECTED BIBLIOGRAPHY

Black News, Vol. 3, No. 20, October 1977.

See photographs page 465.

WINGARD, JONNI MAI
active Los Angeles, 1980s

WITHERS, ERNEST (1922–   )
active Memphis, Tennessee

Born in Memphis, Tennessee., Withers began photographing at the age of fourteen. For over twenty-five years, he maintained a studio on world-renowned Beale Street. His photographs include individuals and groups active in the civil rights movement. They have appeared in *Time, Newsweek, Ebony, Jet, The New York Times, Washington Post* and the *Chicago Defender*. Most recently, his works appeared in the PBS documentary "Eyes on the Prize." In 1968 he received an award from the National News Association for the "Best Photograph of the Year." Withers operates a photographic studio; his works continue to appear in books and exhibitions.

Withers wrote in an article entitled "Photo-Journalism As History": "Photography is a collection of memories. . . . When I go through the negatives with various images out of the past, it has a tendency to jog my mind. The average person who doesn't go through such images doesn't have their minds as refreshed about the past. It renews your memory. It starts you to thinking retrospectively. . . . In my Civil Rights photographs, I want people to see the conditions of the times. I want them to be a reflection of what transpired. . . ."

His most noted subjects include Dr. Martin Luther King, Jr., Rev. Jesse Jackson, Rosa Parks, composer W. C Handy, and entertainer Elvis Presley.

SELECTED EXHIBITIONS:

1987. "Let Us March On," The University of Mississippi, Jackson, Mississippi

See photographs pages 466–467.

WOODEN, LENNY
active New York City, 1970s

WOODSON, LEROY
active New York City, 1970s

WRIGHT, MEL (1942–)
active New York City

Wright is a commercial and portrait photographer in New York City. He studied photography at the New York Institute of Photography and opened his commercial studio in 1970. Wright's work has been published in *Family Circle, Encore* and *Rock Magazine,* among others. Since 1970, his work has been exhibited in such New York galleries as the Studio Museum in Harlem, the Schomburg Center for Research in Black Culture and the Adam Clayton Powell, Jr., State Office Building Gallery.

Since 1965, Wright has traveled throughout the world, photographing the human condition and "capturing the splendor and visual essence of these diverse cultures." Many of his photographs reflect his journeys through such places as Venezuela, Ecuador, Brazil, Malaysia, India and Vietnam.

COLLECTIONS

Schomburg Center for Research in Black Culture, New York Public Library, New York, New York

See photographs pages 468–469.

YEARWOOD, LLOYD
active New York City, 1960–present

Yearwood has been active in photographing the Harlem community since the early 1960s. He was a major contributor to the Metropolitan Museum of Art exhibition "Harlem on My Mind." His photographs have been published on book jacket covers, in major publications and periodicals. He has received numerous citations for his photographs from camera clubs and organizations such as the Photographic Society of America and the Metropolitan Camera Club Council. A lecturer on photography, Yearwood has exhibited his works in galleries in the New York area as well as in the branch libraries of the New York Public Library.

His subjects include Malcolm X, Martin Luther King, Jr., and poets Gwendolyn Brooks, Nikki Giovanni and Sonia Sanchez among others. He has also photographed the cultural and political events in Harlem over the last twenty years.

THE PHOTOGRAPHS

O'NEAL LANCY ABEL

Malcolm X, Percy Sutton, Hulan Jack,
Harlem; New York, 1963
*Courtesy of the Schomburg Center for Research in Black
Culture, The New York Public Library*

O'NEAL LANCY ABEL

Dick Gregory at microphone, Gordon Parks, Malcolm X,
Hulan Jack; New York, 1963
*Courtesy of the Schomburg Center for Research in Black
Culture, The New York Public Library*

BILLY ABERNATHY (FUNDI)

Untitled, Chicago, ca. 1962
Courtesy of the photographer

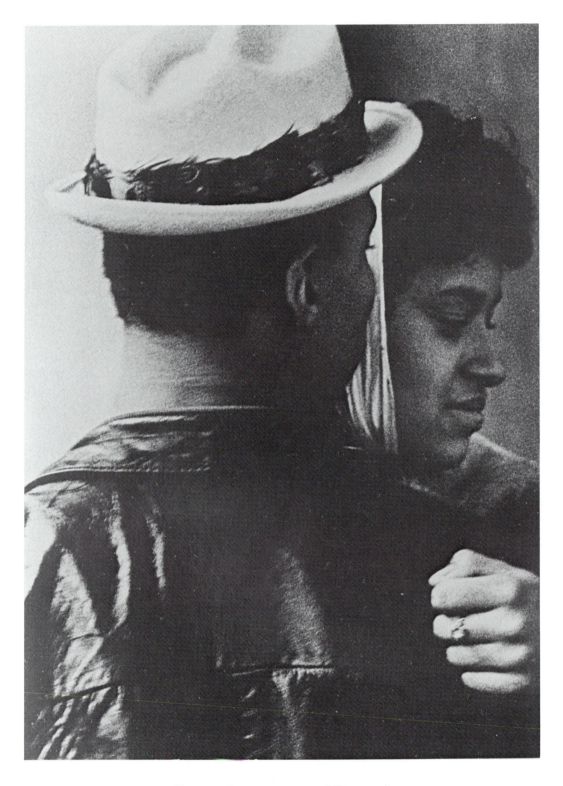

BILLY ABERNATHY (FUNDI)

Untitled [man and woman], Chicago, ca. 1962
Courtesy of the photographer

SALIMAH ALI

Portrait of Ella Baker, civil rights leader, 1980
Courtesy of the photographer

VANCE ALLEN

Untitled, 1985
Courtesy of the Schomburg Center for Research in Black
Culture, The New York Public Library

VANCE ALLEN

Curtis Balls and James White, New York City, 1986
Courtesy of the photographer

VANCE ALLEN

Doorway, Harlem, 1967
Courtesy of the Schomburg Center for Research in Black
Culture, The New York Public Library

VANCE ALLEN

Portrait of Joseph Attles, entertainer, 1980
Courtesy of the photographer

VANCE ALLEN

Marijuana Day, New York City, 1974
Courtesy of the photographer

BERT ANDREWS

Scene from *The Toilet* by LeRoi Jones. Cast shown:
Antonio Fargas, Gary Bolling, Jamie Sanchez, 1960
*Courtesy of the Schomburg Center for Research in Black
Culture, The New York Public Library*

BERT ANDREWS

Scene from *A Soldier's Play* by Charles Fuller. Cast
shown: Adolph Caesar, Denzil Washington, 1982
*Courtesy of the Schomburg Center for Research in Black
Culture, The New York Public Library*

BERT ANDREWS

Scene from *Big Time Buck White* by Joseph Solan Tuotti. Cast shown:
Dick Anthony Williams, Kirk Kirksey, Ron Rich, 1968
Courtesy of the Schomburg Center for Research in Black
Culture, The New York Public Library

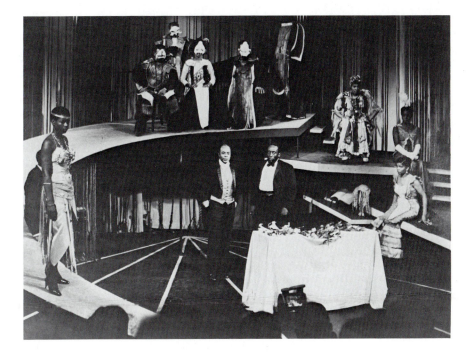

BERT ANDREWS

Scene from *The Blacks* by Jean Genet. Cast shown: Cicely
Tyson, Roscoe Lee Browne, Godfrey Cambridge, 1961
Courtesy of the Schomburg Center for Research in Black
Culture, The New York Public Library

BERT ANDREWS

Scene from *For Colored Girls Who Have Considered Suicide
When the Rainbow Is Enuf* by Ntozake Shange. Cast shown:
Alfre Woodard, Trazana Beverly, Carol Mallard, 1978
*Courtesy of the Schomburg Center for Research in Black
Culture, The New York Public Library*

OMOBOWALE AYORINDE

"Theocratic Rasta," Bull Bay, Jamaica, 1980
Courtesy of the Schomburg Center for Research in Black
Culture, The New York Public Library

O MOBOWALE A YORINDE

"Mi Nevt Idren," St. Ann's, Jamaica, 1980
Courtesy of the Schomburg Center for Research in Black
Culture, The New York Public Library

OMOBOWALE AYORINDE

University of West Indies, Jamaica
[group of men and women], 1984
Courtesy of the photographer

OMOBOWALE AYORINDE

Dancer, Oyotunji Village, Beaufort, South Carolina, 1985
Courtesy of the photographer

ANTHONY BARBOZA

Dakar, Senegal, ca. 1974
Courtesy of the photographer

Ornette Coleman — musician — 85

ANTHONY BARBOZA

Portrait of Ornette Coleman, musician, 1985
Courtesy of the photographer

Lester Bowie — musician — '79'

ANTHONY BARBOZA

Portrait of Lester Bowie, musician, 1979
Courtesy of the photographer

James Baldwin — writer — '75'

ANTHONY BARBOZA

Portrait of James Baldwin, writer, 1975
Courtesy of the photographer

Norman Lewis   painter '76'

ANTHONY BARBOZA

Portrait of Norman Lewis, painter, 1976
Courtesy of the photographer

ANTHONY BARBOZA

Self-Portrait entitled "Introspect," 1982 (original in color)
Courtesy of the photographer

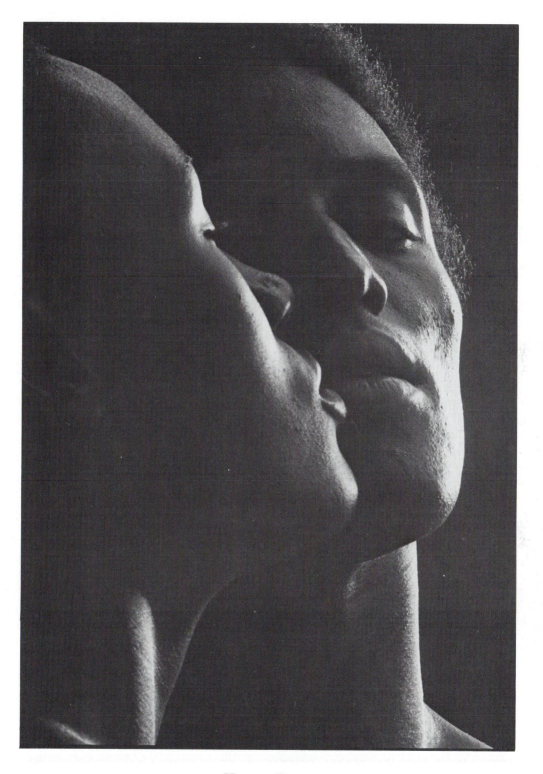

HUGH BELL

Untitled, [portrait of a man and woman], ca. 1975
Courtesy of the photographer

HUGH BELL

Portrait of Beverly Johnson, model, ca. 1980
Courtesy of the photographer

HUGH BELL

Untitled, [musicians], ca. 1980
Courtesy of the photographer

DAWOUD BEY

Harlem Series [child standing in front of a Millie Jackson poster], ca. 1980
Courtesy of the Schomburg Center for Research in Black
Culture, The New York Public Library

DAWOUD BEY

Untitled, Syracuse, New York, 1985
Courtesy of the photographer

DAWOUD BEY

"At the Bus Stop," Syracuse, New York, 1985
Courtesy of the photographer

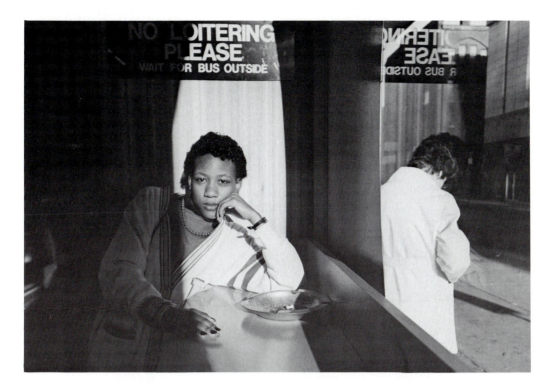

DAWOUD BEY

Portrait of a girl waiting in luncheonette, Syracuse, New York, 1985
Courtesy of the photographer

DAWOUD BEY

Portrait of a girl working at McDonald's, Syracuse, New York, 1985
Courtesy of the photographer

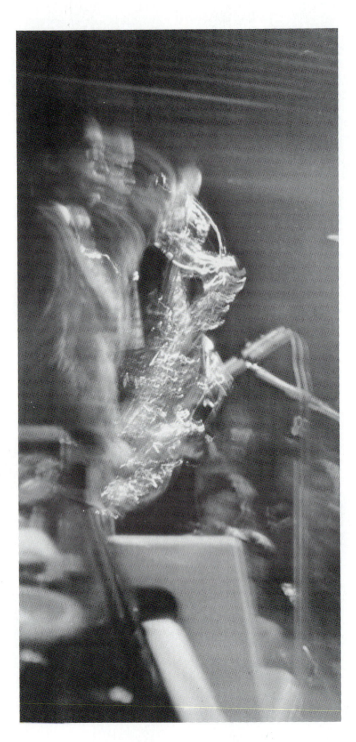

HART LEROY BIBBS

Portrait of Archie Shepp, Paris Jazz Series, No. 1, 1979
*Courtesy of the Schomburg Center for Research in Black
Culture, The New York Public Library*

ANTHONY BONAIR
Portrait of a man entitled "Dignity," 91st and Broadway, 1980
Courtesy of the photographer

HARRISON BRANCH

Untitled, Ajijie, Mexico, n.d.
Courtesy of the photographer

HARRISON BRANCH
Untitled, n.d.
Courtesy of the photographer

KWAME BRATHWAITE

Portrait of Captain Thomas Sankara, President of
Burkino Faso, Africa, 1986
Courtesy of the photographer

KWAME BRATHWAITE
Portrait of Stevie Wonder, in Jamaica, 1975
Courtesy of the photographer

KWAME BRATHWAITE
Portrait of singing group "Labelle" in performance, ca. 1975
Courtesy of the photographer

JOE BROOKS
Portrait of Kionna, 1981
Courtesy of the photographer

JOE BROOKS
Storefront preacher, Washington, DC, 1981
Courtesy of the photographer

MILLIE BURNS

Weeping willow, 1984
Courtesy of the photographer

MILLIE BURNS

Trellis, 1981
Courtesy of the photographer

MURIEL BUSH
"Merry Christmas" [portrait of two girls with dolls], ca. 1950
Courtesy of June Cross

MURIEL BUSH
"Merry Christmas" [portrait of a young boy reading a book], ca. 1950
Courtesy of June Cross

MURIEL BUSH

Portrait of a woman, inscribed "Min," ca. 1930
Courtesy of June Cross

MURIEL BUSH

Portrait of a woman wearing lace collar and pearls, ca. 1940
Courtesy of June Cross

LEONARD BYRD

Pond in Autumn, 1986 (assemblage series; original in color)
Courtesy of the photographer

DENNIS OLANZO CALLWOOD

La Quincenera No. 2, 1982
Courtesy of the photographer

DENNIS OLANZO CALLWOOD

La Quincenera No. 3, 1983
Courtesy of the photographer

DENNIS OLANZO CALLWOOD
Portrait of a woman reaching for photographs, 1982
Courtesy of the photographer

DENNIS OLANZO CALLWOOD

Portrait of a young couple, 1983
Courtesy of the photographer

ROLAND CHARLES

The shoeshine boy works the streets of the French Quarter
in New Orleans, Louisiana, 1973
Courtesy of the photographer

ROLAND CHARLES

A Penacostal Minister sits on his front porch near Dillard
University in New Orleans, Louisiana, 1973
Courtesy of the photographer

R OLAND C HARLES
Antebellum housing styles typical of the low income Black
sections of "uptown" New Orleans, 1973
Courtesy of the photographer

ALBERT CHONG

"The Sisters," 1986
Courtesy of the photographer

ALBERT CHONG

"Knife and Fork and Feather," 1986
Courtesy of the photographer

ALBERT CHONG

"Chair-full," 1987
Courtesy of the photographer

ALBERT CHONG

"Sadie," 1985
Courtesy of the photographer

ALBERT CHONG

"Natural Mystic," 1982
Courtesy of the photographer

ALLEN E. COLE

Hub-Bub record shop booth at the Exhibit of Progress,
Cleveland, Ohio, 1946
Courtesy of the Western Reserve Historical Society

ALLEN E. COLE

Mrs. George Anderson's recreation room, ca. 1945
Courtesy of the Western Reserve Historical Society

ALLEN E. COLE

Freeman Ensemble [later Evelyn Freeman Swing Band],
Cleveland, Ohio, ca. 1940
Courtesy of the Western Reserve Historical Society,
Cleveland, Ohio

ALLEN E. COLE

Bible School outing, Lakeview Mission and
Christian Center, Cleveland, Ohio, 1941
Courtesy of the Western Reserve Historical Society

ALLEN E. COLE

Lane Metropolitan Church Senior Missionary Society,
Cleveland, Ohio, 1947
Courtesy of the Western Reserve Historical Society

JIM COLLIER

The Jones's decenium, 1979
Courtesy of the photographer

JIM COLLIER

Portrait of a woman entitled "Another Heritage," 1971
Courtesy of the photographer

JAMES CONNOR

Untitled, [window with religious statues], ca. 1975
Courtesy of the photographer

ADGER W. COWANS

Ocean view, Bahia, Brazil, 1970
Courtesy of the photographer

ADGER W. COWANS

"Duke Delivers," Bear Mountain, New York, ca. 1970.
Courtesy of the photographer

ADGER **W.** COWANS

Self-portrait, ca. 1965
Courtesy of the photographer

ADGER **W.** COWANS

"The Studio," 1975
Courtesy of the photographer

ADGER W. COWANS

Elizabeth Street, New York, 1970
Courtesy of the photographer

ROBERT CRAWFORD

Castro's newsstand, Chicago, 1970
Courtesy of the photographer

CARY BETH CRYOR

Jazmin I, 1985
Courtesy of the photographer

CARY BETH CRYOR

Grandma and Grandad, 1975
Courtesy of the photographer

TERE L. CUESTA

Jibaro Cubana, Habana, Cuba, 1985
Courtesy of the photographer

FIKISHA CUMBO

Bob Marley, Don Kinsey, Judy Mowatt at
the Apollo Theatre, 1979
Courtesy of the photographer

COLLIS H. DAVIS, JR.

Portrait of a Haitian "boat person" at the Brooklyn, New York
Immigration Detention Center, 1982
Courtesy of the photographer

COLLIS H. DAVIS, JR.
"A" Train Bluesman, Euclid Avenue Station, Brooklyn, New York, 1979
Courtesy of the photographer

COLLIS H. DAVIS, JR.
Portrait of Curtis Lundy and Gary Bartz entitled
"Tin Palace Dreams," 1979
Courtesy of the photographer

COLLIS **H**. **D**AVIS, **J**R.

Portrait of actress Hattie Winston as "Claire" from the
production, *A Photograph: A Study in Cruelty* by Ntozake Shange, 1977
Courtesy of the photographer

GRIFFITH J. DAVIS

Across from the Bowery flophouse, New York, New York, 1949
Courtesy of the photographer

GRIFFITH J. DAVIS

Workman on Liberia's first railroad during the rainy season, 1950
Courtesy of the photographer

GRIFFITH J. DAVIS

Portrait of Arna Bontemps and Langston Hughes,
co-editors of *The Negro in Poetry*, 1949
Courtesy of the photographer

GRIFFITH J. DAVIS

Portrait of Juanita Hall, the original "Bloody Mary," 1949
Courtesy of the photographer

GRIFFITH J. DAVIS

Portrait of C. A. Scott, publisher of the *Atlanta Daily World*, 1948
Courtesy of the photographer

GRIFFITH J. DAVIS

Portrait of artist Hale Aspacio Woodruff working on the
California Centennial Mural, 1948
Courtesy of the photographer

GRIFFITH J. DAVIS
Portrait of Duke Ellington, the composer, 1950
Courtesy of the photographer

GRIFFITH J. DAVIS
Portrait of Langston Hughes, 1947
Courtesy of the photographer

GRIFFITH J. DAVIS
Portrait of President William Tubman with the
Tubman Monument, Liberia, 1951
Courtesy of the photographer

PAT DAVIS

Self-portrait, ca. 1977
Courtesy of the photographer

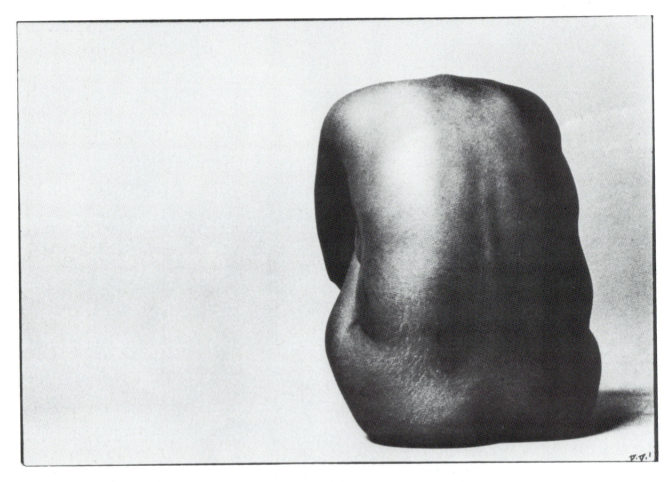

PAT DAVIS
Body sculpture, 1975
Courtesy of the photographer

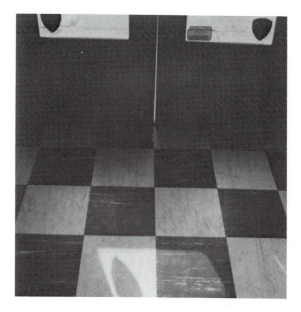

C. DANIEL DAWSON

Stairway, Studio Museum in Harlem, New York, 1981
(original, color SX 70 Poloroid)
Courtesy of the photographer

C. DANIEL DAWSON

Untitled, 1982. (original, color SX 70 Polaroid)
Courtesy of the photographer

BILL DOGGETT

Composition: canvas in brick, Los Angeles, California, 1980
(original in color)
Courtesy of the photographer

BILL DOGGETT

Composition: Meter after Antonioni, Los Angeles, California,
1979 (original in color)
Courtesy of the photographer

LYDIA ANN DOUGLAS

Portrait of Sherrie Knight, Talking Drums, ca. 1986
Courtesy of the photographer

LOUIS DRAPER

"John Henry," Lower East Side, New York, New York, 1960
Courtesy of the photographer

LOUIS DRAPER

"Congressional Meeting," Greenwich Village, New York, New York, ca. 1961
Courtesy of the photographer

LOUIS DRAPER

"Playground Series," Lower East Side, New York, New York, 1961
Courtesy of the photographer

LOUIS DRAPER

"Boy Daydreaming," Lower East Side, New York, New York, ca. 1963
Courtesy of the photographer

LOUIS DRAPER

"Soccer Game," Dakar, Senegal, 1978
Courtesy of the photographer

JOAN EDA

Portrait of Tish and Mother, 1985
(hand-colored black and white, mixed media print)
Courtesy of the photographer

JOAN EDA

Portrait of Brenda and Grandfather, 1987
(hand-colored black and white, mixed media print)
Courtesy of the photographer

SULAIMAN ELLISON

Sunset on the Niger River, Mali, 1980
Courtesy of the photographer

SULAIMAN ELLISON

Seydou and Musa, Mali, 1977
Courtesy of the photographer

SULAIMAN ELLISON

Portrait of Carmen McRae, 1985
Courtesy of the photographer

SULAIMAN ELLISON

Portrait of Sarah Vaughan, 1971
Courtesy of the photographer

SHARON FARMER

Morgan State University Choir, Washington, DC, 1984
Courtesy of the photographer

SHARON FARMER

"Peace Be Still," 1983
Courtesy of the photographer

SHARON FARMER

"Freedom Fighter," 1983
Courtesy of the photographer

JEFF FEARING

Untitled, [landscape], California, 1984
Courtesy of the photographer

JEFF FEARING

Tree No. 1, Maryland, 1978
Courtesy of the photographer

VALERIA "MIKKI" FERRILL
Fourth of July parade, Alameda, California, 1986
Courtesy of the photographer

VALERIA ''MIKKI'' FERRILL

Body builder, Oakland, California, 1986
Courtesy of the photographer

VALERIA ''MIKKI'' FERRILL

Annual Black Cowboy Parade
[Cowboy in Jessie James Duster], Oakland, California, 1986
Courtesy of the photographer

VALERIA "MIKKI" FERRILL

Blind woman in front of employment office, Chicago, 1972
Courtesy of the photographer

BOB FLETCHER

Lowndes Co. Freedom Organization Headquarters, n.d.
Courtesy of the Schomburg Center for Research in Black
Culture, The New York Public Library

COLLETTE FOURNIER

Portrait of Cousin George in New York, 1980
Courtesy of the photographer

COLLETTE FOURNIER

Sweet, Bo and friends, Jamaica, 1983
Courtesy of the photographer

COLLETTE FOURNIER

Sid and Clive, Jamaica, 1982
Courtesy of the photographer

JACK FRANKLIN
Martin Luther King, Jr., and Rev. Ralph Abernathy on flat
bed truck, in Philadelphia, 1963
Courtesy of the photographer

JACK FRANKLIN

Roy Wilkins (NAACP), Cecil Moore (NAACP-Philadelphia,)
and Judge Herbert Mullen, 1965
Courtesy of the photographer

JACK FRANKLIN

Congressman Adam Clayton Powell, Jr., with Cecil Moore at
NAACP rally, 1964
Courtesy of the photographer

JACK FRANKLIN

March on City Hall by the NAACP, 1963
Courtesy of the photographer

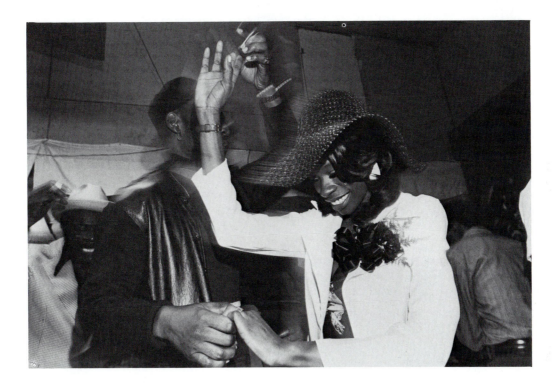

ROLAND FREEMAN

"Dancing in Jazz Alley," Chicago, Illinois, 1974
Courtesy of the photographer

ROLAND FREEMAN

"Arabing" (street vending), South Baltimore, 1970
Courtesy of the photographer

ROLAND FREEMAN

"Gilbert Hall Sr., Jr., and III," 1986
Courtesy of the photographer

ROLAND FREEMAN

Quilter Victoria Bennett, Mississippi, 1976
Courtesy of the photographer

Tyrone Georgiou

Untitled [silver print with acrylic paint], 1981
Courtesy of the photographer

Tyrone Georgiou

"So They Told Me," (A diorama: silver print, mat board and
plastic), 1986
Courtesy of the photographer

TYRONE GEORGIOU

Untitled [Polaroid construction], 1979
Courtesy of the photographer

TYRONE GEORGIOU

Crushed Architecture Series, 1977
Courtesy of the photographer

BERNADETTE GIBSON

Portrait of Madeline and son in Chino, California, 1980
Courtesy of the photographer

FRANCIS GILES

Egyptian prisoners of war, Near Suez, Egypt,
Yom Kippur War, 1973
Courtesy of the photographer

FRANCIS GILES

"At last . . . will on aging," New Mexico, 1987
Courtesy of the photographer

ANTHONY GLEATON

"Sylvia Waits for Me," Oaxaca, Mexico from "Sange Pura:
Mexico's African Legacy," 1985
Courtesy of the photographer

ANTHONY GLEATON

"Sea of Dreams," Oaxaca, Mexico from "Sange Pura:
Mexico's African Legacy," 1985
Courtesy of the photographer

ANTHONY GLEATON

"Soledad," Guerrero, Mexico from "Sange Pura: Mexico's
African Legacy," 1985
Courtesy of the photographer

ANTHONY GLEATON

"Three Sisters," Guerrero, Mexico from "Spimal," 1985
Courtesy of the photographer

DAVID A. GORDON
Untitled [with minister], from "Hold," 1984
Courtesy of the photographer

DAVID A. GORDON
Untitled [with two women], from "Hold," 1984
Courtesy of the photographer

276

HUGH GRANNUM

Portrait of Samuel Cobb, horse trainer, Detroit, Michigan, 1983
Courtesy of the photographer

HUGH GRANNUM

Samuel Cobb with the palomino show horse Lloyd
Highland on Belle Isle, Detroit, Michigan, 1983
Courtesy of the photographer

HUGH GRANNUM
Boy and cloth, Dakar, Senegal, 1985
Courtesy of the photographer

HUGH GRANNUM

School Girl, Dakar, Senegal, 1985
Courtesy of the photographer

MILTON GRANT

Nobel Peace Prize winner Bishop Desmond Tutu of South Africa
meeting with the United Nations Correspondents Association, 1984
Courtesy of the United Nations Photo Department

MILTON GRANT

Prime Minister Maurice Rupert Bishop of Grenada, meeting
with the press at United Nations Headquarters, 1979
Courtesy of the United Nations Photo Department

MILTON GRANT

Kamanda wa Kamanda, Security Council President
for the month of April, 1982
Courtesy of the United Nations Photo Department

MILTON GRANT

Commander Daniel Ortega Saavedra, co-ordinator of the
governing Junta of National Reconstruction of Nicaragua,
speaking at his United Nations Headquarters press conference, 1982
Courtesy of the United Nations Photo Department

MILTON GRANT

Family, Dominican Republican, ca. 1984
Courtesy of the United Nations Photo Department

TED GRAY
"Snow Phantom," Chicago, 1977
Courtesy of the photographer

TODD GRAY

"Odysseus" (black and white silver print with
charcoal and conte), 1983
Courtesy of the photographer

TODD GRAY

"Anti-Hero No. 2" (black and white silver print with
charcoal and conte), 1984
Courtesy of the photographer

TODD GRAY

"History Repeating'Itself" (black and white silver print with
charcoal and conte), 1987
Courtesy of the photographer

TODD GRAY

"When is now" (black and white silver print with
charcoal and conte), 1987
Courtesy of the photographer

S TANLEY G REENE

Street corner, Maroc, 1980
Courtesy of the photographer

STANLEY GREENE

Jesse Jackson Presidential campaign, surrounded by children, 1986
Courtesy of the photographer

STANLEY GREENE

Ku Klux Klan rally, ca. 1980
Courtesy of the photographer

GEORGE HALLETT
Portrait of Wole Soyinka, playwright and author, Nigeria, 1981
*Courtesy of the Schomburg Center for Research in Black
Culture, The New York Public Library*

GEORGE HALLETT
Portrait of a woman from District Six, South Africa, 1970
*Courtesy of the Schomburg Center for Research in Black
Culture, The New York Public Library*

GEORGE HALLETT

Portrait of Ousmane Sembene, film maker, Senegambia, ca. 1982
Courtesy of the Schomburg Center for Research in Black
Culture, The New York Public Library

GEORGE HALLETT

Portrait of Gavin Tantyes entitled "We Are in a Manner of Speaking Freedom Figh-
ters on the Battlefield of Culture," 1984
*Courtesy of the Schomburg Center for Research in Black
Culture, The New York Public Library*

GAIL HANSBERRY

George Washington Bridge, New York, 1973
Courtesy of the photographer

GAIL HANSBERRY

Crater Lake, Ethiopia, 1972
Courtesy of the photographer

GAIL HANSBERRY

Portrait of young girl with pails, Nigeria, 1972
Courtesy of the photographer

GAIL HANSBERRY

Portrait of a woman with basket, Haiti, 1975
Courtesy of the photographer

INGE HARDISON

Untitled [Harlem newspaper boy], ca. 1949
Courtesy of the photographer

INGE HARDISON

Untitled [Expectant mother], ca. 1950
Courtesy of the photographer

INGE HARDISON

Untitled [Harlem construction worker with wheel barrel], ca. 1952
Courtesy of the photographer

INGE HARDISON

Untitled [Harlem two boys peering in storefront window], ca. 1955
Courtesy of the photographer

INGE HARDISON

Untitled [Paul Robeson], ca. 1950
Courtesy of the photographer

DOUG HARRIS

"First Vote" [portrait of a woman holding voting certificate
for the State of Alabama], 1965
*Courtesy of the Schomburg Center for Research in Black
Culture, The New York Public Library*

THOMAS HARRIS

Portrait of a woman from the "Woman in Church" series, 1987
Courtesy of the photographer

JAMES HARRISON

Portrait of a woman entitled "Wisdom," 1983
Courtesy of the photographer

JAMES HARRISON

The Key of Life, Egypt, 1983
Courtesy of the photographer

JAMES HARRISON

Morgan State Band, "getting down" at the African American
Day Parade, Harlem, New York, 1987
Courtesy of the photographer

ALEX HARSLEY
Lower East Side, New York, New York, 1986
Courtesy of the photographer

ALEX HARSLEY

9th Street Children's Program, New York, New York, 1987
Courtesy of the photographer

ALEX HARSLEY

125th Street and 8th Avenue, New York City, 1973
Courtesy of the photographer

RICHARD HAYNES

Untitled [cathedral entrance with standing figure], 1985
Courtesy of the photographer

RICHARD HAYNES

Untitled [interior with statue], 1985
Courtesy of the photographer

LEROY HENDERSON

Portrait of Rosa Parks, ca. 1974
Courtesy of the photographer

LEROY HENDERSON

Bobby Seale, Jesse Jackson, and Richard Hatcher, ca. 1970
Courtesy of the photographer

LEROY HENDERSON

Richard Roundtree, actor, ca. 1972
Courtesy of the photographer

LAURENCE HENRY

Malcolm X with interviewer in France, 1965
*Courtesy of the Schomburg Center for Research in Black
Culture, The New York Public Library*

LAURENCE HENRY

The Selma March with Dr. Martin L. King, Jr., Coretta Scott
King, Bayard Rustin, A. Philip Randolph, Ralph Abernathy, Ralph Bunche, ca. 1966
*Courtesy of the Schomburg Center for Research in Black
Culture, The New York Public Library*

LAURENCE HENRY

Marchers in the Selma-Montgomery March with young girl
leading carrying the American flags, ca. 1966
*Courtesy of the Schomburg Center for Research in Black
Culture, The New York Public Library*

CHESTER HIGGINS, JR.

Untitled [Ghana], ca. 1974
Courtesy of the photographer

CHESTER HIGGINS, JR.

Untitled [Ghanian Girl], ca. 1974
Courtesy of the photographer

CHESTER HIGGINS, JR.

Untitled [Clarence Holt in his library], 1986
Courtesy of the photographer

CHESTER HIGGINS, JR.

Untitled [Bob Marley], 1981
Courtesy of the photographer

CHESTER HIGGINS, JR.
Portrait of photographer, James VanDerZee, ca. 1981
Courtesy of the photographer

CHESTER HIGGINS, JR.
Portrait of dancer, Carmen DeLavellade, ca. 1980
Courtesy of the photographer

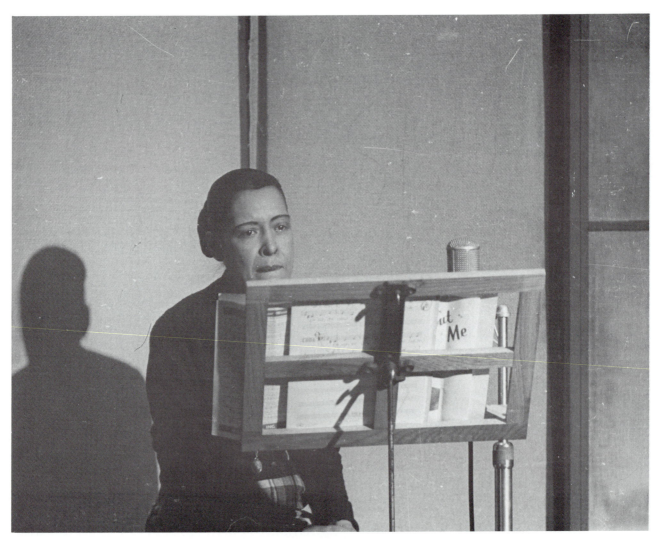

MILT HINTON

Portrait of Billie Holiday at her last recording session, 1958
Courtesy of Milt and Mona Hinton/David G. Berger

MILT HINTON

Portrait of Count Basie, 1957
Courtesy of Milt and Mona Hinton/David G. Berger

MILT HINTON
Portrait of Lester Young, 1957
Courtesy of Milt and Mona Hinton/David G. Berger

BOBBY HOLLAND

Portrait of Richard Pryor, 1986
Courtesy of the photographer

LEON HOLLINS

"Lone Protest," Wiltshire and Normandie Avenues, Los
Angeles, California, 1987
Courtesy of the photographer

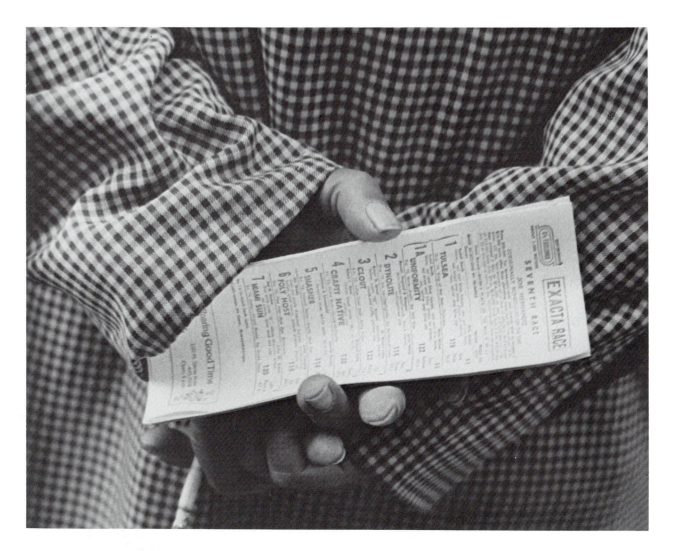

LEON HOLLINS
"The Gambler," Hollywood Park, California, 1983
Courtesy of the photographer

STEPHEN HOPKINS

Dona Nadine, Salvador, Bahia, 1985
Courtesy of the photographer

STEPHEN HOPKINS

Untitled [portrait of woman with braids], Salvador, Bahia, 1985
Courtesy of the photographer

STEPHEN HOPKINS

Untitled [portrait of Bahian woman with traditional dress],
Salvador, Bahia, 1985
Courtesy of the photographer

STEPHEN HOPKINS

Untitled [portrait of two women], Salvador, Bahia, 1985
Courtesy of the photographer

BILL HOWELL

Woman at window with boar, West Africa (hand-colored
black and white photograph), 1974
Courtesy of William and Melvina Lathan

EARLIE HUDNALL
Portrait of a woman entitled "Another Day," 4th Ward
Houston, Texas, 1985
Courtesy of the photographer

EARLIE HUDNALL

The Fourth Ward, Houston, Texas, 1985
Courtesy of the photographer

EARLIE HUDNALL

"Friday night" [two dancers, Houston, Texas, 1983
Courtesy of the photographer

EARLIE HUDNALL

Portrait of a family in Thomason, Georgia, 1984
Courtesy of the photographer

EARLIE HUDNALL

Portrait of a guitar player, 1982
Courtesy of the photographer

LAWRENCE HUFF

Gallery: Villa Montalvo, Saratoga, California (platinum/palladium print), ca. 1986
Courtesy of the photographer

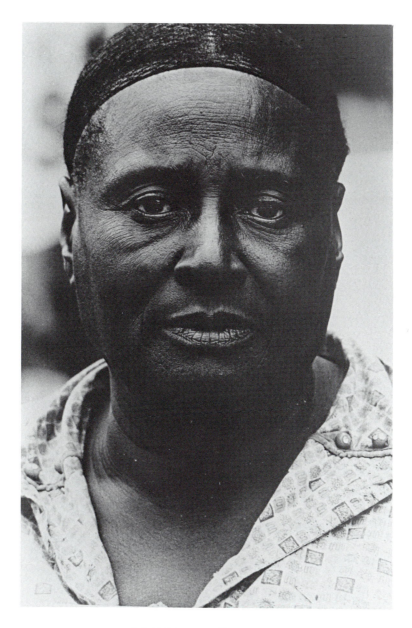

ADEOSHUN **I**FALADE

Portrait of a man, Chicago, ca. 1968
Courtesy of the photographer

REGINALD L. JACKSON

"Unity (Umoja)," Ghana, West Africa, 1970
Courtesy of the photographer

REGINALD L. JACKSON

"Wisdom," Ghana, West Africa, 1970
Courtesy of the photographer

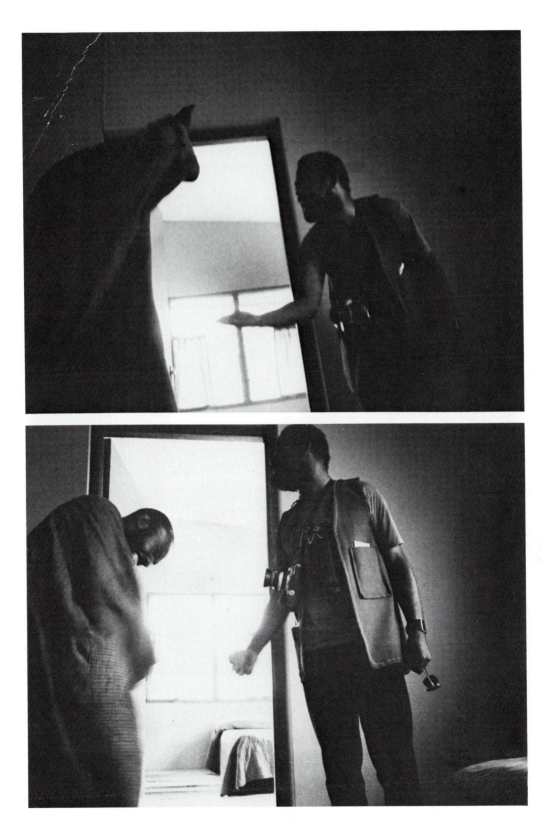

REGINALD L. JACKSON
"Home Again," Accra, Ghana, West Africa, 1970
Courtesy of the photographer

LOUISE JEFFERSON

An Old New England home, Litchfield, Connecticut, n.d.
Courtesy of the photographer

LOUISE JEFFERSON

Going home from the laundry, Lagos, Nigeria, ca. 1970
Courtesy of the photographer

LOUISE JEFFERSON

Louis Armstrong in concert in Central Park, New York, n.d.
Courtesy of the photographer

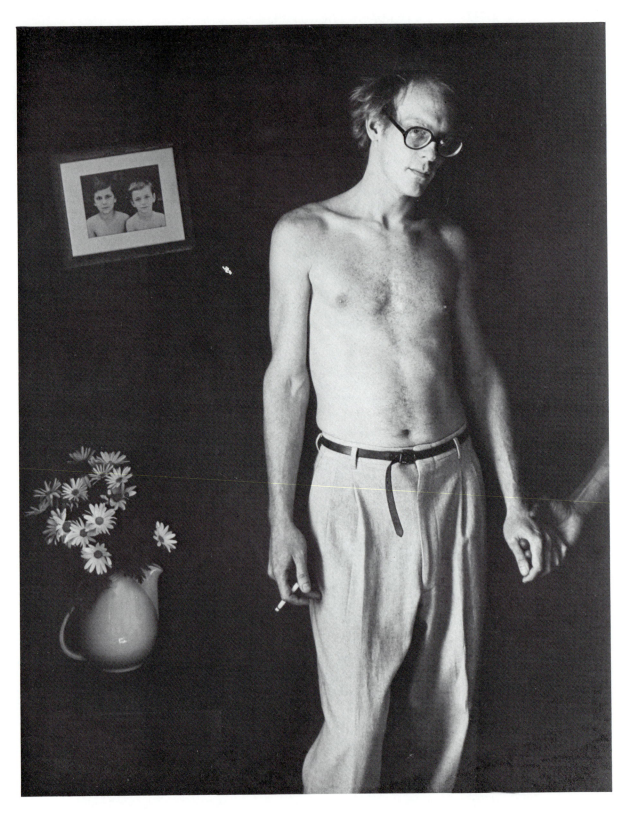

CHRIS JOHNSON

Portrait of Rob Kame (original in color Polaroid), 1976
Courtesy of the photographer

BRENT JONES

First day of voluntary school integration, lone black girl on
school bus in Milwaukee, Wisconsin, 1976
Courtesy of the photographer

BRENT JONES

Portrait of Chicago Mayor Harold Washington, 1983
(original in color)
Courtesy of the photographer

BRENT JONES

Portrait of minister Louis Farrakhan, Chicago, 1985
Courtesy of the photographer

BRENT JONES

A teenager looking out of a window,
Cabrini Green Housing Project, Chicago, 1972
Courtesy of the photographer

BRENT JONES

Young boy with dog, Chicago, 1974
Courtesy of the photographer

BRIAN V. JONES

"Corpuscular Light," "Illinois Farms" series, 1981
Courtesy of the photographer

BRIAN V. JONES

"The Guardians," Chicago lakefront, 1981
Courtesy of the photographer

BRIAN V. JONES

"Man, Boy, Swing," Chicago lakefront, 1981
Courtesy of the photographer

BRIAN V. JONES

Store mannequins, Washington, DC, 1987
Courtesy of the photographer

JULIA JONES

Presidential candidate Rev. Jesse Jackson addresses the press
team from the White House Rose Garden upon the successful completion of his diplomatic mission to Syria to free U.S.
Navy Lt. Robert Goodman, January 4, 1984
Courtesy of the photographer

JULIA JONES

Congressional Delegate Walter Fauntroy, Candidate for
President of the U.S. Jesse Jackson; Washington, DC, Mayor
Marion Barry and DC City Councilmember Frank Smith,
Washington, DC, April 15, 1984
Courtesy of the photographer

MARVIN **T**. **J**ONES
Commencement, Howard University, 1985
Courtesy of the photographer

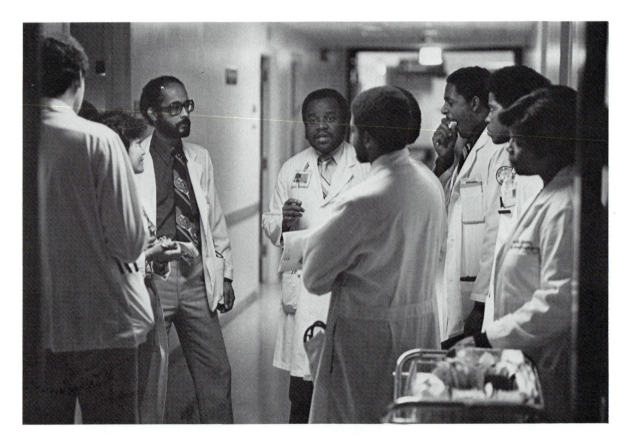

MARVIN **T**. **J**ONES
Six A.M. rounds for medical interns,
Howard University Hospital,
Washington, DC, 1982
Courtesy of the photographer

LEAH JAYNES KARP

From the Fan Series, 1985
Courtesy of the photographer

LEAH JAYNES KARP

"Chattahouchee River from Atlanta Children's Notebook," 1983
Courtesy of the photographer

OMAR KHAREM

Shadows, New York, 1969
Courtesy of the photographer

LUCIUS KING

Portrait of a man entitled "Remember When," 1983
Courtesy of the photographer

LUCIUS KING

Portrait of a woman entitled "Salma," 1981
Courtesy of the photographer

R OMULO L ACHATANERE

"Eastside I," ca. 1951
Courtesy of Diana Lachatanere

ROMULO LACHATANERE

"Boys in a Small Village in Puerto Rico," ca. 1951
Courtesy of Diana Lachatanere

R OMULO L ACHATANERE

"Portrait of Sara," ca. 1950
Courtesy of Diana Lachatanere

R OMULO L ACHATANERE

"Eastside II," ca. 1951
Courtesy of Diana Lachatanere

GEORGE **R.** LARKINS
Still life entitled "High Class Blues," 1985
Courtesy of the photographer

ARCHY LaSALLE

Jamaica, West Indies, 1983
Courtesy of the photographer

ARCHY LaSALLE

Nice, France, 1985
Courtesy of the photographer

ARCHY LASALLE

Jamaica, West Indies, beachfront, 1983
Courtesy of the photographer

ARCHY LASALLE

Plum Island, Massachusetts, 1984
Courtesy of the photographer

SA'LONGO LEE
"Water Spirit No. 1, I am the Past, The Present, The Future," 1974
Courtesy of the photographer

CARL LEWIS

Still Life entitled "Where's a Good Stud When You Need One?!" 1986
Courtesy of the photographer

ROY LEWIS

Portrait of a man entitled "Get Your Paper Brother," Black
Power Conference, Philadelphia, Pennsylvania, 1968
Courtesy of the photographer

ROY LEWIS

Portrait of Gwendolyn Brooks, The People's Poet, 1986
Courtesy of the photographer

R O Y   L E W I S

Portrait of Larry Neal, writer, 1978
Courtesy of the photographer

FERN LOGAN

Portrait of Romare Bearden, artist, 1983
Courtesy of the photographer

FERN LOGAN

Portrait of Adolph Caesar, actor, 1984
Courtesy of the photographer

FERN LOGAN

Portrait of Elizabeth Catlett, artist, 1986
Courtesy of the photographer

FERN LOGAN

Portrait of Gordon Parks, photographer, 1983
Courtesy of the photographer

EDIE LYNCH

Portrait of a woman and two boys entitled
"You Are the Keeper of My Secrets," Jamaica, 1982
Courtesy of the photographer

EDIE LYNCH

Group portrait of small Jamaican children entitled
"Sissy Didn't Want Her Picture Taken. She Ran Away," 1982
Courtesy of the photographer

JIMMIE MANNAS

Untitled [children with chair], ca. 1967
*Courtesy of the Schomburg Center for Research in Black
Culture, The New York Public Library*

RICHARD MASSIE

Seventh Avenue, Harlem. African American Day Parade, ca. 1969
Courtesy of the photographer

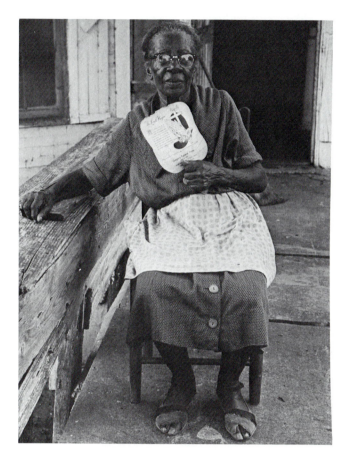

MICKEY MATHIS
Untitled [Woman with "The Lord's Prayer" fan], ca. 1979
*Courtesy of the Schomburg Center for Research in Black
Culture, The New York Public Library*

MICKEY MATHIS
Untitled [Portrait of Pop Mathis], ca. 1980
*Courtesy of the Schomburg Center for Research in Black
Culture, The New York Public Library*

IN THIS TEMPLE
AS IN THE HEARTS OF THE PEOPLE
FOR WHOM HE SAVED THE UNION
THE MEMORY OF ABRAHAM LINCOLN
IS ENSHRINED FOREVER

BERTRAND MILES

Group portrait of Civil Rights Leaders including Whitney Young,
A. Philip Randolph, Martin L. King, Jr., Roy Wilkins, et al. Washington, DC, 1963
*Courtesy of the Schomburg Center for Research in Black
Culture, The New York Public Library*

BERTRAND MILES
Portrait of Mary Church Terrill, ca. 1950s
Courtesy of the photographer

BERTRAND MILES

Portrait of Adam Clayton Powell, Jr., ca. 1966
Courtesy of the photographer

BERTRAND MILES

Portrait of Ethel Waters, ca. 1954
Courtesy of the photographer

BERTRAND MILES
Portrait of the Photographer's Mother, ca. 1950
Courtesy of the photographer

HOWARD MOREHEAD

Portrait of Dexter Gordon at the California Club, one of the
early Los Angeles jazz clubs, 1958
Courtesy of the photographer

HOWARD MOREHEAD

Portrait of Billie Holiday (this photograph appeared on her
album "Body and Soul"), 1957
Courtesy of the photographer

HOWARD MOREHEAD

Portrait of Paul Robeson superimposed with the front page
of the *California Eagle*, 1947
Courtesy of the photographer

HOWARD MOREHEAD

Meru Women and children in East Africa, n.d.
Courtesy of the photographer

John W. Mosely

Morgan State runner at the Penn Relays, Philadelphia,
Pennsylvania. 1954
*Courtesy Charles L. Blockson/Dr. Richard Beards,
Temple University, Philadelphia, Pennsylvania*

JOHN W. MOSELY

Untitled [World War II Recruits], 1943
Courtesy Charles L. Blockson/Dr. Richard Beards,
Temple University, Philadelphia, Pennsylvania

JOHN W. MOSELY

Untitled, Church leader, ca. 1956
Courtesy Charles L. Blockson/Dr. Richard Beards,
Temple University, Philadelphia, PA

JOHN W. MOSELY

Untitled [birthday celebration], ca. 1957
Courtesy Charles L. Blockson/Dr. Richard Beards,
Temple University, Philadelphia, Pennsylvania

JEANNE MOUTOUSSAMY-ASHE

Susie standing next to Holy Picture,
Daufuskie Island, South Carolina, 1980
Courtesy of the photographer

JEANNE MOUTOUSSAMY-ASHE

Mary at her breakfast table,
Edisto Island, South Carolina, 1979
Courtesy of the photographer

JEANNE MOUTOUSSAMY-ASHE
Ma Taylor's Funeral, South Hill, Virginia, 1979
Courtesy of the photographer

JEANNE MOUTOUSSAMY-ASHE
Josette's Wedding, Queens, New York, 1981
Courtesy of the photographer

OZIER MUHAMMAD

A child waits to be fed by the Red Cross, Makalle, Ethiopia, 1984
Courtesy of the photographer

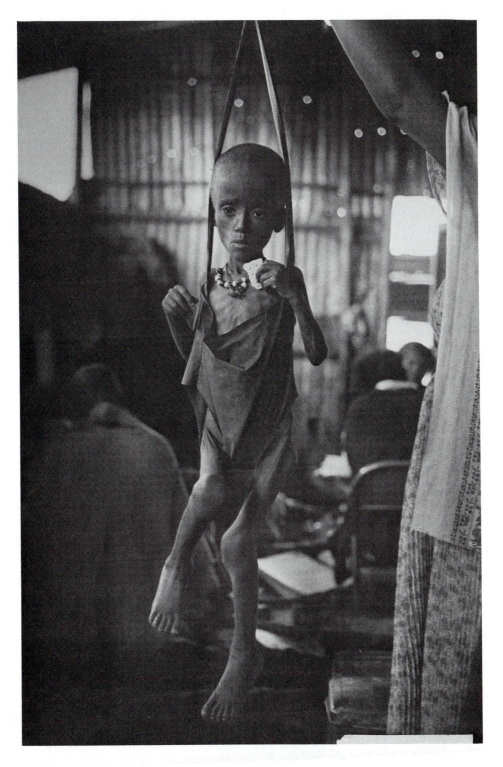

OZIER MUHAMMAD

Small girl at weekly weigh-in clutches a biscuit,
Korem, Ethiopia, 1984
Courtesy of the photographer

OZIER MUHAMMAD

Portrait of two boys entitled "D's Love," Chicago, Illinois, 1970
Courtesy of the photographer

OZIER MUHAMMAD

Muhammad Ali recites a poem, Dearborn, Michigan, 1976
Courtesy of the photographer

OZIER MUHAMMAD

Hilliard McMoore, 106 years old with his 1929 Model "A"
Ford, Rock Hill, South Carolina, 1974
Courtesy of the photographer

MANSA K. MUSSA

The Bucket Dance Theatre, 1983
Courtesy of the photographer

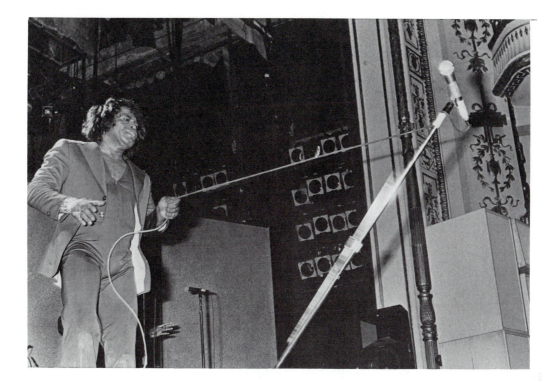

HAKIM MUTLAQ

James Brown at the Apollo Theatre, New York, 1987
Courtesy of the photographer

HAKIM MUTLAQ

Party, New York, 1987
Courtesy of the photographer

MARILYN NANCE

Baba Ishangi, Queens, New York, 1986
Courtesy of the photographer

MARILYN NANCE

Portrait of Al and Ali, Brooklyn, New York, 1981
Courtesy of the photographer

MARILYN NANCE

Nigeria Festac, Lagos, Nigeria, 1977
Courtesy of the photographer

NGE

Portrait of Phyllis Hyman, New York, ca. 1985
Courtesy of the photographer

NGE

Portrait of James Brown, New York, ca. 1980
Courtesy of the photographer

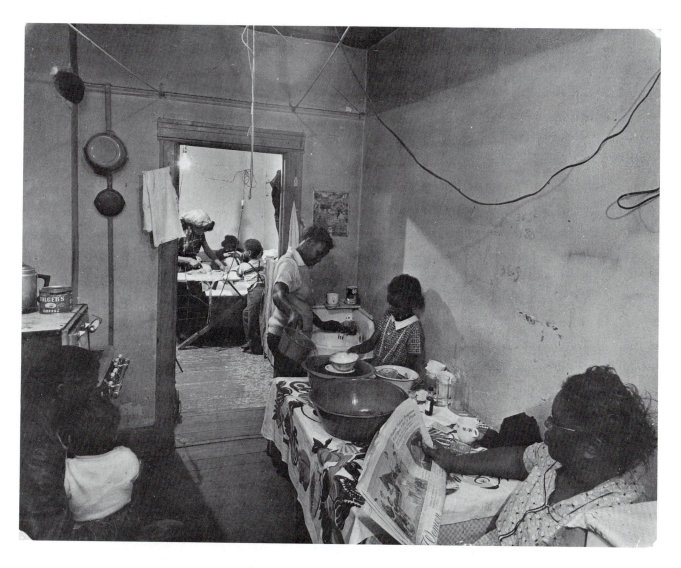

D WOYID G. O LMSTEAD

Interior kitchen, Pittsburgh, Pennsylvania., ca. 1945
*Courtesy of the Schomburg Center for Research in Black
Culture, The New York Public Library*

REG PATRICK

Black Fireman, 1977
Courtesy of the photographer

R EG P ATRICK

The Natural Blues, 1985
Courtesy of the photographer

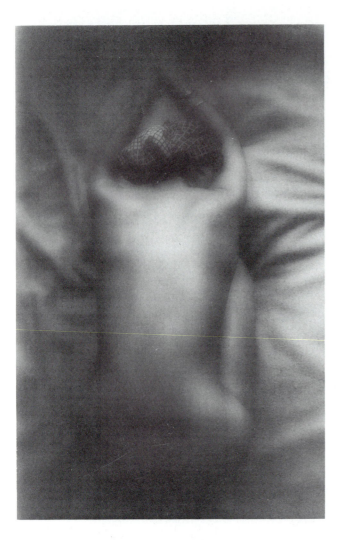

BILL PERRONEAU

Nude Series No. 1, 1975
Courtesy of the photographer

BILL PERRONEAU

Still Life Series No. 1, 1976
Courtesy of the photographer

JOHN PINDERHUGHES

Untitled [Shadyside portfolio, chair], ca. 1980
*Courtesy of the Schomburg Center for Research in Black
Culture, The New York Public Library*

JOHN **P**INDERHUGHES
Portrait of Charles Madison, Warrington, Virginia, ca. 1975
Courtesy of the photographer

TED PONTIFLET
"Poetic Reflections," 1986
Courtesy of the photographer

WAYNE PROVIDENCE
Roy Brooks of M-Boom at St. John the Divine Cathedral,
1981
Courtesy of the photographer

WAYNE PROVIDENCE
The World Saxophone Quartet at the Guggenheim
Museum, New York, 1984
Courtesy of the photographer

ROBERT A. ROBINSON
Untitled [Rodeo Series, 1978–79, Rider No. 223]
Courtesy of the photographer

ROBERT A. ROBINSON
Untitled [Rodeo Series, 1978–79, rodeo clown with bull]
Courtesy of the photographer

RUDOLPH ROBINSON

Black French Boy, 1987
*Courtesy of Museum of the National Center of
Afro-American Artists, Boston, Massachusetts*

CYRIL RYAN

Sons of Harlem, 1982
Courtesy of the photographer

CYRIL RYAN

New Mexico, 1977
Courtesy of the photographer

CYRIL RYAN

Flying Saucer House, Brazil, 1974
Courtesy of the photographer

JUMA SANTOS

Marcus Garvey Day Parade, Harlem, New York, 1986
Courtesy of the photographer

RICHARD SAUNDERS
Young girl with umbrella, University of Pittsburgh, 1952
Courtesy of Emily Saunders

RICHARD SAUNDERS
Man sitting on railing in New York, 1950
Courtesy of Emily Saunders

RICHARD SAUNDERS

Malcolm X with his wife, Betty, and their two children at
home in Long Island, New York, 1955
Courtesy of Emily Saunders

JEFFREY SCALES

Portrait of a woman, Amsterdam Avenue, Harlem, New York, 1985
Courtesy of the photographer

JEFFREY SCALES

Portrait of a man entitled "Easter, Harlem, New York," 1985
Courtesy of the photographer

J EFFREY S CALES

Central Park, 110th Street, Harlem, New York, 1986
Courtesy of the photographer

J EFFREY S CALES

Portrait of Christ, Harlem, New York, 1987
Courtesy of the photographer

JEFFREY SCALES
Portrait of Chi Chi and Coco, Harlem, New York, 1987
Courtesy of the photographer

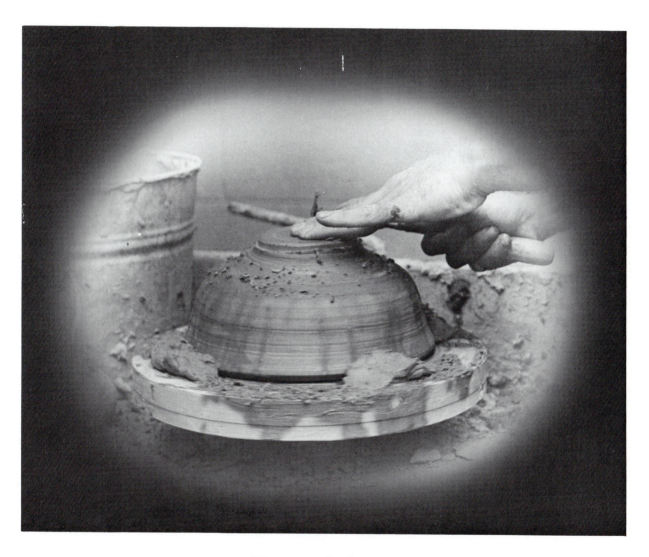

WILLIAM J. SCOTT

Potter's Hands, 1958
Courtesy of the photographer

GEORGE H. SCURLOCK

Portrait of Senator Edward Brooke, 1967
Courtesy of the photographer

GEORGE H. SCURLOCK

Duke Ellington receiving honorary doctorate degree at
Howard University, 1971
Courtesy of the photographer

GEORGE H. SCURLOCK

Portrait of Willie Brown, Don King, Alex Haley, 1970
Courtesy of the photographer

R OBERT S. S CURLOCK

Portrait of Lois Mailou Jones, artist, 1983
Courtesy of the photographer

R OBERT S. S CURLOCK

Touch Football, 1969
Courtesy of the photographer

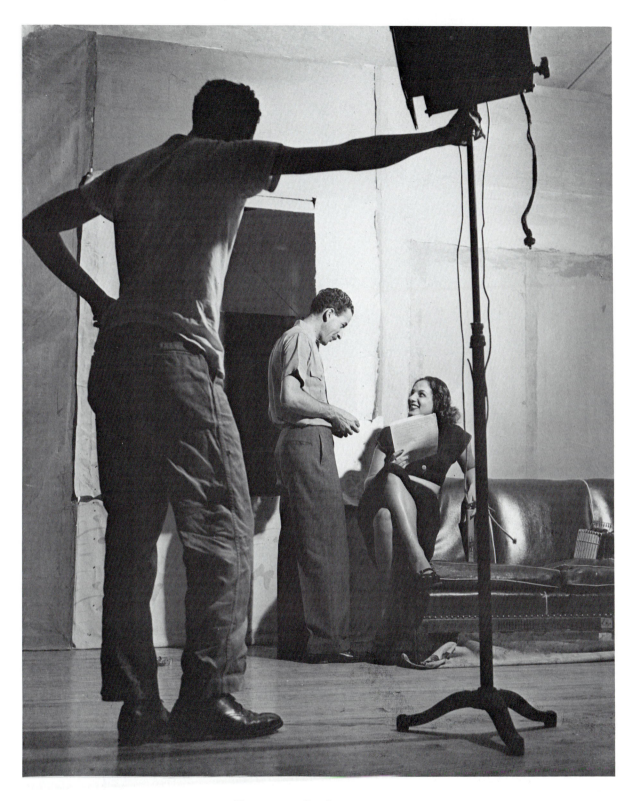

ROBERT S. SCURLOCK

Drama Coach, 1948
Courtesy of the photographer

R OBERT S ENGSTACKE

Portrait of Dr. Martin Luther King, Jr., 1966
Courtesy of the photographer

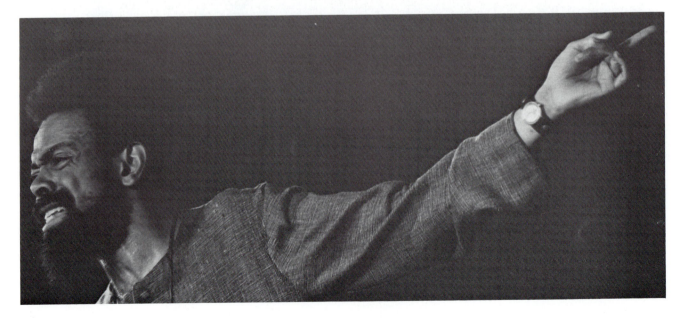

R OBERT S ENGSTACKE

Amiri Baraka, poet, 1970
Courtesy of the photographer

ROBERT SENGSTACKE

Portrait of a young boy entitled "Street Warrior," Chicago, 1966
Courtesy of the photographer

ROBERT SENGSTACKE

Kitchen scene, Mississippi plantation house, 1971
Courtesy of the photographer

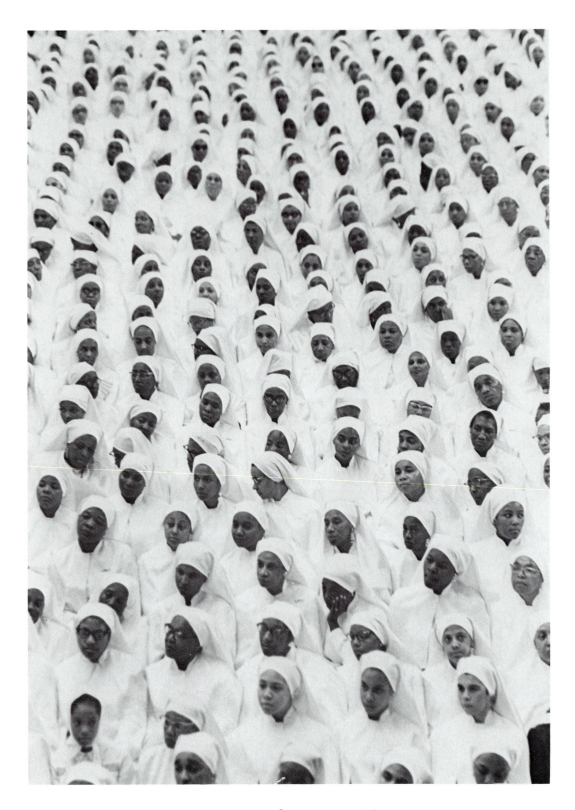

ROBERT SENGSTACKE
Savior's Day, Women's Section, Chicago, 1966
Courtesy of the photographer

CHERYL SHACKELTON

Untitled, Man seated in automobile, 1978
Courtesy of the photographer

ED SHERMAN

"Count Bassie's," silver print, ca. 1968
Courtesy of the photographer

ED SHERMAN

"What's in the Bag?" silver print, ca. 1968
Courtesy of the photographer

COREEN SIMPSON

Portrait of Richard, 1985
Courtesy of the photographer

COREEN SIMPSON

Portrait of Barry, 1985
Courtesy of the photographer

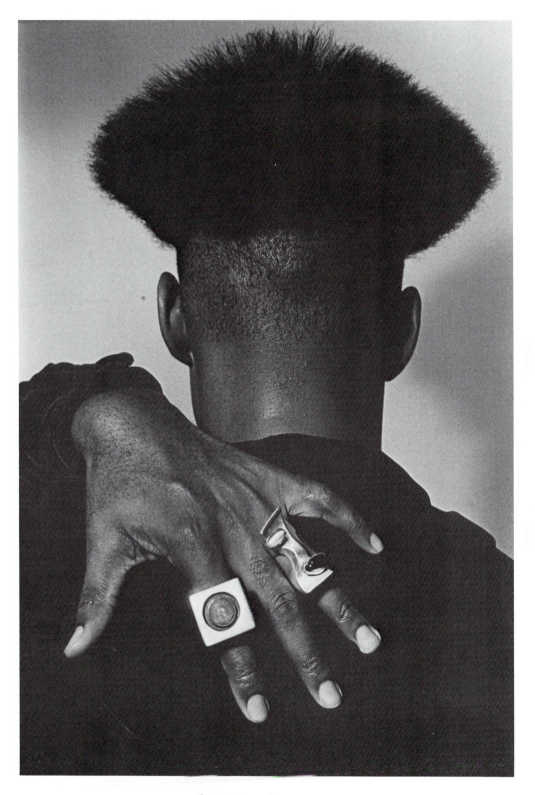

COREEN SIMPSON

Portrait of Vic, wearing jewelry designed by Arthur Smith, 1986
Courtesy of the photographer

COREEN SIMPSON

Portrait of Velma Jones, 1978
Courtesy of the photographer

sometimes Sam stands like his mother

LORNA SIMPSON

Gestures/Reenactments, "Sometimes Sam Stands like His
Mother," 1985
Courtesy of the photographer

MONETA SLEET

Mrs. Coretta Scott King and her daughter Bernice at the
funeral of Dr. Martin Luther King, Jr., Atlanta, Georgia,
1968
Courtesy of Johnson Publishing Company, Inc

MONETA SLEET

Portrait of Billie Holiday, 1956
Courtesy of Johnson Publishing Company, Inc

MONETA SLEET

Jackie Robinson at his induction into the Baseball Hall of
Fame with Branch Rickey, Rachel Robinson and mother,
Maille Robinson, Cooperstown, New York, 1962
Courtesy of Johnson Publishing Company, Inc

MONETA SLEET

Nigerian youngsters at independence celebration,
Lagos, Nigeria, 1960
Courtesy of Johnson Publishing Company, Inc

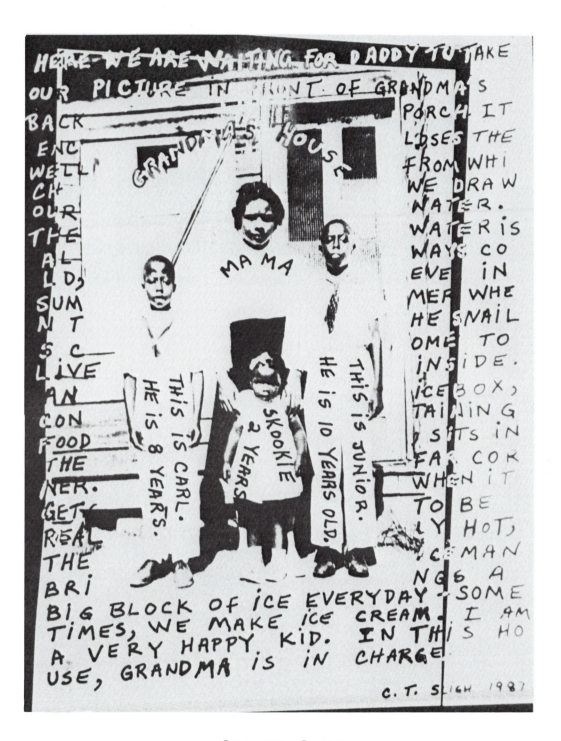

CLARISSA SLIGH
"Waiting for Daddy" (Van Dyke print), 1987
Courtesy of the photographer

CLARISSA SLIGH

"Lay on Top of Me" (Van Dyke print), 1984
Courtesy of the photographer

CLARISSA SLIGH

"House" (Van Dyke print), 1985
Courtesy of the photographer

422

CLARISSA SLIGH

"Bee Bee Gun" (Van Dyke print), 1984

Courtesy of the photographer

BEUFORD SMITH

Man with roses, 1968
Courtesy of the photographer

BEUFORD SMITH

Boy on subway train, 1984
Courtesy of the photographer

BEUFORD SMITH

Woman and flag, Harlem, 1966
Courtesy of the Schomburg Center for Research in Black
Culture, The New York Public Library

BEUFORD SMITH

Portrait of Barry Harris, musician, 1985
Courtesy of the photographer

Jamyl Smith

Portrait of David Murray, musician, ca. 1   6
Courtesy of the photographer

JAMYL SMITH

Untitled [two swimmers], ca. 1985
Courtesy of the photographer

JAMYL SMITH

Untitled [landscape], 1986
Courtesy of the photographer

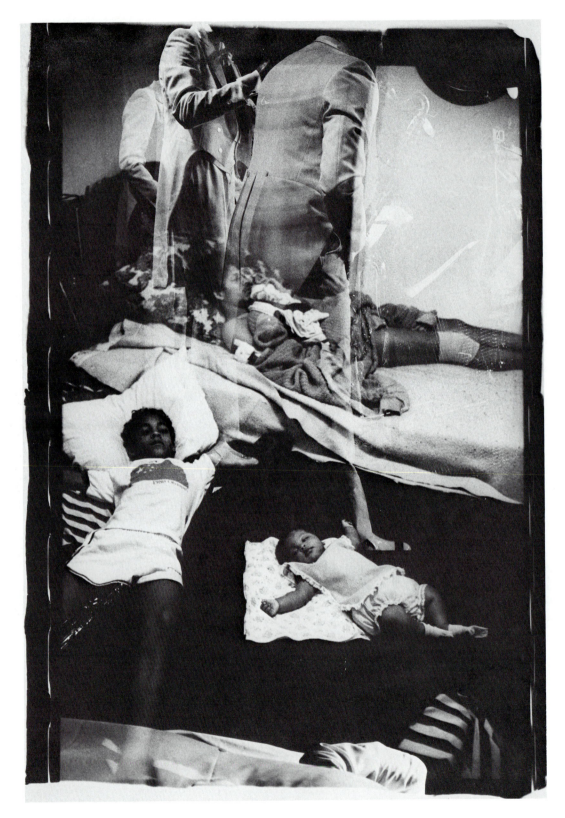

MING SMITH

"Save the Children," ca. 1979
Courtesy of the photographer

MING SMITH

"American Seen," ca. 1980
Courtesy of the photographer

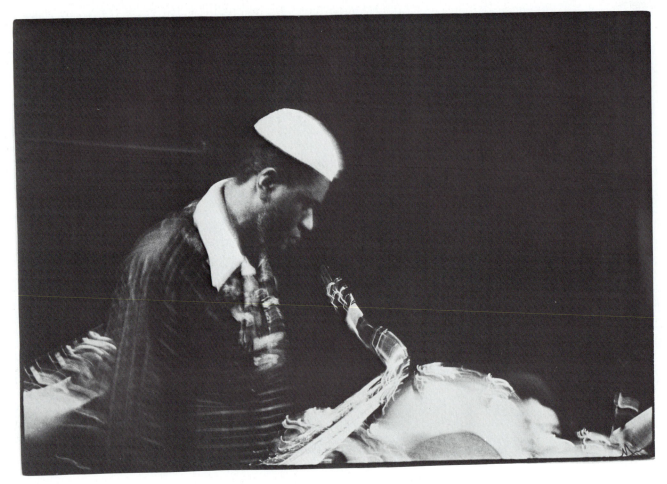

MING SMITH

Portrait of Pharoah Sanders, ca. 1978
Courtesy of the photographer

OTIS SPROW

"Eloquent Fall," 1983
Courtesy of the photographer

OTIS SPROW

Untitled [doorway and window], ca. 1985
Courtesy of the photographer

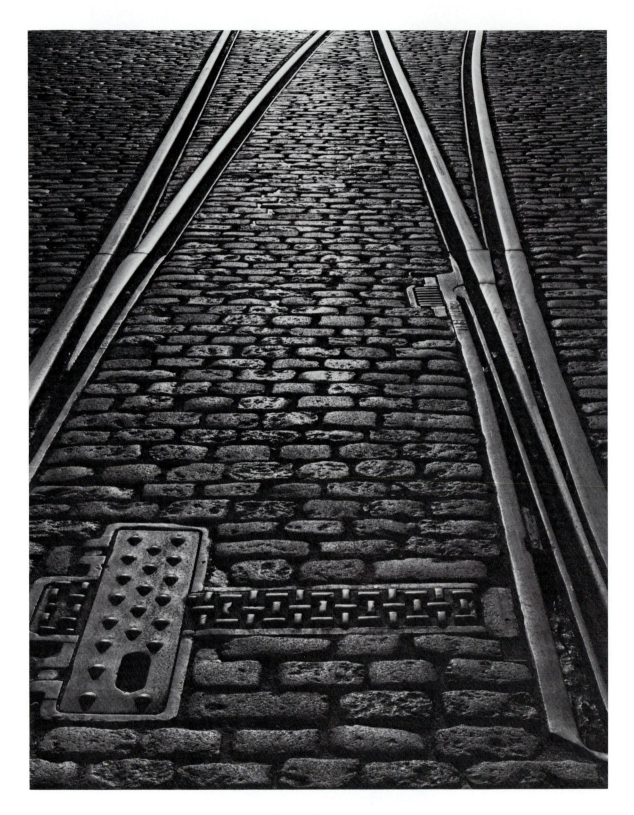

OTIS SPROW

Untitled [tracks], ca. 1982
Courtesy of the photographer

OTIS SPROW

Part 1, Picture 5, ca. 1984
Courtesy of the photographer

C HUCK S TEWART

Portrait of Eric Dolphy, 1964
Courtesy of the Schomburg Center for Research in Black
Culture, The New York Public Library

CHUCK STEWART

Portrait of John and Alice Coltrane, 1966
*Courtesy of the Schomburg Center for Research in Black
Culture, The New York Public Library*

CHUCK STEWART

Portrait of Billie Holiday, 1955
Courtesy of the Schomburg Center for Research in Black
Culture, The New York Public Library

FRANK STEWART

Untitled [street scene], 1978
*Courtesy of the Schomburg Center for Research in Black
Culture, The New York Public Library*

FRANK STEWART

Untitled [young boy standing near police motor brigade], ca. 1979
*Courtesy of the Schomburg Center for Research in Black Culture,
The New York Public Library*

FRANK STEWART

Easter Sunday, Harlem, 1977
*Courtesy of the Schomburg Center for Research in Black
Culture, The New York Public Library*

ELISABETH SUNDAY

Self-Portrait, Kenya, 1987
Courtesy of the photographer

ELISABETH SUNDAY

Profile, Kenya, 1987
Courtesy of the photographer

ELISABETH SUNDAY

Dogon mother, Mali, 1987
Courtesy of the photographer

LAWRENCE F. SYKES

Barbershop, Decatur, Alabama, 1970
Courtesy of the photographer

LAWRENCE F. SYKES
Cap Haitien Morning, Haiti, 1972
Courtesy of the photographer

BRUCE TALAMON

Portrait—father and son, Chicago, 1986 (from the photo
documentation project *A Day In the Life of America*)
Courtesy of the photographer

BRUCE TALAMON

Jesse Jackson with national press coordinator Frank Watkins,
New York City, 1984
Courtesy of the photographer

BRUCE TALAMON

Portrait of Ron Carter, Locarno, Switzerland, 1983
Courtesy of the photographer

BRUCE TALAMON

New Year's Day, Gabon, West Africa, 1981
(Bob Marley gave a New Year's concert in Gabon
the year he died and asked Talamon to document the tour;
these four boys were at the sound check)
Courtesy of the photographer

JACQUELINE PATTEN VAN SERTIMA

Untitled [Two young girls with musical instruments] n.d.
Courtesy of the photographer

JACQUELINE PATTEN VAN SERTIMA

Untitled [Four women play cards], ca. 1979
Courtesy of the photographer

SHAWN WALKER

Untitled [gathering in front of the RKO], 1963
Courtesy of the photographer

SHAWN WALKER

Untitled [portrait of two men wearing white hats], New York, 1972
Courtesy of the photographer

SHAWN WALKER

Untitled [portrait of man with child], New York, 1964
Courtesy of the photographer

SHAWN WALKER

Untitled [veteran with tuba], 1986
Courtesy of the photographer

WILLIAM ONIKWA WALLACE

Untitled [window frame], n.d.
Courtesy of the photographer

WILLIAM ONIKWA WALLACE

Untitled [portrait of a woman], n.d.
Courtesy of the photographer

SHARON WATSON-MAURO

Untitled [model in white], 1985
Courtesy of the photographer

CARRIE WEEMS
"Momma and Willie are always trying to make ends meet . . . ," ca. 1985
Courtesy of the photographer

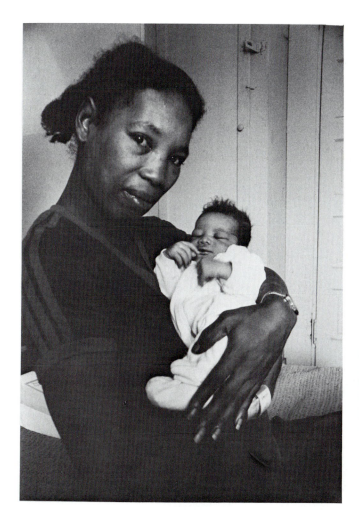

C ARRIE W EEMS

"At least four babies is what Dorothy wants . . . ," 1984
Courtesy of the photographer

C ARRIE W EEMS

Untitled [interior Church of God in Christ], ca. 1986
Courtesy of the photographer

WENDEL WHITE
Untitled [building with cross], 1986
Courtesy of the photographer

WENDEL WHITE

Untitled [landscape], Texas, 1983
*Courtesy of the Schomburg Center for Research in Black
Culture, The New York Public Library*

PAT WARD WILLIAMS

"Ghosts that Smell Like Cornbread" (window frame,
cyanotype, VanDyke brown prints, silver prints, family snap-
shots, fabric, stones, broken cup), 1987
Courtesy of the photographer

There's something going on here. I didn't see it right away. After all, you see one lynched man you've seen them all. He looks so helpless. He doesn't look lynched yet. What is that under his chin? How long has he been LOCKED to that tree? Can you be BLACK and look at this? Life magazine published this picture. Could Hitler show pics of the Holocaust WHO took this this picture? Couldn't he just as easily let the man go? Did he take his camera home and then come to keep the back with a blowtorch? Where do you TORTURE someone JEWS in line. BURN off an ear? Melt an eye? A screaming mouth with a blowtorch How can this photograph exist? WHO took this picture? Oh. God Life answers — Page 141 — no credit. Somebody do something

PAT WARD WILLIAMS

"Accused/Blowtorch/Padlock" (window frame, magazine
photo, silver prints, film positive, paint text), 1987
Courtesy of the photographer

WILLIAM EARLE WILLIAMS

Untitled [woman with Marilyn Monroe mask], Philadelphia, 1983
Courtesy of the photographer

WILLIAM EARLE WILLIAMS

Untitled, [waiter], Philadelphia, 1981
Courtesy of the photographer

ALPHONSO WILLIS

Portrait of The Willis Family, ca. 1952

Courtesy of the photographer

DEBORAH WILLIS

"A Homegoing," Florence, South Carolina, 1978
Courtesy of the photographer

DEBORAH WILLIS

"A Church Reunion,"
Shady Grove, Orange County, Virginia, 1980
Courtesy of the photographer

CURTIS WILLOCKS

March Against South Africa, Harlem, 1986
Courtesy of the photographer

CURTIS WILLOCKS

Candlelight Walk, Harlem, 1986
Courtesy of the photographer

CURTIS WILLOCKS

Veteran's Day, New York, 1986
Courtesy of the photographer

GILBERTO WILSON

Untitled [woman standing with white hat], ca. 1985
Courtesy of the photographer

GILBERTO WILSON

Untitled [church choir], ca. 1986
Courtesy of the photographer

GILBERTO WILSON

Untitled [baptism], ca. 1985
Courtesy of the photographer

GILBERTO WILSON

Untitled [woman reading the Bible], ca. 1985
Courtesy of the photographer

SULE GREG WILSON

Still Life: Muga's Sewing Room, Takoma Park, Maryland, 1979
Courtesy of the photographer

SULE GREG WILSON

"The Last Winter in Oberlin," Oberlin, Ohio, 1977
Courtesy of the photographer

ERNEST **G.** WITHERS

The Chauffer's Service Club, Inc., Memphis, ca. 1965
Courtesy of the photographer

ERNEST **G.** WITHERS

Main Street, Memphis—The march on April 8, 1968
Courtesy of the photographer

ERNEST **G.** WITHERS

Mississippi March, with Martin Luther King, Jr., Floyd McKisick,
Dr. Green, Stokely Carmichael, and Bernard Lee, 1966
Courtesy of the photographer

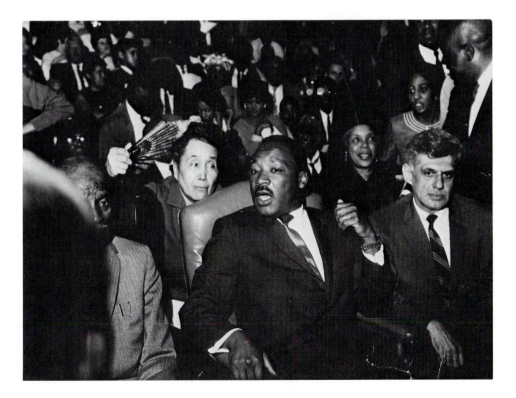

ERNEST **G.** WITHERS

Dr. Martin L. King, Jr. at the Rally for Memphis Sanitation
Workers, Mason Temple National Headquarters, Memphis, Tennessee, 1968
Courtesy of the photographer

MEL WRIGHT

Cuzco, Peru, 1976
Courtesy of the photographer

MEL WRIGHT

Kathmandu, Nepal, 1981
Courtesy of the photographer

AFTERWORD

White American critics . . . have always vacil-
lated between a tendency to exclude blacks
altogether from the world of art and an inclina-
tion to include them as infants of the spring.

HOUSTON A. BAKER, JR.

The Journey Back: Issues in
Black Literature and Criticism

In her two volumes *Black Photographers, 1840–1940* and the current *An Illustrated Bio-*
Bibliography of Black Photographers, 1940–1988, Deborah Willis-Thomas provides a body
of information to refute the standard misconceptions, such as those noted above, vis-à-vis
photographic history. Though modestly proposed as a "working resource" and the "basis"
for future critical inquiry, Willis-Thomas' work documents an amazing 150 years of activity
among photographers of African descent, from Jules Lion, who first introduced the daguerreotype to New Orleans circa 1840, to Lorna Simpson whose large-scale images with
text function in the post-modern arena of the 1980s. Though what the author has published
is necessarily selective, the accomplishments of over 300 black photographers have been
systematically recorded, some unearthed and taking their rightful place in history for the
very first time. In research that has spanned more than fifteen years, Willis-Thomas has
taken on one of the most arduous tasks of scholarship—the culling of primary source
material—and produced a collection that will remain an important resource for generations to come.

Black photographers of the last fifty years can be discussed in terms of two distinct
approaches to the medium, that of "straight" or documentary style and the use of the
symbolic or metaphoric image.

Documentary photography has its roots in the American regionalist art of the 1930s and the Farm Security Administration photographs of that era. These pictures contain useful/recognizable information about the specific subject under study; yet they are still subjective interpretations where artistic faculties are used to give, as Whitman said, "vivification to fact." While documentary photography as a movement lost its impetus with World War II, it became the essence of contemporary photojournalism, a style advanced by the availability of hand-held cameras and fast film that brought both photographer and viewer to the scene as never before. Straight photography combines all these antecedents.

In the work of many black photographers straight photography is synonymous with "street-photography," largely urban landscapes capturing the beauty of ordinary black people in their day-to-day existence. Gordon Parks and Roy DeCarava, working in the 1940s and 1950s, are often considered the progenitors of this genre, and whether in print or as mentors, have influenced generations of photomakers. Those currently working in this mode include Billy Abernathy, Robert Sengstacke, Frank Stewart, Dawoud Bey, Shawn Walker, Marilyn Nance, Beuford Smith, Jeanne Moutoussamy-Ashe and Jeffrey Scales among others.

Under the loosely knit artists organizations of the 1960s, particularly the Kamoinge Workshop in New York and the Organization of Black American Culture (OBAC) in Chicago, black photographers came together and defined a new black aesthetic. A primary concern was reaching the black audience. As Willis-Thomas states in the introduction to this volume, the photographers who were molded by the socially conscious 1960s and 1970s set a new standard in photography, providing it with a new index of meanings; so that while Adger W. Cowans, Dan Dawson and Ming Smith came through the Kamoinge Workshop, they did not become practitioners of street-photography, for which that collective was known. Cowans' photographs even from the first years of the 1960s attest to his early interest in metaphor. Dawson's recent color work of Brazilian architecture and horizons reveals a vigorous sense of abstract composition. Ming Smith's long-exposure photographs, particularly of jazz musicians, have a distinctly surreal quality. This work is allusive, connotative, gestural and, like "art photography" of the late nineteenth century, perhaps draws more from painting than from the documentary photographic tradition.

The latest generation of photographers, coming of age in the 1980s, utilizes both the straight and the metaphoric image, sometimes combining them. Dawoud Bey's recognizable/realistic black-and-white images, pervaded by an amazing quality of light, can be read as both document and allusion. The works of Wendel White and Wayne Providence use long exposures to create forceful and evocative movement. Albert Chong, a native of Jamaica, West Indies, in a series titled "I-Traits," uses the technique of *tableau vivant* to create allegories of ancient African heritage and its contemporary spiritual manifestations, and his recent large-scale prints are shrinelike still lifes that draw the viewer into their ritual. Lorna Simpson also works with big pictures, but in nontraditional formats that border on the sculptural. Using somewhat disjunctive narrative devices, Simpson critiques human gestures; themes of race and gender are prevalent. Text accompanies the images at once corroborating and complicating them.

These are just some of the many black photographers who, in the words of Rodger Birt, possess the "active consciousness to command our attention, to wake us up to the wider possibilities of the world and our own lives."* They are artists, architectural historians, documenters, witnesses, photojournalists and portraitists, and, above all, part of the history of the photographic medium. Robert Sengstacke and Billy Abernathy are black photographers whose contemporary imagery can stand toe to toe with that of their white counterparts Robert Frank, Gary Winogrand and Lee Friedlander. Coreen Simpson's "Transvestites" and "B-Boys" series compare with Diane Arbus' visions of those on the fringes of society. The photographs of Carrie Mae Weems are narrative dramas like those of Duane Michals. Yet there remains an urgent need for documentation of the activities of black photographers, and a scarcity of writers and critics who have taken up the task. We who have contributed to this volume—scholars and artists alike—hope to inspire both those within and outside the field toward understanding and action.

KELLIE JONES
January 1988

*Rodger Birt, "Coreen Simpson: An Interpretation," *Black American Literature Forum* (Terre Haute), Vol. 21, No. 3 (1987), 289.

AFTERWORD

BIBLIOGRAPHY

Books

Alinder, James. *Roy DeCarava Photographs.* Carmel, Calif.: The Friends of Photography, 1981.

Baraka, Amiri, and Abernathy, Billy. *In Our Terribleness.* New York: Bobbs-Merrill Company, 1970.

Barrow, Thomas; Armitage, Shirley; Tydeman, William. *Reading into Photography: Selected Essays, 1959–1980.* Albuquerque: University of New Mexico Press, 1982.

Barthes, Roland. *Camera Lucida: Reflections on Photography.* New York: Hill and Wang, 1981.

Bunch, Lonnie III. *California Black Photographers, The Tradition Continues.* Los Angeles: California Museum of Afro-American History and Culture, 1983.

Campbell, Mary Schmidt; Driskell, David; Lewis, David; Willis-Ryan, Deborah. *Harlem Renaissance: Art of Black America.* New York: The Studio Museum in Harlem and Harry N. Abrams, 1987.

———. *Tradition and Conflict, Images of a Turbulent Decade, 1963–1973.* New York: The Studio Museum in Harlem, 1985.

Capa, Cornell. *The Concerned Photographer.* New York: Grossman Publishers, 1972.

Coar, Valencia Hollins. *A Century of Black Photographers: 1840–1960.* Providence: Museum of Art, Rhode Island School of Design, 1983.

Cole, Ernest. *House of Bondage.* New York: Random House, 1967.

Crawford, Joe. *The Black Photographers Annual, Vol. 1.* Brooklyn, N.Y.: Black Photographers Annual Inc., 1972.

———. *The Black Photographers Annual, Vol. 2.* Brooklyn, N.Y.: Black Photographers Annual Inc., 1974.

———. *The Black Photographers Annual, Vol. 3.* Brooklyn, N.Y.: Another View, Inc., 1976.

———. *The Black Photographers Annual, Vol. 4.* Brooklyn, N.Y.: Another View, Inc., 1980.

DeCarava, Roy, and Hughes, Langston. *The Sweet Flypaper of Life.* Washington, D.C.: Howard University Press, Reprint 1984.

DeCock, Liliane, and McGhee, Reginald. *James Van Der Zee*. Dobbs Ferry, N.Y.: Morgan and Morgan, 1973.

Dodson, Owen, and Billops, Camille. *The Harlem Book of the Dead James Van Der Zee*. Dobbs Ferry, N.Y.: Morgan and Morgan, 1978.

Dover, Cedric. *American Negro Art*. Greenwich, Conn.: New York Graphic Society, 1960.

Driskell, David. *Two Centuries of Black American Art*. New York: Los Angeles County Museum of Art and Alfred A. Knopf, 1976.

Fax, Elton C. *Black Artists of the New Generation*. New York: Dodd Mead, 1971.

Fox, Ted. *Showtime at the Apollo*. New York: Holt, Rinehart and Winston Inc., 1983.

Grabowski, John J., and Martin, Olivia. *Somebody, Somewhere, Wants Your Photograph*. Cleveland: Western Reserve Historical Society, 1980.

Greene, Carroll. *Afro-American Art: 1986*. Washington, D.C.: The Visions Foundation, 1987.

Hamalian, Leon, and Hatch, James V. *Artist and Influence, 1986*. New York: Hatch Billops Collection, 1986.

Hansberry, Lorraine. *The Movement, Documentary of a Struggle for Equality*. New York: Simon and Shuster, 1964.

Higgins, Chester Jr., and Coombs, Orde. *Some Time Ago: A Historical Portrait of Black Americans, 1850–1950*. New York: Anchor Press/Doubleday, 1980.

Hoffman, Michael. *Aperture, 92*. New York: Silver Mountain Foundation, 1983.

International Center of Photography. *Encyclopedia of Photography*. New York: Crown Publishers, 1984.

Johnson, Chris. *The Practical Zone System*. Stoneham, Mass.: Focal Press, 1986.

Johnson, Thomas L., and Dunn, Phillip C. *A True Likeness: The Black South of Richard Samuel Roberts: 1920–1936*. Columbia, S.C.: Bruccoli and Clark, 1986.

Levinson, Sandra. *Center for Cuban Studies 15th. Anniversary Journal*. New York: Town Crier for Performing Arts, 1987.

———. *Cuba: A View from Inside, 40 years of Cuban Life in the Work and Words of 20 Photographers*. New York: A Multimedia Project of the Center for Cuban Studies, 1985.

Livingston, Jane. *P.H. Polk*. Washington, D.C.: Corcoran Gallery of Art, 1981.

Lomax, Pearl Cleage. *P.H. Polk, Photographs*. Atlanta: Nexus Press, 1980.

Long, Worth W., and Reagon, Bernice Johnson. *We'll Never Turn Back*. Washington, D.C.: Smithsonian Performing Arts, 1980.

McQuaid, James. *An Index to American Photographic Collections*. Boston: G.K. Hall, 1982.

Magubane, Peter. *Magubane's South Africa*. New York: Alfred A. Knopf, 1978.

Mapplethorpe, Robert. *Portraits*. New York: Twelvetrees Press, 1985.

Moutoussamy-Ashe, Jeanne. *Daufuskie Island: A Photographic Essay*. Columbia: University of South Carolina Press, 1982.

———. *Viewfinders: Black Women Photographers*. New York: Dodd Mead and Company, 1986.

Newhall, Beaumont. *The History of Photography*. New York: Museum of Modern Art, 1982.

Parks, Gordon. *A Choice of Weapons*. New York: Harper & Row, 1966.

———. *Born Black*. Philadelpia: Lippincott, 1971.

———. *Moments Without Proper Names*. New York: Viking Press, 1975.

Rowell, Charles. *Callaloo, A Journal of Afro-American and African Arts and Letters, Vol. 9*. Baltimore, Md.: The Johns Hopkins University Press, 1986.

Schoener, Allon. *Harlem on My Mind: Cultural Capital of Black America 1900–1968.* New York: Random House, 1968.

———. *Harlem on My Mind: Cultural Capital of Black America 1900–1979.* New York: Dell, 1979.

Stewart, Charles, and Harrison, Paul. *Jazz Files.* Boston: New York Graphic Society, 1985.

Stewart, Frank, and Jennings, Corinne. *Contemporary African-American Photography of the 60's and 70's, Two Schools: New York and Chicago.* New York: Kenkeleba House, 1986.

Willis, John. *Theater World, 1979, Vol. 14.* New York: Crown Publishers, 1980.

Willis-Thomas, Deborah. *Black Photographers, 1840–1940, An Illustrated Bio-Bibliography.* New York: Garland Publishing, 1985.

Wilmer, Valerie. *The Face of Black Music.* New York: Da Capo Press, 1976.

Wright, Richard, and Rosskam, Edwin. *12 Million Black Voices, A Folk History of the Negro in the United States.* New York: Viking Press, 1941.

ARTICLES

Adelman, Bob. "Harlem on My Mind: 'Lawrence Welk Plays The Blues.'" *Infinity: American Society of Magazine Photographers,* March 1969.

Allen, Vance. "The Black Photographers Annual, 1973." *Photo Newsletter,* January–February 1973.

———. "Exhibition by Beuford Smith." *Photo Newsletter,* June 1972.

———. "Focus on Bob Fletcher." *Photo Newsletter,* June 1972.

———. "Portfolio by B. Brisset." *Photo Newsletter,* Fall 1973.

———. "Shawn Walker, Photographer." *Photo Newsletter,* March 1973.

Ashley, Dolores. "The Black Woman Photographer." *Photo Newsletter,* January–February 1973.

Barboza, Anthony. *Photo District News,* June 1987.

Bardagjy, Andrew M. "Photographs by Richard Saunders." *An African Portfolio, Topic Magazine,* U.S. Information Agency, 1986.

Battle, Thomas C. "'For Women Only,' an Exhibition of Local Black Women Photographers." Howard University exhibition catalog, 1983.

Bey, Dawoud. "Images—Six Black Photographers in Focus." *American Arts,* September 1982.

"Big Crowds Force Museum to Cut Off 'Harlem' Show Line." *New York Times,* January 26, 1969.

Birt, Rodger C. "A True Likeness—The South of Richard S. Roberts, 1920–1936." *American Visions,* April 1987.

———. "Coreen Simpson: An Interpretation." *Black American Literature Forum,* Vol. 21, No. 3, Fall 1987.

Campbell, Crispin Y. "History of Blacks in Photography Brought to Light." *The Washington Post,* February 16, 1985.

Capar, Judith. "Star-Struck Trolley Driver Has Right Drops for Hobby." *Staten Island, New York, Advance,* December 1981.

Cohen, Daniel. "Gordon Parks: Plot, Poetry & Pictures." *Photo District News,* March 1987.

Colby, Joy H. "Moving Metaphors Abound in Photos by Black Artists." *Detroit News,* September 12, 1982.

Davis, Angela. "Photography and Afro-American History." *Ten.*8, 1987.

Garver, Thomas H. "Larry Chatman: The Path Not Taken." *Framework*, A Journal of Images and Culture, Vol. 1, No. 1.

Giddons, Gary. "The Young Bloods: A New Generation in Jazz." *The Village Voice*, June 25, 1985.

Gomez, Jewelle. "Showing Our Faces: A Century of Black Women Photographed." *Ten.*8, 1987.

Greene, Cheryll Y. "International Black Photographers: Where We're Coming From." *International Black Photographers Newsletter*, Winter 1981.

"Harlem: Sold Out by Massa Hoving???" *Modern Photography*, 1969.

Hellman, Peter. "Harlem on Their Minds." *New York*, 1969.

Jones, Duane. "A Portfolio of Dance Photographs." *Caribe.*

Jones, Kellie. "No Second Fiddles." *The Village Voice*, April 14, 1987.

June, George. "P.H. Polk." *Photo Works*, July–September 1982.

Kubler, George. "The Black Photographer." *Photo Newsletter*, Fall 1973.

Lipson, Karin. "News Photographs That Catch The Black Experience." *Newsday*, July 27, 1986.

McGhee, Reginald. "Edward Steichen, 1879–1973." *Photo Newsletter*, March–April 1973.

Morris, Kathy. "Women in Photography Conference: The Click of Connections." *The Ithaca Times*, October 16, 1986.

"Moseley Photos in Tyler Black History Show." *Temple Times*, February 19, 1987.

Perry, Regina. "A Black Photographer's Annual, 1973" (a review). *Photo Newsletter*, March–April 1973.

Pincus, Robert L. "Affirmation of Ethnicity in 2 Shows." *Los Angeles Times*, January 2, 1984.

Rothstein, Arthur. "The Critical Eye." *Travel & Camera*, April 1969.

"A Salute to Black Photographers." *Ebony*, October 1971.

Sorlien, Sandy. "Black Photographer Gets Overdue Exposure." *Philadelphia Daily News*, February 17, 1987.

Taubman, Bryna. "Some Visitors to Met Don't Mind Harlem." *New York Post*, January 24, 1969.

Thornton, Gene. "P.H. Polk's Genius Versus Modernism." *New York Times*.

Trend, David. "Black & White Photography: The Object & Subject in Black Photography." *After Image*, May 1986.

Vestal, David; DeCarava, Roy; Francis, Ray; Mann, Margery. "Can Whitey Do a Beautiful Black Picture Show?" *Popular Photography*, May 1969.

Williams, Ted, and Brown, Oscar, Jr. "In Memoriam." *Time Capsule*, Spring 1981.

Willis-Ryan, Deborah. "Remaking the Past to Make the Future. The Photograph Collection of the Schomburg Center for Research in Black Culture." *Ten.*8, 1987.

Wilmer, Val. "Beuford Smith: In The Humane Tradition." *Ten.*8, 1987.

———. "Black Image." *Ten.*8, 1987.

———. "Coreen Simpson: Taking Care of Business." *Ten.*8, 1987.

———. "Evidence: New Light on Afro-American Images." *Ten.*8, 1987.

Wilson, Melba. "Viewfinder: Black Women Photographers by Jeanne Moutoussamy-Ashe." *Ten.*8, 1987.

SELECTED EXHIBITIONS 1969–1987

1987

ALLENSWORTH: AN ENDURING DREAM
California Afro-American Museum, Los Angeles,
California

**ARIZONA ARTIST OF THE BLACK
COMMUNITY**
Yuma Art Center, Yuma, Arizona

ARTISTS' INSTALLATIONS
Jamaica Arts Center, Jamaica, New York

HERSTORY, HER SPACE, HER MOMENTS
Castillo Gallery, New York, New York

AUTOBIOGRAPHY: HERSTORY
The Rotunda Gallery, Brooklyn, New York

BLACK PHOTOGRAPHERS: 1840–1940
Albright-Knox Gallery, Buffalo, New York

CARIBBEAN ARTISTS' CONNECTION
843 Studio Gallery, Brooklyn, New York

**EIGHTH ANNUAL BLACK ARTIST
EXHIBITION**
Speed Art Museum, Louisville, Kentucky

**FIELD TO FACTORY: AFRO-AMERICAN
MIGRATION 1915–1940**
National Museum of American History,
Smithsonian, Washington, DC

FIVE VIEWPOINTS ON BLACK AMERICA
African-American Museum, Hempstead, New York

GORDON PARKS: A RETROSPECTIVE
New York Public Library, Gottesman Hall, New
York, New York

**HARLEM RENAISSANCE: ART OF BLACK
AMERICA**
Studio Museum in Harlem, New York, New York

**IN CELEBRATION OF AFRO-AMERICAN
HISTORY MONTH**
John Jay College Gallery, New York, New York

**JOHN W. MOSELEY, PHOTOGRAPHS,
1936–1967**
Temple University, Tyler School of Art, Elkins
Park, Pennsylvania

**LARGE AS LIFE: CONTEMPORARY
PHOTOGRAPHY**
Jamaica Arts Center, Jamaica, New York

**THE LEGENDS: PORTRAITS OF AFRO-
AMERICAN AND LATIN MUSICAL ARTISTS**
Caribbean Cultural Center, New York, New York

LET FREEDOM RING
Du Sable Museum of African American History,
Chicago, Illinois

NATIONAL URBAN LEAGUE ART EXPO
1987
Thomas Convention Center, Houston, Texas

NEW VISIONS
Soho 20 Gallery, New York, New York

9 UPTOWN
Harlem School of the Arts, New York, New York

PART III, "PHOTOGRAPHY AND
COMMUNITY"
The Institute of Art and Urban Resources, New
York, New York

A PHOTO-JOURNALISM PORTFOLIO
FROM EAST AFRICA
The Artbanque Gallery, Minneapolis, Minnesota

RACE AND REPRESENTATION: ART/
FILM/VIDEO
Hunter College Art Gallery, New York, New York

THE 7TH. ANNUAL ATLANTA LIFE
NATIONAL ART COMPETITION AND
EXHIBITION
Atlanta, Georgia

SIX BLACK PHOTOGRAPHERS: 1920–1980
Cooper Union, New York, New York

SOUTH AFRICA: THE CORDONED HEART
Museum of Cultural History, UCLA, Los Angeles,
California

STREET LIFE AND ROCK N ROLL
Evergreen 7, Williamsburg, New York

TRADITION AND CONFLICT: IMAGES OF
A TURBULENT DECADE 1963–1973
(TRAVELING)
David and Alfred Smart Gallery, University of
Chicago, Chicago, Illinois

THE WEST, A MULTI-ETHNIC
PORTRAIT
The Bridge Gallery, Los Angeles, California

1986

AMERICA: ANOTHER PERSPECTIVE
Photo Center Gallery, New York University,
New York, New York

BLACK VISIONS' 86
Tweed Gallery, New York, New York

EXPRESSIONS' 86: AFRICA IN AMERICAS
Aaron Davis Hall, City College, New York, New
York

ON FREEDOM: THE ART OF
PHOTOJOURNALISM
The Studio Museum in Harlem, New York, New
York

PLACES AND FACES
The Education Gallery, The International Center
of Photography, New York, New York

RICHARD S. ROBERTS: 1920–1936
The Columbia Museum, Columbia, South
Carolina

SEEING IS BELIEVING?
Alternative Museum, New York, New York

THE STONE CHURCHES OF ETHIOPIA
The Studio Museum in Harlem, New York, New
York

A STORM IS BLOWING FROM PARADISE!
Castillo Center, New York, New York

24 EXPOSURES
Union Square Gallery, New York, New York

2 SCHOOLS: NY & CHICAGO, AFRICAN-
AMERICAN PHOTOGRAPHY OF THE 60'S &
70'S
Kenkeleba Gallery, New York, New York

WOMEN OF COLOR: DEFINED AND
REDEFINED
Unicorn Gallery, Newark, New Jersey

1985

THE BLACK PHOTOGRAPHER: AN
AMERICAN VIEW
Chicago Public Library Cultural Center, Chicago,
Illinois

BRIDGE ACROSS THE MIND
Grinnell Gallery, New York, New York

THE BROOKLYN LANDSCAPE
Rotunda Gallery, Brooklyn, New York

CARIBBEAN EXPLORATIONS
Grinnell Gallery, New York, New York

CLASSIC ATTITUDES & EXPRESSIONS
CONTEMPORARY PORTRAIT
PHOTOGRAPHY
Mills House Visual Arts Complex, Santa Ana
College, Santa Ana, California

GESTURES
Multicultural Arts & Humanities Center, San
Diego, California

IT LOOKS LIKE YESTERDAY TO ME
Port Washington Public Library, Port
Washington, New York

NINETEENTH CENTURY IMAGES OF
BLACKS IN SOUTH AMERICA AND THE
CARIBBEAN
Schomburg Center for Research in Black Culture,
New York, New York

PHOTO COLLECTIVE
Studio Gallery Inc., New York, New York

ROY LEWIS: PHOTOJOURNALIST
The Afro-American Historical & Cultural
Museum, Philadelphia, Pennsylvania

SOUTHERN ROADS/CITY PAVEMENTS
Studio Museum in Harlem, New York, New York

TRACES OF RITUAL
Irvine Fine Arts Center, Irvine, California

TRADITION AND CONFLICT: IMAGES OF A
TURBULENT DECADE 1963–1973
Studio Museum in Harlem, New York, New York

VARIATIONS OF FOUR PHOTOGRAPHERS
Castillo Gallery, New York, New York

1984

BLACK IMAGES IN FILM
Schomburg Center for Research in Black Culture,
New York, New York

FUNDI: A PHOTOGRAPHIC ESSAY
Afro-American Studies and Research Program,
University of Illinois–Urbana, Illinois

LEWIS: A PHOTOGRAPHIC ESSAY
Afro-American Studies and Research Program,
University of Illinois–Urbana, Illinois

MODERN BRIDE AND PLEASURES OF
CHILDHOOD
Moonmade Space, New York, New York

SHARRIEFF: A PHOTOGRAPHIC ESSAY
Afro-American Studies and Research Program,
University of Illinois–Urbana, Illinois

WAVELINES/MARTHA'S VINEYARD,
RECENT PHOTOGRAPHS
Gallery 62, New York, New York

1983

AFRICAN MOSAICS
The 4th Street Photo Gallery, New York, New York

THE BLACK AND WHITE SHOW
Kenkeleba Gallery, New York, New York

A CENTURY OF BLACK PHOTOGRAPHERS:
1840–1960
Museum of Art, Rhode Island School of Design,
Providence, Rhode Island

CONTEMPORARY AFRO-AMERICAN
PHOTOGRAPHY
Allen Museum, Oberlin College, Oberlin, Ohio

DAWOUD BEY, RECENT PHOTOGRAPHS
Cinque Gallery, New York, New York

EVIDENCE FROM 12 PHOTOGRAPHERS
Henry Street Settlement, Louis Abrons Arts for
Living Center, New York, New York

FOR WOMEN ONLY
Founders Library, Howard University,
Washington, DC

14 PHOTOGRAPHERS
Schomburg Center for Research in Black Culture,
New York, New York

GEORGE HALLETT
The Gallery of Art, College of Fine Arts, Howard
University, Washington, DC

INTROSPECT: THE PHOTOGRAPHY OF
ANTHONY BARBOZA
Studio Museum in Harlem, New York, New York

INQUIRIES
The 4th Street Photo Gallery, New York, New
York

SCENES FROM THE 20TH CENTURY
STAGE: BLACK THEATER IN
PHOTOGRAPHS
Schomburg Center for Research in Black Culture,
New York, New York

SENGSTACKE: A PHOTOGRAPHIC ESSAY
Afro-American Studies and Research Program,
University of Illinois–Urbana, Urbana, Illinois

THE SOUND I SAW: THE JAZZ PHOTOGRAPHS OF ROY DECARAVA
The Studio Museum in Harlem, New York, New York

THE TRADITION CONTINUES: CALIFORNIA BLACK PHOTOGRAPHERS
California Museum of Afro-American History and Culture, Los Angeles, California

THE YOUNG LORDS PARTY: 1969–1975
Caribbean Cultural Center, New York, New York

1982

THE ART OF JAZZ
Schomburg Center for Research in Black Culture, New York, New York

8 CONTEMPORARY PHOTOGRAPHERS IN THE SCHOMBURG CENTER COLLECTION
Schomburg Center for Research in Black Culture, New York, New York

THE GOODRIDGE BROTHERS, SAGINAW'S PIONEER PHOTOGRAPHERS
Saginaw Art Museum, Saginaw, Michigan

PHOTOGRAPHY: IMAGE AND IMAGINATION
Jazzonia Gallery, Detroit, Michigan

1981

BLACK AMERICAN LANDMARKS
Gordon Library, Worcester Polytechnic Institute, Massachusetts

A HISTORY OF BLACK PHOTOGRAPHY, 1850–1950
Jamaica Arts Center, Jamaica, New York, New York

MAYNARD
Black Woman Collaborative Gallery, Chicago, Illinois

MOMENTS
Greene Street Gallery, New York, New York

THE PHOTOGRAPHS OF HARVEY JAMES LEWIS, 1878–1978
Black Woman Collaborative Gallery, Chicago, Illinois

P. H. POLK
Corcoran Gallery of Art, Washington, D.C.

SIX PHOTOGRAPHERS
Western Electric Company, New York, New York

1980

COREEN SIMPSON, JACQUELINE LA VETTA PATTEN
Gallery 62, New York, New York

JULES ALLEN, BEUFORD SMITH, FRANK STEWART
Gallery 62, New York, New York

ONE MAN SHOW, GEORGE MINGO
Cinque Gallery, New York, New York

SELF PORTRAIT
Studio Museum in Harlem, New York, New York

SOMEBODY, SOMEWHERE, WANTS YOUR PHOTOGRAPHY
Western Reserve Historical Society, Cleveland, Ohio

STILL PHOTOGRAPHS
Chicago Public Library Center, Chicago, Illinois

VANTAGE POINTS
Benin Gallery, New York, New York

WE'LL NEVER TURN BACK
Smithsonian Institute, Washington, DC

1979–1969

THE BLACK PHOTOGRAPHER, 1908–1970: A SURVEY
The Addison Gallery, Andover, Massachusetts   1971

HARLEM ON MY MIND: 1900–1969
The Metropolitan Museum of Art, New York, New York   1969

JAZZ PHOTOGRAPHS OF ROBERT ELLISON
The Alternative Center for International Arts, New York, New York   1977

P. H. POLK
Studio Museum in Harlem, New York, New York   1976

ROY DeCARAVA, PHOTOGRAPHER
Sheldon Gallery, University of Nebraska at Lincoln, Lincoln, Nebraska   1970

SIX CONTEMPORARY BLACK PHOTOGRAPHERS
San Francisco Camerawork, San Francisco, California   1979

WOMEN ON THE SCENE
Brockman Gallery, Los Angeles, California   1979